The Electricity *of* Every Living Thing

The
Electricity
of
Every
Living
Thing

One Woman's Walk
with Asperger's

This edition first published in Great Britain in 2018 by
Trapeze
an imprint of the Orion Publishing Group Ltd
Carmelite House
50 Victoria Embankment
London EC4Y 0DZ
An Hachette UK Company

1 3 5 7 9 10 8 6 4 2

A CIP catalogue record for this book is available
from the British Library.

ISBN: 978 1 4091 7250 5
Ebook ISBN: 978 1 4091 7252 9

Typeset by Input Data Services Ltd, Somerset

Printed and bound in Great Britain by Clays Ltd, St Ives plc

www.orionbooks.co.uk

For Bertie

Contents

Contents

'The universe is full of magical things patiently
waiting for our wits to grow sharper.'

Eden Phillpotts, *A Shadow Passes*

'. . . walking too far too often too quickly is not safe at all.
The continual cracking of your feet on the road makes a
certain quantity of road come up into you.'

Flann O'Brien, *The Third Policeman*

A Note on Chapter Illustrations:

*The lines at the beginning of each chapter plot
the shape of my walking route.*

Prologue

The Isle of Thanet, November

Late afternoon in November, and it's dark already. I'm driving. To my left is the sea at Westgate; to my right, the low sweep of Pegwell Bay. Not that I can see either of them in the gloom, but I know this stretch of road well. The land feels spacious when the sea's nearby, and this is the furthest tip of Kent, the jutting hound's nose where you're suddenly surrounded by water.

I'm late. I hate being late. I switch on the radio for company. A man is interviewing a woman. She is talking about the intensity of everything around her; the way all her senses are heightened to light, noise, touch and smell. They make her anxious. I turn on the windscreen wipers and clear myself two arcs in the drizzle. She finds people hard to understand; she would prefer it if they said what they meant. *Too true*, I think. *Good luck with that.*

Then the interviewer says that his son is on the autism spectrum too, and he needs to write everything down or else he won't be able to take it in, and I think, *Yes but I'm like that, too.* I hate plans made on the hoof; I know I won't remember them. I can't ever recall names unless I see them in writing. Mind you, I can't remember faces, either. People just fade in and out of the fog, and I often have no sense of whether or not I've met them before. My life consists of a series of clues that I leave in diaries, and address books, and lists, so that I can reorient myself every time I forget.

It's like that for everyone, though. We're all just trying to get by.

'All autistic people suffer from a degree of mind-blindness. Is that true of you?' asks the interviewer.

'To some extent,' says the woman. 'I'm better at it than when I was young, because I'm more conscious of it as an issue. I'm constantly searching for clues in people's faces and tone of voice and body language.' *Thank God for my social skills*, I think. *Thank God I can get on with anyone.* There's a twinge of discomfort there, as I push away the sense of what that costs me, of how artificial it all feels. *I am good at this*, but I have to qualify it with *nowadays*.

'By and large, do you tend to think visually more than you think in language?' he says.

'Yes,' says the woman, 'I have an eidetic memory.'

I certainly don't have one of those. Although I suppose I do remember whole pages of books sometimes, like an imprint on my eyelids. At school, my French teacher laughed as I recalled pages of vocabulary: 'You're cheating!' she said. 'You're just reading that from the inside of your head.' And me, at thirteen, squirming in my seat, because I couldn't work out if this was a compliment – in which case, I should laugh along – or an accusation.

'Were you interested in other children, as a child?' says the man.

'No, I just didn't see the point. When I got a bit older, I would try to play with other people, but I wouldn't get it right. By the time I got to seventeen I had a breakdown, because I couldn't deal with all the stuff that was going on.'

The memory surges up of those blank days when I thought I might just give up talking for ever, because the words seemed too far away from my mouth; of the red days when I would hit my head against the wall just to see the white percussive flashes it brought; of the sick, strange days when the drugs made everyone else say I was nearly back to my old self again, but I could feel them in my throat, tamping everything down so that it didn't spew back up . . .

'One cliché about autism is that romantic relationships are very, very difficult,' he says. 'You're married. How did courtship work for you?'

. . . And I find myself nearly spitting at the radio, saying, out loud, 'How fucking dare you? We're not completely repellent, you know . . .'

And that word, *we*, takes me quite by surprise.

PART ONE

Desolation Point

....

Minehead Sea-Front, August

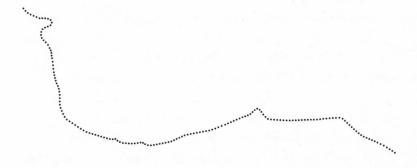

We arrive far too late in Minehead.

We meant to leave Whitstable at 5.30 a.m., and this was accompanied by a whimsy that we would wrap the boy in a blanket and bundle him, sleeping, into his car seat. He would awake, by our reckoning, just as we were approaching Bristol, and we would stop somewhere stylish and enjoy a picturesque family breakfast. I would have my feet on the South West Coast Path by lunchtime.

I'm not sure when we will learn that planning is futile in our household. We are awoken at eight by Bert yelling *DAAAAAADDDDDDDYYYYY* from his bedroom, and quickly realise that we neglected to set that five o'clock alarm. We finally leave at nine after a great deal of bickering, just in time to catch the worst of the August Bank Holiday traffic. Everyone, it seems, is heading down to the West Country for a last hurrah before school starts. There is little for us to do but to queue bad-temperedly, and make numerous stops at service stations along the way.

We finally roll into Minehead at three. 'Are we in Devon yet?' asks Bert, and I say, 'Yes,' because I can't be bothered to introduce him to a whole new county this late in the game. We are actually in Somerset, but he already knows Devon, and if everything goes to plan, I will cross the border tomorrow afternoon.

'We are in Devon,' I say, 'and it's beautiful.' I perch on the edge of the open boot of my car and lace up my walking boots. I can see Minehead Butlins across the grey shingle beach. I wonder if this will be my path, the one I've been craving, the wild one. I can't imagine it somehow. Maybe this is a misstep; maybe this isn't what I want after all.

A giant metal map in a pair of giant metal hands marks the start of the path. I pose for a photo with Bert, and then flick through the pictures on my phone, meaning to post one on Twitter with something jaunty, like *Here I go!* But I'm too appalled by how fat I look, and I post one of Bert instead, grinning impishly from between the folds of the map. Always better to post pictures of him than me these days, I find.

'I've really got to make a start,' I say to H. 'I'll never get there.' I can feel the first threads of agitation winding around me. I need to get going. Everyone else is alarmingly slow, and I am running on fast time today.

'Go on then,' he says. 'Where do you need to go?'

'I don't know. I suppose I just follow the coast. Keep the sea to my right.'

'Can't go far wrong,' he says. 'Even you.'

'Even me.'

'We'll see you on your way.'

We dawdle along the sea-front, past a pub and a cafe and an ice-cream shop. Bert wants a lolly. H is looking for a public toilet. I am getting increasingly irritable. It feels like we could all just wander endlessly around the outskirts of Minehead, and I'll eventually have to accept that this was a stupid idea that was never going to happen. I've got nine miles to cover before the sun goes down, and I have no idea whether I can even walk nine miles anymore.

But then Bert gets distracted by a playground and I am suddenly ahead of them both, and I turn back to say, 'Bye! See you in Porlock Weir!' and I am off, alone, on the South West Coast Path, on my own two feet.

The South West Coast Path is a difficult, craggy and bloody-minded walking route that hugs the coastline between Minehead in Somerset and Poole Harbour in Dorset, taking in the seaboards of North and South Devon, and the entire perimeter of Cornwall along the way. I call it bloody-minded because it exhibits a wilful refusal to provide any kind of short cut, even where it's obvious that any sane person would take one. Walkers routinely find themselves climbing perilously down into a cove, only to make a steep ascent immediately afterwards, and often with a far more sensible, level path in full sight.

Such is the brutal glory of the SWCP. For its entire 630 miles, it clings as close to this island's crinkled edge as possible; so close, in fact, that chunks of it regularly fall into the sea. There are moments when it feels as though it was designed with mountain goats in mind, rather than humans.

Its original users – before the path had a name and a nifty set of acorn-embossed waymarkers – were coastguards, who created a series of routes that allowed them to check for smugglers in isolated coves. This perhaps justifies the exhausting pattern of rise and fall, but I detect something more in its design, too. There is a kind of landscape geekery embedded in the SWCP. Whenever I walk it, I get the sense that someone else understands my urge to know the full extent of my world; to trace its boundaries with my feet; to take the longest, hardest way round.

It may not be obvious from what I've said so far, but I adore the SWCP; I crave it, particularly the stretch between Bantham and Start Point in the South Hams of Devon. It has seen my best of times and worst of times; I have kicked back in Devon at the most triumphant moments of my life, and scuttled down there in terror when my life was in shreds. It always seems to replenish me.

I first discovered the SWCP on honeymoon, after secretly getting married in Maidstone Registry Office. Our plan was to run away to a West Country thatched cottage, and to send out a set of breezy postcards to proclaim our matrimonial status to our friends. This wasn't the only misjudged part of the plan. When we arrived, we were greeted by an elderly woman bent double over a walking stick, who told us that her previous guests were 'something of a mystery' as they had disappeared in the middle of one night, never to be seen again. The reason for this soon became clear. The bathroom smelled of stale urine, spiders abseiled from every surface, and, every time we turned off the lights, an unnerving scuffling would start up in earnest. We endured it for two sleepless nights before throwing ourselves on the mercies of the Kingsbridge Tourist Information Office.

The woman behind the counter tutted and said, 'These awful old cottages!' Then she picked up the phone and, after a short conversation with an unknown third party in which we were described, enticingly, as a 'lovely young couple', announced that we were extremely lucky to have found anywhere at this short notice, but that she thought we'd be happier there.

We drove over to Salcombe – a town we didn't know – in some trepidation, working over a plan to simply give up and go home if the B&B turned out to have nylon bedspreads and portraits of Jesus on the walls. What greeted us instead was a vision of perfection: a high Edwardian villa with pale walls, seagrass flooring, and a wonderful landlady who spent the rest of the week pointing us out to passers-by as we sat on our balcony, and squealing, 'These two have eloped! To my place! I've got two proper runaways!'

We didn't mind. We were too busy admiring the view over the estuary, where hundreds of white boats bobbed in the blue, with the fields of East Portlemouth in the distance. We bought our first Ordnance Survey map that week, and attempted our first proper walk (an abortive foray onto Dartmoor, where we promptly got lost in a sudden, dense, mid-July fog which we later learned was totally normal). We studied our map for beaches where I could swim, and inched the car down narrow lanes, high-sided with bracken, to pristine coves with wild seas.

One evening, at dusk, we found the clear sea at Thurlestone full of jellyfish, and perhaps it was then – I can't be sure – that we tried to get a better look at the famous rock archway, and ended up following the South West Coast Path to Hope Cove. On the way, we discovered red cliffs and watched swallows swooping over a river to drink. I couldn't believe my luck at finding such a path, so different from anything in our native Kent. I adored our shingle beaches and flat sands, of course, but here was something entirely different, where a little effort on foot would reward you with crenellated bays full of the sea-caves and rock pools we knew only from childhood picture books. We were enchanted.

That enchantment has never worn off. I am obsessed with South Devon; I crave it. And yet the last time I made it down there, I didn't walk the path at all. It seemed impossible with Bert around. I suppose other mothers would have fashioned some manner of papoose and carried their child with them along the clifftops; but then, I learned a long time ago that I don't seem to be like other mothers. It's not just the physical discomfort that bothers me (or the danger; I am not sure-footed). It's something far more unspeakable: I don't want to walk with a child on my back. I want to return to the days when I would wander with H for hours and return home with my skin radiating the sun's heat, feeling like we'd set the world to rights. Better still, I want to walk alone. I thought I wasn't entitled to do that anymore.

I don't know what changed, then, to get me here.

A few things shifted in my mind, I suppose. Something about being nearly thirty-eight and my brow-line suddenly sagging to meet my eyelids. Something about the stiffening of my limbs and the thickening of my middle. Something about the feeling that I am probably now halfway through my life; that time is running out; that it's now or never.

Other things, too. We went to Devon in July and visited Gara Rock, which sits above my favourite beach in the world. For the first time, we stayed in the cafe at the top instead of taking the steep path down to the cove itself. It was just easier to do that than to schlep all the way down there. I was ashamed of myself, but also exhausted, lazy, and more than a little reluctant to carry a toddler back up at the end of the afternoon. I was worried about the possibility of sunburn, about my inappropriate footwear.

Even so, sitting under glass eating scones and jam, I knew I'd lost ground. When I had Bert, I dreamed of giving him something different from this: long days camped out on the beach; sleeping in the car on the way home; growing up to crave the seaside like I do, but perhaps being robust enough to cope with the sand and the breaking of routines. I couldn't understand why I was unable to deliver this. Like so many things since he'd been born, there was an invisible barrier between what I intended to achieve, and what I was able to do in practice.

Nevertheless, we finished our cakes and our tea, and decided to go home. As we began to walk back to the car park, Bert turned to face the extraordinary view, narrowed his eyes, and started to sing:

All the clouds are in the sky,
And the wind, the wind, the wind
To blow us away!

I've told everyone I know about that moment and they all say, 'Yes, they do make up funny little songs at that age.' But to me, it was more than that. My little boy – all three and a quarter years of him – gazed out at the sea and reflected my own thoughts back at me. The clouds. The sky. The wind. The simple awe of those things. I didn't know he was capable of feeling such wonder.

And then, a week later, I got lost in the woods. I stopped off for a short stroll around the Blean on my way back from work, but found a group of Japanese schoolchildren about to set off on my usual circular path. They were chattering noisily, and a couple of them pulled faces at my car as I passed. People carry electricity for me; they have a current that surges around my body until I'm exhausted. It's hard to pinpoint what it is, exactly; something about their noise, their unruly movement, the unpredictable demands they might make on me. It makes the air feel thick, like humanity has . . . not a scent, but a texture. It makes me feel like I can't breathe. I had come to the woods to escape that, and yet here it was, following me. I considered turning back, unable to bear the thought of all that chaos happening within earshot as I tried to clear my head. But then I was struck with the genius idea of simply following the trail backwards, and so I set off in the opposite direction.

I am an idiot. I'm not sure how early on I took a wrong turning, but pretty soon I found myself at the beginning of what looked like a faerie path, covered in thick moss and cobwebs. Clearly no one else had visited that part of the woods for quite some time. The sensible thing would have been to retrace my steps at that point, but no. I thought I'd be clever, and rejoin my intended route just as soon as I'd explored this untouched part of the forest.

Three hours later, I emerged thirsty and dead-limbed, having ranged all over the ancient woodland, disturbed a man taking photos of his girlfriend's breasts (I didn't like to ask him for directions, given the circumstances), and wondered whether I'd have to dig for water. I'm not sure how I managed to convince myself that I had any sort of a sense of direction; this has never been the case. Google Maps wouldn't load. I spent some time trying to identify where the sun was in the sky in order to navigate, but the only answer available seemed to be 'up', so I just had to trust that I'd eventually reach civilisation if I walked in a consistent direction. I had to text a friend to ask him to pick up Bert from nursery, and it took at least twenty attempts and waving my phone in the air at the top of a hill before the message would even send.

The thing was, once Bert was accounted for, I felt fantastic. I was free to get confused and exhausted. It was funny. It was liberating. There was one point, deep into the woods, when I stopped to see if I had a phone signal and slowly became aware of a noise like the crackle of static. I put my phone back in my pocket and listened. All around me, the forest was alive, growing and shifting, and drawing up water from the soil, and putting on new growth, and letting go of its dead. It was so loud, so absolute. If I were ever to believe in a god, I would have found it right there. It was exquisite.

That was the moment I realised how much I'd lost of myself. No, that's wrong: I'd already realised that, over and over again. I'd fought it and suffered it and mourned it. This was new. This was the moment I realised that it was necessary to get myself back again. This was the moment I realised that, as the mother of a young child, the world was never going to give me permission to be on my own, but that I needed it anyway.

So I got home, endured a fair amount of ribbing for having no sense of direction, applied blister plasters to most areas of my feet, and quietly made plans to walk the entire South West Coast Path before I turned forty.

I told all my friends before I told H, because I was certain he would say it was impossible. But, in the event, he didn't. He said, 'Okay then,' and, 'Can I do some of it with you?' and we left it at that.

I didn't think to wonder why he gave in so easily; but then, it would be three months before I heard the voice on the radio that changed everything I knew about myself. All I knew was that something wasn't right. I thought, perhaps, that I could walk it off.

So: Minehead on August Bank Holiday Saturday. I am in Somerset rather than Devon, and the landscape I'm craving is at the opposite end of the path – about 450 miles away, by my reckoning. My planned schedule will get me there in eighteen long months' time. No matter. I am here, and I am breathing the air, and it smells of pine forest, chips with vinegar, and the brackish taint of the sea. I can see the Welsh coast, grey-blue across the water.

This is time on my own. This is an adventure. Maybe it will set me straight again.

2

....

Minehead to Foreland Point, August

Heading west out of Minehead, I quickly realise that my concerns about physical conditioning are entirely founded.

The first two miles take me uphill through woodland, jack-knifing on a steep path whose purpose is to rise as high and fast as is possible without a ladder. I'm not sure why I didn't detect this on my Ordnance Survey map; I'm certain I covered contour lines in year eight geography, just before I dropped it altogether. I drag myself up an endless steep incline, panting and stopping every time the path dog-legs, pretending to myself that my bootlaces need tightening, my hair needs tying back more firmly. I can't do this. I know I can't. I'm not fit enough. I just don't have it in me anymore.

H took me down paths like this in my second day of labour. The only book we'd got around to reading said it would help to visualise being somewhere else, somewhere familiar and wonderful. The pain rumbled into focus and, in desperation, he talked me along the route from Sharpitor to Bolt Head in South Devon, a narrow alley opening up into a wild headland, where I could remember the grass bristling with thrift, and the russet flash of a kestrel diving between the cliffs. It was an inspired piece of improvisation, just familiar enough to occupy all my senses during the ragged, other-worldly intervals that the contractions brought. *It's not like pain as you know it*, I remember telling him; *it's like a tidal wave, a spirit possession.*

As the next rolled in, he talked me along the path again, and this time I saw blackberries ripening on the brambles around me, and felt warm gusts of early September air. Every imagined journey along that path became more luminous. It was, at the same time, scathingly unpleasant and exhausting and vile, but it was improved by this conjuring of the coast path, and by the intimacy of having someone with you who knew that it would be just the right thing.

There is a moment today when I wonder whether visualising contractions would help propel me up this never-ending hill, but I'm pretty certain it won't work that way around. At least I'm choosing this agony, though; at least I'm in control.

After some time the path delivers me onto Exmoor, where everything is changed. I imagined that the transition into moorland would be gradual, but it's sudden, like passing through a doorway into another room. The ground bumps around my path, met by a deep duvet of grey cloud. Everything is covered in purple heather and yellow gorse, spiked with bracken. Brambles tangle at the margins, and the blackberries are at their autumn blackest. The air is alive with birds. I feel very far away from Minehead, and abundantly free. I am alone, and it is quiet and beautiful, but far from serene: the colours blare loudly, and the sky is all menace. I love it. It fills my head, and pushes out everything else.

Now I'm on the flat, I can pick up speed, and I begin to

stretch my legs to their full extent, letting the air rush across my bare arms. The sun was already past its peak when I left Minehead, and now it is low in the sky, but warm and clear. I walk and walk. There is no sense in feeling guilty at this abundant solitude, in turning back and heading home. I can only go forward. Forward is all I have. I barely see another soul, except for a man who tries to chat with me as I overtake. I don't slow down. I'm on a roll. I yomp past him, dipping down towards the sea at Hurlestone Point, a slope so steep and rocky that my thighs sing with pain. By the time I'm at the bottom, I'm exhausted. A switch has been flipped: my legs have realised how far they've travelled, and the soles of my feet feel bruised. I'm dreaming of a cup of tea now, a hot shower, and the chance to tell everyone that I've done it, all by myself.

Still two miles to go. I skirt the bay at Bossington, and then pass onto Porlock Marsh. It's six o'clock, and the low water is full of wild flowers, cragged by the skeletons of trees. I wish I could convey the scent, somehow: sharp and green, like a florist's early in the morning. There are people on the path now, walking dogs and strolling with children, and I'm suddenly an oddity, jelly-legged, the evidence of sweat in my hair. I have to nearly drag myself across the huge, shingle plates of Porlock beach, my feet raging at me. I'm tempted to unlace my boots right there and soak my aching soles in the cold, smooth water, but I know I will never be able to lace them back up again, and anyway, the end is in sight, my husband and son just a few strides away.

By the time I reach them in the garden of Miller's hotel, all I can talk about is the marsh, its smell, the yellow and purple on Exmoor, the sea, the clouds, the wind. I feel like the survivor of a Shakespearean shipwreck, stumbling ashore in a tangle of seaweed and telling of a magical island, where nature is uncanny in ways they can't understand. I am wild with wonder.

But then Bert unearths a broken spade from the sandpit, and soon I am my irritable self again. *Don't eat the sand! Don't throw things! Do you want a time out?*

Nine miles covered today. Twelve planned tomorrow. It can't come soon enough.

We go to bed early the night of my first walk, unsure of what else to do, given that we're sharing a hotel room with a three-year-old. I'm dog-tired anyway, and so secretly grateful to be allowed to pass out at half past nine. Two hours later, I wake from the first cycle of sleep to find my whole body on fire with pain: my feet, calves, knees, hips and thighs are jangling with the stress I've suddenly imposed on them. Even my arms and shoulders join in, indignant at hauling a backpack so far. I try to blanket them under sleep, but they refuse, pushing themselves to the front of my consciousness with burning insistence. Eventually, I get up and grope around for my handbag, where I find a blister pack of ibuprofen among the crumbs and hairpins.

This, at least, affords me some sleep. But when we are awoken the next morning by Bert thudding heavily out of bed, I am almost rigid, and can only watch H rush to gather him up and bundle him in between us. It takes me a long time to get up, to bend to put my clothes on, to ease myself down into the hard chair in the breakfast room.

'Do you think you'll be okay today?' says H.

'I'll manage,' I say, taking grim care to consume enough calories. 'I'm sure I'll loosen up when I get started.'

I have greater concerns than the rigidity of my legs: the weather is not looking good. Nevertheless, I lace on my boots, H drives me back to Porlock Weir, and we make arrangements to meet up for lunch at a walkers' car park on Exmoor, around midday.

I feel a little lonelier today. It's colder and greyer, and my feet are sore. H is playing Marlena Shaw in the car as he drops me off, and the outside air seems pale without her. Still, I'm surprised how well my muscles warm up for the trudge uphill to Culbone, past a gated toll road that's still in operation and a tiny, remote church. I cross into woodland, where a sign reminds me of the dangers of Lyme disease, and I make a mental note of how to remove a tick, should I have the misfortune to acquire one.

It's all going rather well; there's plenty more of that grand Exmoor scenery, with squat, hairy ponies whose coats seem to mimic the wiry grass. I even have no problem identifying the short path up to the main road where H will be waiting for me. My map-reading is, by my own reckoning, pretty impressive. In fact, I'm worried I will be early.

But then, the short path on the map reveals itself to be a steep, zig-zagging track in real life, which takes me the best part of an hour to climb. Ten minutes in, it begins to rain, harder and harder until I have to stop to put on my cagoule. I start to climb again, leaning into the slope, panting hard. A river has gathered itself, and it's rushing down the path in slippery ribbons. It's gruelling. Rain and sweat are dripping off my face. I just don't have enough breath for this, enough energy in my thighs. I become aware that I am muttering to myself, whispering curses as I climb. The rain splutters off my lips.

Perhaps I'm hungry, I think, and haul a cereal bar out of my backpack, choking it down as I continue up the path. It's too late, though. My brain is already a dark, rattling space, empty of any perspective but full of futile anger at inanimate things: maps, stones, mud, rain. I am angry at the incline, and I am angry at remoteness. I am angry that I am here. I am angry that this is my choice. The only way I can manage to continue is to count my steps in groups of one hundred, and then of fifty, and then, ultimately, of ten. I start to lose the numbers after ten anyhow.

When I see our car waiting at the top of the track, I try to pick up speed, but I only seem to move slower. I feel like a zombie in a cheap horror film, lurching, incoherent, and laughably feeble. I slump into the car and groan like the undead. Bert is asleep in the back. The windows are steamed up.

'Not great?' says H.

'Fucking awful,' I say.

We find a pub for lunch, but I've got no appetite. I'm just cold and tired. It's still pouring down outside. We pay up and get back in the car. Bert is now petitioning – unfathomably – for crazy golf. H drives me back to the car park where he picked me up, and says, 'Chin up. Just keep the sea to your right and you can't go wrong.'

It takes me a dispiriting half-hour to walk back onto the coast path, despite it being downhill. My map marks a direct track down a slope, but in practice this turns out to be a near-vertical muddy bank, covered in brambles and nettles. I scramble back up the few metres I've travelled, and strike off for the longer, slower path I'd sought to avoid.

I need a break nearly as soon as I've found the actual SWCP again. I shouldn't have diverted off the route for lunch. I should have brought sandwiches with me, and not got distracted by the promise of a warm, dry pub with my family to talk to. It was a weak instinct; I can see that now. The path has become wooded and narrow, barely the width of my tread, and it is cut into a steep embankment that drops two hundred metres into the sea. Several times, my feet slip, and I imagine how I'd knock into each tree like a pinball on my way down.

I cross over a gushing stream, swollen by the rain, and then sit on a wet log and drink all the tea in my flask. As an afterthought, I decide to indulge in my favourite woodland pastime of taking a 'nature wee' (Bert's term), making my own little stream down the drenched slope. Then, I stand up and immediately slip over in it. I stay on the ground for a few moments, examining the grazed palms of my hands, but nothing is really amiss. The only thing dislodged is my dignity, and there's no one here to see. Back on my feet. Forward. Onward.

I begin to tread gingerly over the sodden path. I've already proven myself unsteady; now I begin to feel genuinely at risk. I cross over five more streams, and a ritual seems to introduce itself, whereby I have to dip my hand into each one and anoint my forehead with the water. I must pay my homage to the rivers for my safe passage. I feel like this is all I have.

The backs of my knees begin to ache with the stress of bracing myself to stay on the track. Checking my map, I find that I've reached Desolation Point, close to a hamlet that is simply called Desolate. I allow myself a grim laugh, and text H to tell him to meet me at Countisbury instead of Lynmouth; it's a couple of miles closer, maybe less than that. I can catch up tomorrow. I'm at the bottom of my resources.

H doesn't reply to my text. After half an hour, I call him and leave a voicemail. By then, I have reached the start of Foreland Point, a crag of bracken that juts out into Lynmouth Bay. I walk on down a steep tarmac road, hoping he will get back to me. He doesn't. When I reach the end of the headland only to realise I have missed my path by half a mile, I lose my temper entirely and fire off a text that I can only be grateful my phone fails to send. I gaze at the white lighthouse for a few moments, and then turn back and start to climb the hill again. It's getting dark, and I had arranged to be in Lynmouth by now. It is only once I have climbed the best part of a hundred and twenty metres onto the top of the headland that my phone rings, and I get a panicked H on the end of the line.

'You are not my favourite person,' I say.

He's been trying to get a signal for hours. I attempt to explain where I am over a crackly line, and then walk back up to the road, where I sit on my backpack and wait. It is only then that I check my map and realise that I had been ten minutes from Countisbury, and also that I have probably added an extra two miles to my route through wrong turns and that stupid deviation for lunch.

I expect to be angry with H when he arrives, but even as I hear the diesel chug of our Skoda rounding the bend at the top of the hill, I know that I'm nothing but grateful. I have a support team, albeit one with intermittent mobile reception.

'You did the right thing,' he says as I get into the car. 'It's dangerous out there.' I look up and see that we're encased in thick fog, so dense that I can't make out the sides of the road. I'm not sure when that arrived, or whether I had been walking in it. And, despite being a couple of miles short of my target, I'm almost high with relief.

'You've covered twenty miles over the last two days,' says H. 'People do a couple more than that and call it a marathon.'

'They're running,' I say.

'Some of them are walking.'

'And they do it in a day.'

'That's not the point.'

'God, I'm unfit. I'm ashamed of how unfit I am.'

'You know the only way to get fitter?' says H. 'Doing the kind of walk you just did. It won't be so hard next time.'

Easy for him to say. I hunch down into the car seat and pull my cagoule hood around my face.

3

Foreland Point to Ilfracombe, September

On my thirty-eighth birthday, I refuse to take part in any celebrations until I have completed my grudge match with Foreland Point.

We set off early, leaving Bert with friends who will join us later. Late morning we drive past Minehead, where last month's walk started, and soon we are crossing the distinctive Exmoor landscape of yellow gorse and purple heather. H suggests that we park in Countisbury, the other side of the headland that proved my nemesis last time.

'No,' I say, 'I'm going to start where I gave up.'

'But you walked the extra miles when you got lost. There's no need.'

'I don't care.'

'Well, we can't park there. We'll have to walk a mile just to get to the right place on the path.'

'I'm not going to start skipping bits for the sake of fifteen minutes' walking.'

I would never have guessed that walking together would be one of the losses I'd tot up when Bert arrived, but it's actually one of the most profound. We started walking when I was at university, and needed to fill dull Sundays when all the shops were closed; we bought a book of pub walks and truly believed we'd earned a few pints after a three-mile circular stroll. H is not a natural walker. His size-thirteen feet are – in the words of the orthopaedic surgeon he saw after breaking a metatarsal – 'constructed like flippers' and 'just within the range of normal'. Apart from providing hilarious phrases with which to periodically taunt him, this means in practice that he gets awful blisters every time we walk. This is not – and it has taken me a very long time to accept this – his fault.

We park up, and he fusses with two pairs of socks and various tensions of lacing. I know he'll stop in a few metres anyway to start the process all over again. Still, the sea is pale blue and spotted with the shadows of clouds, and the bracken is already turning the hills rusty.

First of all we zig-zag down the road to the coast path (H stops twice), and then climb up onto the headland. I can't remember how far I got before I turned round and gave up last time, but I can now see that I'd done the worst of it. I wish I'd had the faith to push on, rather than doubting that I could manage that last piece of effort. I could have at least reached Countisbury, and that would have felt like a proper destination, instead of a roadside.

Up on the high moor, we pass a herd of grazing Exmoor ponies, and repeatedly have to stop to avoid treading on the shiny black beetles that seem to congregate along the path. The air is full of birds that I wish I could identify. It takes an hour and a half of moderate walking to reach Lynmouth – nothing, really. Some of it is even a little dull, hugging roadsides and skirting playing fields. When we arrive, we sit in the garden of the Rock House Hotel and I toast my birthday with a pint of Tribute and a bag of crisps. Soon, Bert is running over the West Lyn footbridge to greet me, shouting, 'Mummymummymummy!' and everything is set straight again.

In the days – and then weeks – following my first walk, I was troubled by the thought that I didn't cope.

I don't mean in terms of fitness; I expected that. I never took so much as a vitamin before I had Bert, but pregnancy broke me. I developed high blood pressure that caused pointless stays in hospital, and had asthma for the first time in my life. I endured horrific nosebleeds and nausea that remained stubbornly in place into the third trimester. There was a week, between Christmas and New Year, when I felt fantastic and rearranged all the kitchen cupboards for three days in a row. But then I woke up the next morning with chest pains and it all started again.

I still find myself returning to my GP every four months to check my raging blood pressure. My stomach valve, apparently, is stretched out of shape; the constant acid reflux has made my voice crackle. I swallow a little pile of pills every morning to deal with both problems. I'm aggrieved at these incursions into my otherwise robust health, but I also realise that I would be a fool to ignore them. That doesn't stop me resenting the daily parade of tablets; I feel more aged by the box of blister packs by the toaster than I ever have by the lines around my eyes or the gentle sagging of my jaw.

My right hip is wrong now, too. I dislocated it while I was giving birth – not that I noticed at the time, given my comprehensive approach to self-administering an epidural. I wasn't taking any chances. However, the first time I tried to walk, I felt a distinct looseness in the joint, which only got worse over the weeks that followed, well into the time when people were telling me that a walk would do me good. *Take baby out in the pushchair, get a bit of fresh air. Meet people. You'll feel better.* It's not such a great prospect when you feel like a rickety chair, and when contact with people makes you physically, tearfully nauseated.

'It happens, I'm afraid,' said my doctor, and referred me to a physiotherapist who lectured me on how he gets out on his bike three times a week, even if it's 11 p.m., and despite having three kids. Bully for him. I asked him how many books he'd written and he looked at me blankly. He already thought I was stupid at that point, anyway, because I could somehow never recall the exercises he gave me, even a few minutes after he'd shown me them.

'I don't remember that at all,' I would say, in a kind of wonder at the memory-blank I found for the preceding few moments of my life.

'But I took you through it,' he would say, in a different kind of wonder – the dark kind that teachers feel towards students who simply will not learn. 'You did it with your own body.'

My own body. That was some kind of a joke, surely? My own body that had been poked by unwanted hands for eight months, confined in hospital under guilt-inducing threats that they *could not be held responsible*, strapped to machines that whirred and ticked and chattered.

My own body that could be stopped in Marks and Spencer so that a woman could gaze into my pram and say she hoped I was breastfeeding; that could be scolded for holding my baby for too long, or for not enough time; that really ought to be sleeping alongside my child in the same bed – or in a Moses basket, depending on who was insisting at the time – rather than separately, quietly, in a different room.

My own body, that should be carrying my boy rather than pushing him in that pram, because the woman in the grocer's did when hers were small, and it was good for her back, and the prams take up such a terrible amount of space in the shop.

My own body, that didn't even smell right anymore, and which had this terrible new landscape of sags and puckers below the neckline, and which didn't quite seem to be able to behave in a way that would attract approval.

This man, who had three children of his own, and so *knew what it was like*, would have to excuse me if I had entirely taken leave of my own body by that point, and all the things it could and could not do, because otherwise I would lose the last shreds of my sanity.

My lack of fitness, then, was no surprise. It was deliberate, planned, protective. I'm not even ashamed. In the end, it was easier to let go of fitness than to hand over my body, and my stuttering, inadequate brain, to somebody else's judgemental hands. I had to haul in my sails, or be wrecked on the rocks. Every other person we know is a triathlete these days; it seemed easier to be nothing at all, rather than to tread the awkward, halfway path of compromise.

But the truth is, I coped, physically, with the walking. It surprised me that I made it at all. I found it difficult, and I was exhausted afterwards, but my knees didn't fall from under me, and I made it up steep ascents and over long distances. No. What troubles me is the way that my mind seemed to unravel under duress; the way that I muttered dark things as I dragged myself up Glenthorne in the rain to meet H; the way that I lost myself in obsessive rituals at Desolation Point, anointing my head with the water of every stream I crossed, asking their nymphs for safe passage. I was hungry, yes. I didn't eat enough. I let my glucose levels fall too low, and then refused to replenish them properly, even after I realised. But then, this became an obsession in itself, keeping myself clean and light as I walked. The hunger wasn't a simple error; it was just another arrow pointing to my defective mind.

I haven't coped with an awful lot of things in the last few years. I didn't cope with being at home, alone, with a baby. I didn't cope with the lack of a job to do, with the absence of a structure to propel me forward. I didn't cope with the other mothers, their obsessive talk of milk and sleep, their earnest discussions of progress, development. The very word 'mother' was enough to make my head spiral: mother, mummy, mum. I wondered vaguely, for a while, if I didn't have some kind of gender disorientation which left me unable to relate these maternal labels to myself. I didn't cope with hospitals and Sure Start centres, with the midwife who handled my breast in the maternity ward, seizing it unexpectedly to squeeze out the pathetic few beads of milk it could manage. All that awful *contact*; all that awful *care*. The world was thick with it.

I didn't cope before that, either. I didn't cope in the early months of pregnancy when I took myself up to London one afternoon, to the Tate gallery. Back to reassuring old territory, to tell myself I wasn't lost. I'm still not sure how I ended up howling in the basement toilets, having to be talked out of there by a kind cleaner who sat me in the canteen and found me a plastic cup of water to drink. So much grief, all of a sudden; so much terror. Perhaps I didn't cope before then. Perhaps this not coping could be connected to other moments, the-same-only-different, stretching back across my whole life.

But no. I was a coper before this. Capable: that was the word most often used to describe me. I always loved the word, like a superhero cape, encasing the world around me in a protective shell. The etymology of cope, too: to strike a blow with one's fist. That's me: a knockabout, bringing everything under my vigorous control. Not this. Not this. Not this sense of overwhelm, all the time.

Overwhelm: to turn upside down, bring to ruins, engulf, submerge, inundate.

Nothing says 'not quite where I hoped to be by now' like a night in a tent on your thirty-eighth birthday. In all fairness, it's glamping rather than camping – in a permanent safari tent with a kitchen and a bed and an electric heater – but I'd be lying if I implied it wasn't the result of a financial compromise.

We drive into the Sandaway Holiday Park past ranks of caravans and a swimming pool with ducks in it, and then turn the corner to encounter the most arresting view of my journey so far. The tent is perched on the edge of a field that overlooks a stunning rocky cove that is not even on the South West Coast Path. This lends it something of an air of exclusivity in my book. After putting Bert to bed, we sit on the deck and drink gin and tonics (in real glasses and with ice from the camp store), and I think I might enjoy this after all.

Fast forward a few hours, and I am already sick of tramping back and forth to the toilet block every time nature calls; and a few hours more, when Bert has insisted on sharing a single bed with me rather than sleeping on his camp-mat on the floor; and a few hours after that, when I foolishly attempt a shower that involves holding in a push-button to maintain water flow while washing one-handed, all the time keeping an eye on the spider crouched in the corner (seriously: wouldn't it be a good idea to brief cleaning staff to remove anything with more than two legs as, you know, *part of the cleaning process*?). None of these things filled me with a love of canvas. But, just for an hour, I got the notion that I could make my peace with sleeping in the Great Outdoors.

The next morning, H drives me and my friend Beccy to Lynmouth so that we can walk the fourteen miles back to camp. Beccy is the most ruggedly outdoorsy person I know, and I am slightly fearful that I am going to embarrass myself – somehow, not sure on the exact manifestation – today. When we arrive at the coast path, however, it is *she* who suggests we take the funicular railway up the first bit, to avoid the climb. I decline, smugly claiming that it would set a bad precedent, at this stage in the game, to start skipping the tough bits.

After fifteen minutes of agonising, heart-pumping walking up a never-ending series of slopes and steps, I come to regret my smuggery. Soon, though, we are walking along the Valley of Rocks (which I insist on calling the Valley of the Shadow of Death, repeatedly, and to no one's amusement), and the whole thing becomes very pleasant. The sun is out, there's a slight September chill in the air, and we're following a level path through craggy Exmoor scenery. By lunchtime, we have solved all the world's problems, and are rather pleased with our progress, so we divert to the Hunter's Inn at Trentishoe for lunch.

I open out the Ordnance Survey map, wondering what time we're likely to reach Combe Martin. Beccy points out that I should calculate my walking time at twenty minutes per mile, plus five minutes per contour line I cross, whether up or down. I didn't realise that it was legitimate to budget extra time for hills; I thought you were supposed to just go up a gear and tough it out. Armed with this expertise, I run my finger along the path, and declare that it's all pretty much flat from here on in, with maybe a little slopey bit towards the end. We should be home in a couple of hours.

Well. It appears that the formula only works if you actually pay attention to what's on the map. After an hour's walking, we come to Holdstone Down, a boggy patch of scrubland that dips alarmingly down towards sea level. 'That can't be the path,' says Beccy, and we stare at the map until we have to admit that it is, indeed, the only way onwards. The ensuing descent is slow, slippery and surprisingly hard on the knees. It's deeply unsatisfying: we feel no sense of achievement at the bottom (after all, gravity would have done a better job than our legs managed) and our only reward is a steep climb afterwards.

We therefore undertake the climb up Girt Down in entirely bad humour, hauling ourselves onwards with the help of affirmations such as, 'Fuck off, you bastard, wanking fucking hill.' I have to stop halfway up because I'm beginning to see spots before my eyes; and then stop again three-quarters of the way up because I can't breathe. When we reach the top, we realise it's just a plateau before another hill begins, and at this point I insist on lying down on the grass for a while, and am hostile to the idea of ever getting up again.

'Don't worry,' says Beccy, 'this is all building up your fitness,' and I tell her to fuck off. At the top of this mound is a Great Hangman Cairn, a pile of stones that perfectly expresses my desire for the sweet release of death. Some wag has poked their walking stick into the top of it, but I doubt very much that this ascent cured anyone of anything.

We add our respective stones to the pile, and then look up to see an old biplane flying overhead. The pilot dips his wing to us and waves from the cockpit, and that suddenly makes me aware of how high we are: the extraordinary view all around, the sea to our right and the moor rising and falling below us, miles into the distance. It's a magical, exhausting privilege to have laboured all the way up here, even if it does seem to have broken me entirely.

We begin the slow descent into Combe Martin, our tired legs making the last mile stretch for hours. It is only later that I realise that this was the highest point of the entire path, and I have conquered it already.

The next morning, I'm about to wash down my customary handful of pills to complete my breakfast, when I realise that I've screwed up. Instead of two types of blood-pressure tablet and one antacid, I've just packed three packets of blood-pressure pills. This is stupid, and even more stupidly, I didn't even notice yesterday. It is almost certainly why I have stomach ache and am burping at comical intervals.

In any case, it's not like I can do much about my antacids as I'm a five-hour drive away. I make a mental note to perhaps seek out some Gaviscon in Ilfracombe and we set off. Beccy, thankfully, is amused by my constant belching. I congratulate myself for having the sort of friends who stick with you through digestive distress.

The sky is blue and the sun is low over the sea. It is clear that we finally left behind Exmoor just west of Combe Martin, and that the coast is in the process of remodelling itself into something new. We walk down a narrow alley, and then along a main road. We get stung by high nettles on narrow paths and slip on mud. There are beautiful views in places – the natural harbour at Small Mouth, complete with a lone, white boat, makes us stand and stare – but somehow this is a frustrating walk; not steep or difficult, just uncomfortable and too close to civilisation.

By the time we round the corner to Hele Bay, I'm tired and irritable. Beccy (who is far fitter than me) wants to push on through to Ilfracombe, but I'm bilious and sore-throated, and pathetically hungry. We stop for a cream tea and sit for a while, watching a group of young women walkers who are perching on the wall with ice lollies. Perhaps walking is all the rage these days; they certainly look more glamorous than us, with their pristine walking gear, patterned head-wraps and a pair of poles apiece. 'Even we weren't lame enough to go on walking holidays when we were that age,' says Beccy, and we allow ourselves a fleeting moment of self-delusion that we were once at all cool.

When we set off again, I do not feel refreshed. I'm dog-tired, and the scone has done terrible things to my digestion. I feel as though it's trying to crawl back out of my gullet. My sense of grievance is not helped by the hulking great hill we have to climb, when there is clearly a road that just cuts around it. I am heartily sick of this sort of self-flagellating zig-zagging. We haul ourselves upwards for a seeming age, and then trot down the other side into Ilfracombe.

Our respective husbands and children are in town today, although I don't know where they are. We plod through the streets, and I wonder if we will spot them. We have planned to press on to Lee or even Woolacombe; that would get me to the ten-mile mark that would mean twenty-five miles' progress this weekend (I'm refusing to count the second attempt at reaching Lynmouth). But my legs are heavy, and my chest is burning from the indigestion. Somewhere nearby, my little boy is playing, and I suddenly want to be part of it. We pass Damien Hirst's flayed, pregnant *Verity*, a vulgar statue in supposed tribute to motherhood that looms above the harbour, and it makes me crave the softness and chaos of actual mothering even more.

'I think I'm going to give up,' I say. 'We can carry on, but it won't be pleasant.'

'Are you sure?' says Beccy.

'Yeah,' I say, and, to demonstrate my exhaustion, I immediately stumble out in front of a car and nearly get myself run over. I text H, and he directs me to Ilfracombe Tunnels Beaches, where we find the children playing with fishing rods made of pampas grass. We follow the Victorian tunnel down to the lovely, secluded sea-bathing pool, and I take off my boots and soak my aching feet.

'I need to work out how to stop getting so tired,' I say. 'This is the second time I've run out of energy.'

'It's just fitness,' says Beccy. 'You'll get there.'

Probably; but I have no idea how. Maybe that isn't the point. Maybe, like the triathletes and midnight cyclists, the aim of this is to bring about tiny, manageable moments of crisis in our lives, so that we're ready when the inundations come again.

4

Ilfracombe to Barnstaple, October

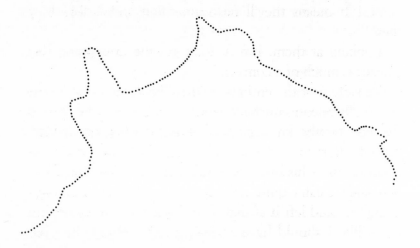

Emma is gripping my hand so tightly that I can feel the bones shifting in my knuckles.

'It's glaring at me!' she says.

'No it isn't.'

'It's going to run at me! I can tell! It's going to run at me!'

I have known Emma for fifteen years, and so I'm allowing her a special dispensation for physical contact in this specific moment of need. I had absolutely no idea she had a cow phobia. Now is a bad time to find out. We have rounded a corner to discover a scattering of peaceful cattle dawdling across the path, seemingly oblivious to our presence.

'Okay,' I say, 'we're going to walk past them.' The pressure on my hand increases. 'It's perfectly all right. There are no calves and no bulls. Just nice lady cows having their lunch.'

At that moment, one of the cows mounts another, and they begin humping enthusiastically. I reflect that perhaps my cow-sexing skills are not what they could be.

'Oh God,' says Emma. 'Now they're shagging!'

'That's a good thing, isn't it?' I say. 'It surely means they're distracted . . .'

'No! It means they'll be furious that we're disturbing them!'

'Looking at them, Em, I don't get the impression that privacy is much of a concern.'

We sidle past the entirely uninterested cows, and Emma eventually releases my hand when we reach the gate. This is the woman who knew me well enough to ring up and say, 'I'll take Bert for a day a week,' when I was in the depths of misery after his birth. She didn't ask first; she just knew. She said, 'I can't quite tell what's wrong, but something's going on,' and left it at that. I realise it's not the same, but I feel like I should have known, in turn, about the cows thing.

'Is it all barnyard animals,' I say, 'or just the cows?'

'Just the cows,' she says. 'Well, chickens are obviously wrong. And I wouldn't want to be in a field with a horse.'

'You have an actual farm phobia. This is incredible!'

'No,' says Emma. 'I have no problem with sheep.'

'Not even menacing sheep?'

'Nope. I reckon I could jump them if they ran at me.'

'Depends on the size of the sheep, surely?'

'I'd just vary my jump. I could hurdle the small ones and leapfrog the big ones.'

I can't tell you how much I needed this walk. I am properly back at work for the first time in about ten years, after a lot of time spent being freelance, contract, self-employed or whatever else you might call my patchwork of a career. I have an office, a salary, a tax code and a set of performance objectives. I am delighted to have it, and I'm exhausted by the sheer number of thoughts in my head. I've been craving the feeling of my feet on the path, and the opening up of a great expanse of water at my right-hand side.

This weekend, I have left Bert at home with H. Time is tight, and the drive is a big ask for a three-year-old. I want to get some miles under my belt without worrying about meeting his needs. This, of course, makes me feel just as bleakly guilty as every other thing I do, but I suppose I've just learned to see that as a background to all things. Go to work: grinding guilt at my absence. Stay at home: grinding guilt at my own impatience. I may as well enjoy myself while I'm feeling guilty.

We take a steep climb out of Ilfracombe, accidentally mixing in with what looks like the walking wing of a local separatist sect, if the preponderance of chinstrap beards is anything to go by. The men march in front, yelling, 'Short, fast steps!' at the women who puff on behind.

'Oh for fuck's sake,' I whisper to Emma. 'Why ruin a place of outstanding beauty by shouting?'

'He's right, though,' she says. 'That's just how you're supposed to do hills.'

It pains me to admit that my hill-climbing was vastly improved by the shouty cult-leader. Soon, I am mincing up every slope in tiny, energy-efficient steps that make me wonder whether last month's battle with Girt Down was a simple matter of poor technique.

We make excellent progress. It is yet again clear that I have a total inability to spot contour lines on a map, but I have come to expect this by now, and I am beginning to feel that it's better for the steep bits to come as a nice surprise, rather than to dread them. Eventually, we reach Morte

Point, where we fall in step with a man and woman who seem to know this part of the path.

'Have you come to see the seals?' he says.

I had no idea there were seals. 'Yes,' I say, 'if we can.'

'I'll show you the right place when we get there.'

True to his word, he calls over to us when we're nearly at the tip of the peninsula, and has us squinting down at the rocks below. 'There,' he says, pointing at a rock. I can see nothing. Emma attaches the zoom lens of her camera, and uses it to scan the shoreline. We climb down the slope a little, and then . . .

Three seals. One enormous black bull, and two slighter ones with golden, spotted pelts. They dive and roll in the shallows, pull themselves onto rocks to sunbathe, and, at one point, appear to kiss. We aren't speechless exactly, but our vocabulary is so dredged by fascination that we have only a few words left: *look, wow, look, oh.* We scrabble around for a shared language of wonder, of awe, of contact with the wild, and then the magic ebbs away, and it's time to move on.

The ground turns sandy at Woolacombe, and the path becomes flatter. We break for the evening at Croyde, and take an eye-wateringly expensive taxi back to our apartment for a takeaway curry and a hot bath each. Tomorrow's walk is another thirteen miles on the flat, following the estuary up to Barnstaple.

'Early start,' I suggest, 'and if we push on, we'll be done by lunchtime.'

I was desperate to get back to work. After I had Bert, I couldn't find my way back in. It wasn't because I didn't want to leave him. Quite the opposite: I needed to get away. It's a terrible thing to say, I know. I am supposed to have wanted to cling to my beautiful baby for as long as was humanly possible. I am supposed to have begged my husband for a few more precious months at home. I didn't. I wanted to get my own brain back, urgently. It's very hard to make people believe that you can feel this way, and still be utterly in love with your child.

I just couldn't process that level of disorder; that's the only way I can describe it. I couldn't process the unpredictability of when a baby cries, and why; the sound of it, the way it would burn through me. I couldn't handle the endless, fiddly routines, the hours spent staring into space while I let him do his thing. The impossibility of reading. The lack of any time to think about things I wanted to think about, to write those things down, to make words. It looks so innocuous laid out like that, but living through it made my heart pound until I felt sick, and many things worse than that, which I try not to remember. Going back to my old habit of banging my head against the wall until my vision went white. Dragging the sharp edge of the tweezers down the inside of my arm until they drew blood. Thinking, endlessly, of how much easier it would be to die than to go on living. Not wanting to die in any active, violent sense; just wanting to disappear, to be obliterated by forces beyond my control. I thought I'd conquered that after the last time my brain dissolved.

Except this time it was different, because I had a tiny person nailing me into the present like a tent peg. Nothing in the world could induce me to hurt him, so I knew I had to stay. I got scolded enough times for saying I was the miserable (read: ungrateful) mother of a young child, as if I wasn't willing to sacrifice enough. Believe me: I sacrificed every last particle of my wits, just so that he would never feel the effects.

There was a period of time – too long for comfort – when I was picking up a scrappy array of freelance work that didn't nearly cover the cost of the childcare that made it possible, but now that is over and I have an actual job. I'm terrified of screwing it up. I have already apologised a few times for my face-blindness and my inability to sit still in meetings. I am making an effort to rein in my entirely inappropriate sense of humour. I am trying hard to stop people from thinking I'm weird this time. I'm not sure I'm always holding it in.

Before I set off for this month's walk, I had to attend a training course on working with dementia sufferers. I'd been dreading it. We were told that it would entail group work and role play, and what with my horror of other people, I thought it might represent a little more interaction than I could manage. The notion of inviting all that terrible contact – that intimacy, that sticky exchange of feelings – left me light-headed. I ought to want this; I ought to want to do the right thing. But it always seems more than I can bear.

The workshop, inevitably, turns out to be nicer than I expected. Everything always does. We spend a luxurious morning wallowing in the pleasant aspects of our childhood – sketching out the shapes of our houses, and sharing the rituals of our family Sunday lunches. The loneliness and alienation that sprawl over most of my early memories don't come into it, not because they're forbidden, but because we focus on the simple, small artefacts of our days: the songs our parents played, and the clothes we wore. I am old enough, it seems, to feel nostalgic about these details.

After lunch, we are invited to take part in a show-and-tell about weddings. We have all been asked to bring something in. Someone shows an Order of Service – 'My Song Is Love Unknown' and Corinthians 13. Another brings a garter of nylon lace, and we all laugh at the quaint frippery, its intimacy eroded by time. I take my wedding dress out of its box rather shyly; I can see, suddenly, that it's different from the rest of the exhibits. An ivory shift with a layer of pewter silk underneath, bought in the Bluewater mall when I was twenty-one. I have kept the receipt: £120. A lot of money, but not enough for a wedding dress. The lace feels dry and brittle, even after this short time. Another ten years and it will surely disintegrate.

'I've brought my wedding dress,' I say, 'because I'm really not sentimental enough to have kept anything else.' I know, suddenly, that it's too much. More people are seeing it today than on its first outing.

'Here,' I say, and I pass it around the circle, watching men and women weigh it awkwardly in their hands.

It's lovely.

Beautiful.

It hasn't dated.

I'm grateful to put it back into its box. That's where it belongs. I had meant, I suppose, to impress them, but I can now see that I have overrun my boundaries by bringing something of real significance. I suspect they feel sorry for me instead. There was some fine-grained implication in the instructions to keep it light, and I missed it. I know it must have been there because everyone else picked up.

We move on to re-enacting a wedding. We are allocated roles: vicar, organist, bride, mother-in-law. I am cast as the groom. I put on my long jacket, and try to look nervous. I hate role play; I hate weddings. We are, in any case, raucous by this point, high on the last remnants of our lunch and too much coffee, unwilling to play this one straight. The wedding we stage is straight out of *EastEnders*; the bride is a bit of a bruiser and someone randomly reallocates herself as a wronged ex-girlfriend who beats the groom with her handbag. I play-act hiding in the corner, grateful that I don't have to engage in anything emotionally meaningful.

'Can we at least manage to pose for a photo properly?' says the facilitator. The group crams themselves together; I try to lurk at the side. 'The groom should be in the middle,' she says, 'holding hands with the bride.'

The bride grins; she's still in character. 'Come on then,' she says, and reaches out her hand. I offer her a gentlemanly elbow, but it isn't enough. She wheedles her fingers along my arm and grips my palm. I try not to tense. Nobody else is bothered by this sort of thing. I attempt to relax, and smile, and enjoy the moment. But the electricity has started. It tingles at first, and then it throbs, and then it jolts to the extent that I feel as though my arm will shoot outwards and we will be thrown apart.

'I'm sorry,' I say. 'I hate holding hands,' and I release myself, rubbing my palm against my hip to let the electricity find its earth. 'With anyone, not you personally.'

What do you say at this point? *It's not you, it's me. One day, you'll find someone worthy of you.* 'I'm just . . . weird like that,' I say. 'I kind of have hot hands.'

You can't do that sort of thing without everyone noticing and wondering what on earth is going on. I get flustered and have to leave the room too quickly, and, hours later, I realise that I left my wedding dress there, in its silver box. But by then, I am already on the road to Devon, and when I get back on Monday, it has disappeared for good.

The next morning, we take a taxi back to Croyde. There are a few disorienting minutes in sepia dawn light, when Emma refuses to back down from her assertion that we're supposed to scramble over a dune system to truly stay on the South West Coast Path. She changes her mind when it becomes clear we're essentially walking on the spot in the thin, dry sand. After that, we positively march along Croyde Sands, and then stride along a particularly boring concrete track that takes us to the mouth of the estuary. We are not here for the scenery, and that's a good thing, as there's little to see. No, we're pitching for speed today, having promised ourselves a roast dinner in Barnstaple before we tackle the drive home.

Don't mess with two women who have realised that they can get home in time to see their children if only they walk fast enough. As the Taw estuary begins to open up, we pause to admire the way the path splits the marsh from the river, but by now Emma has started analysing our speed using an app on her phone, and we become fairly obsessed with doing ten-minute kilometres. This is partly because the ground is flat, and so the only challenge is pace; but it's also because the riverbank scenery is dull compared to the soaring cliffs and white beaches we've grown accustomed to. There is grey marsh grass and mud; there is the odd dilapidated boat to admire. But whereas we couldn't walk ten paces yesterday without Emma stopping to take a picture, we now barely break step when we see a heron. It's good, but just not worth the time penalty. Perhaps we don't have enough awe left today.

When we reach the thirteen-mile mark, we are still far from Barnstaple (my map-reading, again), but we no longer care. We are hungry, our knees are hurting, I am whining, Emma is urging me on (and pointing out that my best chance of roast beef and Yorkshire pudding is in the actual town, rather than by a river); we hear the shrill whistle of curlews at the water's edge and don't even pause to look at them.

We stagger into Barnstaple just after one o'clock, realise that we've walked sixteen miles in four and a half hours, slump into the car without thinking of lunch, and begin to drive home. A weekend in the wild is one thing, but catching bedtime is an entirely different kind of wonder.

As we roll along the M4, Emma says, 'I have to admit, I thought you were completely mad when you told me you were going to do this. But I can see what you mean now. I think I might start doing it myself.'

She thinks for a few moments. 'I might take a bit longer than you, though.'

Barnstaple to Appledore, November

I have been asked two questions over and over again since I started to walk the South West Coast Path.

The first is some variation of 'Are you safe?' This rarely refers to the walking conditions on the path, which is lucky because, given my extreme clumsiness and enhanced ability to fall over, I am probably not entirely safe, but it's best not to dwell on that. Instead, it's pitched at me being a woman, alone, in a remote spot. I tend to brush it aside, and not always in good humour. It's a way of saying 'Don't get raped' in the same, gentle tone as you might say 'Don't catch a cold' when someone goes out in the rain.

Except that we've stopped saying 'Don't catch a cold,' because we've realised that the connection between wet feet and a respiratory virus is, at best, a spurious correlation based on the time of year that they're both most likely to appear. However, we still cling to the quaint notion that sexual violence is somehow brought about by women being in remote places. Those who adhere to this view may wish to note that, statistically speaking, they would be much better off warning me against being alone with any male relative.

My ghoulish leanings also impel me to state that female bodies found in remote locations tend to have been driven there after the event. More to the point, one of the loveliest surprises of the South West Coast Path is the number of women you pass, all of them walking alone. We nod politely and don't bother each other. It's like being part of a discreet, silent community.

The second question has been more of an irritant: 'What will happen when winter comes?' The temptation is to be facetious: our hemisphere will be at its furthest annual point from the sun, and this will result in shortened hours of light and colder temperatures, accompanied by challenging weather conditions such as sleet, fog and snow.

This only betrays my twitchiness around the subject, though. My answer (the one I say out loud) has usually been: 'I'll just layer up and do as much as I can.' I have stopped short of trotting out the old chestnut, *There's no such thing as bad weather; only bad clothing*, because, honestly, I have absolutely no intention of investing the thousands of pounds that 'good clothing' would require in this context. I have neither the budget nor the inclination to kit myself out in the mode of a geography teacher who has finally paid off their mortgage and feels they deserve a little treat.

The truth is, I really don't know how I'll cope with winter. I want to trudge on heroically through all conditions and across all terrains, and I'm resisting the urge to think any more deeply about the matter. I have calculated this walk on twenty-five miles a month, for eighteen months. Even if I can ramp that up to thirty, I still can't afford to skip the winter months. I'm already behind as it is. At this rate, I might have to move down to the South West over the summer and give up on any notion of rest or social contact.

The other challenge is accommodation. Before I started this project, we had never worked out an affordable way to take Bert on a weekend away without compromising on comfort, and that remains the case. I am bleakly aware that I really ought to be camping in the wild, bragging about my ability to do the whole thing on a shoestring, and attempting to inspire everyone else to do the same. But I find life profoundly uncomfortable if it doesn't come with a fitted bathroom. If I don't get to shower in the morning, I feel like my skin doesn't fit. Just because I like walking doesn't mean that I'm remotely rugged.

To be fair, the indoor options aren't all that inspiring either. Family rooms in hotels just mean that we have to go to bed the same time as him. Self-catering is too much of a faff for such short periods of time. This month, I couldn't find anything nearly suitable. In the end, I opted for a heavily discounted suite on a hotel booking site, and comforted myself with the thought that the hotel has a pool and a sauna, so at least I'll be able to relieve my tired muscles, even if it does turn out to be the Crossroads Motel.

On arrival (after a five-hour drive after work on Friday night, with Bert refusing to sleep in the back) we learn that our hotel's definition of a 'suite' is a normal-sized room with an extra camp-bed in it, and, coupled with an unfathomable baby-listening system, this means we are back to the obligation to get into bed with Bert (H inevitably pushed out into the camp-bed while Bert demands to share king-size with me), and try to sleep.

On Saturday morning, I collect the newspaper that's hanging from the doorknob, and read the grim news of a terrorist attack. I then eat a quiet, bewildered breakfast, lace on my boots, and trudge out into grey, squally drizzle, still digesting the appalling events of the night before.

I have been watching the weather all week. There's no doubt about it: it's going to rain, and it's going to rain a great deal. I can't do a lot about that; it has rained all the last four weekends, too, and I will have to brave it if I am going to keep to my schedule. I also know that today's walk won't be the most exciting one on my itinerary – I am essentially walking up the other side of the estuary that I found boring the last time, and there's something dispiriting about the sensation of boots clomping on concrete paths; it's so full of unfulfilled potential. What I hadn't considered, though, was just how miserable the combination of walking fifteen boring miles and battling through oncoming rain would be. You can see absolutely nothing, because your head is angled relentlessly down. Your glasses steam up, but there's no point in wiping them. Your neck begins to ache. Progress is surprisingly slow.

I walk, I think, to let my mind soar around open spaces while my legs get tired. Today, without any stimulating sights or sounds, and with only discomfort to distract me, my thoughts get caught in an obsessive loop that reels around and around everything I've said this week, everything I've written. I sometimes feel as though social relationships are nothing more than a precarious set of plates that I have to spin, and I'm bad at it. People seem to want so much more of my attention than I have to spare. This week, I don't feel like I've kept enough of those plates spinning, enough of the time.

I had few friends as a child, and although I wouldn't say I liked it that way, I can't say it bothered me much either. I enjoyed my own company. The painful part was being conscious of my own difference: I was another species entirely from the little girls in my class, with my big, awkward body and complete inability to relate to anything they said or did.

I used to dream of being able to unpeel my skin to show that underneath I was just like them. I was just dissembling, like in a fairy tale. We would all laugh and learn something in the end.

It's not like that anymore. I have taught myself to be better. I have learned to get on with people. They tend to like me these days. They find me funny and perceptive and endlessly lively. I'm the life and soul; I'm ready for anything. But when I don't quite manage to make the effort necessary to remain likeable, my real self shows through like a garish petticoat.

Like this week, when I overheard H saying to a friend, 'You know how *intense* Katherine gets when she's had a few drinks,' and I thought, *No, I did not know that. I did not know that at all. But apparently everyone else does.* And I'm thinking that perhaps I can't afford to relax like that anymore, because I thought I was just being funny and perceptive and lively, but apparently that's *intense*, and I don't want to be *intense*. I've spent all my life trying not to be *intense*. So I am pushing on through the driving rain, and I suspect that my boots are getting wet on the inside, and I am thinking about the time – only a couple of years ago, still relevant – when a friend said to me, 'Well, of course, people find you a bit . . . Marmitey.'

Marmitey. You either love me or you hate me, right? Except I didn't know that. I feel like I should have known that. I tried to pretend it didn't hurt me to hear it – that I wasn't at all surprised, that I like it that way – ha ha – and then I went home and sobbed about it to H on the sofa. And now, walking in stormcloud light, I'm connecting the two. I am *intense* and I am Marmitey, and at the same time I am profoundly self-indulgent and ungrateful for thinking these things when I am alive and free and walking the South West Coast Path, which is what I wanted, wasn't it?

I keep trying to feel wonder – at the curlews and little egrets picking through the mud, and the flock of goldfinches that flit up the path in front of me – but it all just dissipates into the grey. There are few tastes more bitter than enforced gratitude. By the time I trudge into Bideford at lunchtime, I am conscious that my feet are squelching in my boots, my waterproof is drenched inside and out, and my backpack is heavy with rain. A gust of wind nearly blows me into the road as I cross the famous bridge with its uneven arches like a shifty smile. I walk into the nearest pub, and hear a woman gasp, 'Oh my God, look at her!' I offer a weak smile. I'm drenched. I order a pint of shandy and a plate of nachos and fully intend to give up.

But after forty minutes, I can't think of anything else to do but to press on. I'd be embarrassed to quit again. I text H to ask him to meet me in Appledore. The rain has stopped, and there might be sea in prospect if I can keep going. Now, though, the path turns muddy, and for all my pleasure in seeing the back of the endless concrete cycle path around the estuary, I am slipping and sliding on every tenth step. The ground is soaked. I am soaked. More than this, my thoughts have turned darker still, churning the same worries over and over in my mind, an endless cycle that becomes more paranoid with every rehearsal. I try to reason with myself (*You're worrying about something that hasn't happened yet*), and then to mock my inner voice (*This again? Don't you have anything better to think about?*) but every time, the sense of doom seeps back in. It's funny: I've been nearly desperate for these hours on my own, but now they're here, I'm unable to cope with them.

I finally drip into Appledore to find H telling off Bert

for trying to run into the road. Bert is unrepentant. H is trying to make him listen. It's a relief for my mind to alight on something real. We have coffee and cake, and then drive back to the hotel where I make a pretence of drying my coat and boots on the heated towel rail, knowing that I've really written off tomorrow's walk anyway. It seems I just don't have the heart for all those hours alone.

Once I get back home, I hear that two walkers had to be rescued on that part of the path over the weekend, due to the inclement weather. Perhaps, after all, I was wise to give up, rather than weak. Nevertheless, I decide I need to be better equipped if I'm going to walk through the winter. I focus my reforming zeal on my glasses, which played no small part in my downfall, given that they alternately steamed up, slipped down my nose and collected raindrops throughout my entire walk. I make an appointment at the optician to get new contact lenses – or, failing that, prescription goggles – ready for my next bout.

I hate going to the optician. I hate the amount of touch it entails, the repeated shuffling of instruments around my face, the agonising engagement of being eye to eye with a complete stranger (and one who is breathing on my cheek, at that). I don't find the dentist nearly so bad because those bright halogen lights seem less intimate than the eternal dusk of the optician's office. Dentists don't talk to you; they talk to the nurse in the corner, and that clinical distance is far less electric than the confidential patter of the optician.

I don't go at all unless my glasses disintegrate. My last eye test, three years ago, resulted in a shouting match with the optician that I can't account for even now. I was anxious before I even got there, I suppose. Bert was still a baby, and I'd had to leave him at home with a friend, which seemed like a logistical nightmare to arrange. So, when I got there and was immediately told off for not having my contact lenses in (I couldn't; the prescription was out of date and I could see nothing through them), I suppose I lost my temper more quickly than usual. I'm not sure. It was all a blur, and I felt like I only came back to full consciousness when I was running out of the building in tears, my whole body shaking.

So today, I have to drive over to a different optician in a different town, just to escape the taint of that last experience. I wouldn't bother at all, but I need to make sure that I will not give up on my next walk, or the walk after that, because otherwise I might as well give up altogether and admit it was a stupid idea.

The winter evening is already setting in. I turn on the stereo. You know how the story goes already: the voice on the radio.

The woman describing my own way of seeing the world back to me.

The shifting sands as I listen.

The slow, sudden sense that I am something other than I thought I was.

A name; a label. Asperger syndrome.

But I know what Asperger syndrome is, don't I? Everyone does. It is not me. It is *not* me. It is someone else. It is the boy who is more machine than human, who lists facts, who cannot look at you. Who lives with his mother, still, because he can't cope alone.

It is the man I once sat next to at a conference, who talked over me all day, and, at lunchtime, told me that he cleaned his teeth with a needle. He immediately apologised because he couldn't always tell what he ought to say.

It is the girl I once taught, who needed a fresh checklist

every morning, so that she could remember her bag, her pens, her gym kit; who needed someone else to write down everywhere she needed to be. She excelled in the sciences and maths. She didn't see the point of literature.

None of these things are me – are they?

Are they?

6

Dover to Shepherdswell, December

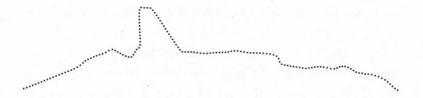

Wind back two years. I am standing on the Bethnal Green Road, having parked on a side street. Bert, a little over eighteen months old, had initially opted to walk to the Museum of Childhood, but is now making this short distance look very long indeed. He wants, I know, to be carried there, but I've already spent the previous afternoon having my shoulder muscles painfully rearranged by a massage therapist, for the fourth time since he was born. We can add it to my list of failings as a mother: I get sick of carrying him around. He doesn't particularly cooperate when I do. Everyone says I should get a cloth baby carrier, but they make me feel as nauseous as every other maternal accoutrement. Too close; too encumbered. I want him – cleanly, distantly – in his pushchair.

Bert has other ideas. He is screeching and flailing his arms and tensing his body into a stiff, straight line that we have come to call 'planking'. Not the amusing internet meme, but the passive-aggressive toddler strategy, applicable to pushchairs, high chairs, car seats and anywhere he doesn't want to be at that specific moment. 'Bert!' I am saying; 'BERT!' and I am trying to make him bend in the middle by slotting him in sideways. I manage to catch his little arm into one of the straps, but he throws it off as soon as I grab for the other. I can feel the blood rising into my head, my ears singing. I am the flustered mother in the street, the one who is unable to deal with her child calmly and competently. I love him. I love him. I want him to be happy. I don't want him to be upset like this. When he cries, I can't hear anything else. It's agony. I lose all perspective.

H, who has been standing quietly behind me says, 'Do you want me to have a go?' and at that moment it breaks, the thing that I was trying to stop from breaking. It's like an atom bomb to the brain: everything turns white, and I am blown into fragments. My ears are full of static and my vision isn't even there. I have crashed. I am rebooting. Stand by. Stand by.

I realise only as I am coming out of my reboot that I am shouting, 'Fuck off! Leave me alone!' at H, who is heartily sick of my shit these days. He crimps his lips together and just walks off, away from me, left standing in the street. I am still shaking and sweating, the adrenal aftermath of the white-out. I am sorry. I am sorry already. It's receding now, but I can feel the crystalline tidemark of it in my throat, a brackish memory.

'Don't!' I call out. 'Please!' and I can see that he's heard me because his shoulders tense into a hard square. I pick up Bert and trot after him down the street, pushing the buggy with one hand, my legs unsteady. 'Stop!' I say. '*Please!*' and I can't grab for his sleeve because my hands are full, so I incompetently crash the pushchair into his legs instead, which only makes him more angry. God only knows what Bert makes of this, of me and my total, pathetic inability to cope with the simplest of tasks. Nobody else seems to find this so hard.

'Please!' I say. 'I'm sorry. I'm sorry. Please stop for a moment.' He suspects me of something here, I can tell. He smells some new shift of self-pity taking over, which he will have to deal with. 'I need to explain. Will you let me just try to explain?'

He takes Bert and I fall into pace beside him, pushing the buggy which is now so light that it skips at every crack in the pavement. 'I need to try to explain what's happening to me when I . . . when I go like that.' Every instinct I have wants to flip this over, to make it H's transgression which we will agree to say no more about. But it is not; it is mine, and I know it is. 'It's like I get taken over,' I say. 'When he's upset, my whole head echoes, and it builds and builds, and then I kind of explode.'

'I noticed,' says H.

'I mean, I explode inside. It's like . . . it's like losing consciousness. It's like the time I hit my finger with a hammer and I woke up flat on my back. It's that much. It's that bad.'

'Everyone feels like that. Everyone finds it awful when they cry.'

'That's just the thing,' I say. 'I don't think it's the same. I've watched other people, and I don't think it's the same. I don't think I'm the same. I don't seem to feel the same as everyone else anymore.'

H sighs.

'I should probably get help,' I say. 'I know I should.'

'Then get it,' he says. He's gruff, but I know he has already forgiven me. He doesn't really have the constitution for arguing, and I'm grateful for that. I lean my shoulder into his arm, and after a while, I feel his hand reach up to rub my back, almost absent-mindedly, almost out of habit.

*

The decision to give up on the idea of getting to Devon in December is an easy one in the end. I watch the forecast on the BBC Weather app obsessively for three weeks, carefully keeping all my weekends free. When the rain looks like it will abate for a few hours, I will pounce, book a cheap hotel for a couple of days, drive down there on my own and make some progress. Problem is, it doesn't stop raining. Every weekend is the same: a monotonous blanket of rain. It's windy, too; the chimney breast in my bedroom whistles every night. I can't face it. I keep telling myself that I will round the corner the next time I walk, and break away from the sheltered estuary to find the sea again. I just can't manage that in battering winds.

It's unseemly to go away in December anyway, when everyone else is carefully signalling how busy they are, the badge of honour of the mother who is going to lay on a Really Good Christmas. I'm not really sure what they find to do with their time. I've ordered all my presents online (they will be wrapped in one fell swoop the night before Christmas Eve, like every other year). Granted, we're having Christmas Day at my dad's, but there's a side of salmon in the freezer to make gravadlax; the Christmas puddings have been steamed and are wrapped up in foil at the back of the fridge. All the meat is ordered for the Boxing Day lunch I'm cooking. I'm really not sure why I'm supposed to pretend that I'm overrun with things to do.

I decide, as an interim measure, to start walking the North Downs Way as well as the South West Coast Path. It's much closer to home, cutting roughly across the middle of Kent, following some of the old pilgrims' route to Canterbury and Dover, and it's therefore much less of a financial risk than getting all the way down to the South West only to discover the weather is making an attempt on my life. Also, I'm rarely happy without a mission to complete, and if I don't start following the North Downs Way, I probably won't walk at all. I just need to keep moving before I can get to Devon again.

I've always lived in Kent, but this path will take me through a part of the county that I barely know at all, which is probably the bit that everyone else would recognise as typically Kentish. I grew up along the northern boundary in Gravesend, and then on the marshes at Chalk, where I could see the cooling towers of the Essex power plants across the Thames. Then I moved on to the Medway towns, and finally to Whitstable. All of these places felt more connected to London than to Kentish-Kent, tied by the electric umbilical cord of the train line and that seep of migration that happens when London natives start to yearn for a garden where they could maybe put a swing.

The path begins on Dover sea-front, where a stone plaque embedded in the promenade says 'START' and, upside down next to it, 'FINISH'. I take a photo of my toes touching it, wearing trainers this time as my beloved boots were completely slain by last month's walk (particularly seeing as I left them wrapped up in a plastic bag for two weeks afterwards, where they went mouldy). From this vantage point, Dover is like a theme park of itself: behind me is a ferry terminal, and then there is a rise of white cliffs, and, on top of that like a cherry on a cupcake, Dover Castle, where H and Bert have encamped after dropping me off. This, right here, is your Dover experience, now that the town has fallen away from its Victorian prosperity. I squint at my Ordnance Survey map, unfamiliar with the necessity to actually navigate rather than to just follow the line of the coast and a set of extremely clear waymarkers at any decision point. There are waymarkers on the North Downs Way too, but it's always hard to keep track of routes through towns, where the signs are diluted by a glut of information.

I take an underpass into the town centre, and then immediately wander off in the wrong direction, only recovering my trail twenty minutes later, after completing a loop around the quiet Sunday streets and having to reorient myself with the help of Google Maps on my phone. It's an unpromising start, but soon I'm climbing uphill through a street of red-brick villas, and then down under a train line and past what my map marks as a former mineshaft. Dover has seen the coming and going of just about every major industry over the years.

Another short climb, and I'm on farmland, the rush of the A2 never far away. I check my OS Explorer map: the route will divert, eventually, from the coast-bound traffic, but I will rarely stray far from civilisation on this path. I unfold the map, and trace the route between all the villages I'll pass through on the way to Canterbury; I only recognise most of their names from road signs. I'm amazed at how little I know of my own home turf; how places connect in ways I didn't understand. There's real pleasure in learning the lie of the land through the soles of your shoes.

The ground is thick clay with chalk underneath; there are moments on the path when so much chalk breaks through, it's as if the land is exposing its bones. But the overall experience is of mud. The ground is drenched after a month of rain. I quickly begin to miss my proper walking boots with their deep soles and high sides. There are several moments when I think I'll lose my trainers altogether as they're sucked into the deep mires I have no choice but to wade through. Higher up on the downs, the drainage is better. The wind is brisk and the skies are a stern, military grey. There are few views or vistas on this part of the walk, just an awful lot of brassica fields and the occasional, sparse copse.

My intention, today, is to walk without too much of a plan, stopping when I get tired and fed up. I want it to be different from my South West Coast Path walk; I'm close to home, and don't have a schedule to keep, so my aim is to be a little freer, a little less goal-oriented. In the back of my mind, though, I'm thinking that I will keep going well into the afternoon, and try to wear away all the thoughts that crowd the front of my mind.

It's a fortnight now since I caught the programme on the radio with the woman and man who seemed to be telling the story of my own inner life. At first I tried to ignore it. I studied psychology at university, and remember our lecturer telling us in the first week, 'Don't be surprised if you diagnose yourself with everything we discuss in this course.' It's part of the mundane normality of mental suffering; everybody knows it. It's all a matter of degree, of spectrum. But then, spectrum has become a danger-ous word in my mind lately. Exactly where on it might I fall?

And anyway, the lecturer qualified his comment on that day: 'Of course, some of you will come to recognise your-self in the more extreme manifestations of these symptoms. If that's the case for you, then now is a good time to seek some help.' And I remember thinking at the time, *But I have sought help.*

I sought help from the hospital consultant at fourteen when I was too exhausted to go to school anymore. He said, 'You're just depressed,' like it was an accusation, like I was taking up his proper, medical time without an actual illness to show for it.

I sought help from my GP at seventeen, when I couldn't find the wherewithal to speak anymore. She said, kindly, 'Your clothes are hanging off you. Are you eating?' and then, less kindly, 'If you don't get on top of this, we're going to have to put you in hospital.'

The panic that brought about. I took the drugs she gave me obediently, even when they made me feel like I was abandoned, panicking, at the bottom of a deep well, and sick with the weight of them; even when I would devote whole afternoons to swallowing every harmful thing I could find in the house, just to see if I would feel anything. I went to the psychiatrist she referred me to, sitting in a thin-walled waiting room at the bottom of Gravesend High Street and hearing all the other clients rehearsing their traumas before I was called in to rehearse my own. Mine didn't really seem so bad, in comparison, and I had given up on speaking by then anyway, so she and I just sat in a room together for an hour, while she let out impatient huffs and checked her watch and made notes (presumably about other people), and I stared into my lap. When I didn't come back a second time, she sent a letter, but even I could tell that it was safe to ignore it.

I sought help other times, too. At university, when my personal tutor said that my worries were nothing compared to hers; at twenty-two, when I saw a counsellor because I just couldn't seem to cope with my job. She signed me off early because she could find nothing that was really bothering me. I felt humiliated: the worried well, failing to cope when everything was fine. Soon, I became too ill to work at all, my joints aching so that I staggered and limped, my head full of cotton wool. My GP diagnosed fibromyalgia, saying, with a sort of a wink, 'That means we don't really know what's wrong with you, but we believe you're not making it up.' It was like being invited in on a dirty joke. You find it distasteful but you laugh along, because what else can you do?

When I went back again at twenty-four, the doctor said that someone like me should look into hiring a private mental-health nurse, as if I were asking for a luxury item, a purely cosmetic procedure on the NHS. *Someone like me*: I didn't understand what that meant. I realised that I didn't fit a pattern somehow, that I just didn't seem quite distressed enough. But I was a master, by then, of the surface appearance. I had watched, carefully, the way that other people behaved, and mimicked it precisely. I had all the social airs and graces – the encouraging smiles and the kind enquiries – and I could chase the lineage of each one of them back to the person I stole them from.

I learned to ask after people's children from a woman on a train. I learned to crack self-effacing jokes from a colleague who always got away with murder. I was a parrot, a mynah bird, and even if I were able to, I wasn't willing to turn it all off just to convince others of my need for care. Underneath that carefully learned set of gestures was raw, boiling chaos. I would cling to the right to cover that for my own dear life. If that meant pretending to be somebody else, then so be it.

I gave up going to the doctors after that. I saw a counsellor at twenty-five who suggested I was simply arrogant and consumed with ambition; another at twenty-eight who said, 'I don't see why all of these things are a problem to you.' We parted company, and I felt embarrassed yet again. There was something going on that was real enough to me, but which I couldn't seem to transmit to anyone else. The only conclusion I could draw was that I was making a fuss over nothing, always. I was clearly just coping badly with perfectly normal things.

I sought help, too, when I was pregnant and the midwife visited, and I told her I was miserable and panicked, and she said, 'But do you feel like that all the time, every day?'

and I had to admit that no, I couldn't quantifiably make that claim. 'Well, then,' she said, and added before she left that she thought it wouldn't do me any harm to have a little glass of wine a few times a week, just to relax a bit.

When the health visitor came after Bert was born, she pulled the Postnatal Depression questionnaire out of her briefcase and hovered it over the table for a few, indecisive seconds before saying, 'No need for this if you're happy not to; I can tell you're fine.' And me, smiling, saying, 'Yes, completely fine, thanks,' and my mind screaming, *Please, God, somebody help me.*

What was the point, anyway, in admitting that something was wrong? I knew by now that it would be futile to challenge the impression she'd already formed, of a happy, content woman, perhaps a little highly strung. It seems to me now that it's not that I fail to manage the simplest challenges, but that I pass too well. I am addicted to passing, and not just in the sense of going unnoticed. I want more than that. I want to be well adjusted to the point of inspiration, hyper-normal. I want to be everyone's favourite. I don't care about the cost, the way it breaks me open and exhausts me and sickens me. Am I willing to dismantle that carefully made passing for something as intangible as self-knowledge? Or is it easier to go quietly on, and brace myself for the storms every few years, when chaos comes again?

Midday on the North Downs Way, and I am beginning to flag. The route is austere, the wind is relentless, and the sun never really seems to have come up. My footwear is not really equal to the task. I feel as though I'm stumbling around in an almost-night which never seems to shift on to the next phase. I text H to see if he wants to come and meet me in the nearest village for lunch, and he replies that they both got sick of the wind at Dover Castle, and are now miles away in a soft-play centre. He's just bitten into a bacon sandwich, he says. Sorry.

No matter. I make it to Shepherdswell by one o'clock, and there, across the village green, is a handsome-looking pub. I dither outside for a few moments before kicking off my muddy trainers at the door and stepping inside. I realise how odd I must look as I enter – a lone woman in green hiking socks with mud splattered up her running tights, asking for a roast dinner and a pint of bitter shandy. But here, on the mud and chalk of the North Downs Way, this seems to be gently accepted.

Isn't that why I walk, anyway: because it gives me permission to go a little bit wild at the edges, and to escape into my own thoughts? I am probably no different from a thousand other walkers who blow in each year, their stomachs empty and their minds still wandering the chalk downs. Here, I am normal in my strangeness. Perhaps walking is the only place where I don't have to pass.

7

Shepherdswell to Canterbury, December

My world is made up of tiny electric shocks. Every living thing carries its own current, and this finds its earth through me. Every unexpected touch, every glance, has a charge. I am a lightning rod, laid out like the red-nosed patient in the game of Operation, eternally braced for the metal-on-metal jolt of contact.

You won't see me shudder anymore, or not often. I've learned my composure, like I learned everything else. I can prepare. I can tell myself, *You'll be going into a room, and people will brush against you*, and then I can be ready. I just need to give my permission. People hug me. People kiss me. I do my best to reciprocate, and try not to stiffen. Some people realise, instinctively, that I'm best off left alone. Those people are paying attention. Most people are not, or don't want to. I was once chased around and around my car by a colleague who refused to let me say no to his friendly embrace. Everyone else had let him, so why not me? 'Come on,' he said, 'give me a hug,' and I just couldn't go along with it, and so I backed away and then began to run, just a little, giggling, 'No! I don't want to! You can't make me!' At least I remembered to laugh. Otherwise, everyone would have felt the horror that I did.

Consent is important to me. Consent doesn't only govern sex. I can go to the dentist or the hairdresser, because there's transaction implicit in our contact. I am paying for their services, and those services entail being touched. I consent. I have the measure of them. In some ways, I think I'm able to surrender more than most. There's no distinction, for me, between having my teeth checked by the dentist and having a smear test. Once I've surrendered the surface of my skin, it makes no difference.

I once embarrassed a consultant gynaecologist by walking away from his examination chair, naked from the waist down. I had been supplied with a sheet, which I had apparently been expected to wrap around myself to cover my modesty. But that modesty was entirely mysterious to me, given that he had just spent the past thirty minutes with his face hovering inches away from my naked genitals. There was, surely, nothing more for him – or, indeed, the clutch of nurses in the room – to see. What on earth was the point in suddenly pretending that my body was a private thing again, to be carefully concealed from view? In this room, it was patently not.

I have no idea how I'm supposed to grasp these shifting rules. In my early twenties, I visited the doctor to have my blood pressure checked, and ended up spending half an hour with a junior GP, who was about the same age as me, and seemed ever so human and friendly in a way that was different from the gruff distance of my usual doctor. He was concerned that my heartbeat wasn't quite right, and I was wearing a dress, so I ended up sitting on his couch in my bra and knickers as he pressed his stethoscope all around my ribcage. When he finished and sat back down at his desk, I suppose I just didn't really think of getting dressed before I sat on the chair opposite him.

It was a failure, on my part, to understand the rules, and I began to realise this when he leaned over and rested his elbows on my bare knees as he spoke to me, as though I was his desk. At that point, the electricity returned again. I may have been naive enough to think that a young doctor would view a near-naked woman in decent lingerie with perfect professional detachment, but I realised, too late, that this was an utter transgression. The problem was that I also realised that the transgression had been mine; I had mis-signalled. I didn't want to embarrass him. The electricity from his arms felt like he was tattooing my legs, but when he asked, 'Do you mind me sitting here like this?' I said, 'No.'

No. It's fine. I don't mind at all. Because it was easier to let this dumb lecher set my skin screaming with his horrifying, rule-breaking *contact* than it was to say, 'Yes I do mind,' and trigger the whole unpredictable hysteria of his defence. At least I understood the rules of this bit. I would have to sit, and smile, and extend the boundaries of my bodily permission for long enough for him to try something a little more concrete, from which I could demur. That would give him the chance to notch it up as a flirtation, the imprint of which he could take into a locked bathroom later on. It wasn't exactly that everyone was a winner, but it did mean that I wouldn't have to deal with anything messy later on.

As it happened, there was a quiet knock on the door a few moments later, and in walked my more usual, paternalistic GP. The trainee jerked back into his seat, and the good doctor widened his eyes at my state of undress and said, 'You can put your clothes back on now.' I have never been more grateful to receive someone's disapproval.

I didn't tell anyone, of course. Not out of a sense of sexual violation, but through a greater shame at my complete inability to read this simple social situation. At that point, it hadn't yet crystallised into a sentiment quite so sharp; but I knew that I was inexpert at these things, and that I ought to be better at them.

And yet, I had somehow managed to forget all of this. I had forgotten that I don't like to be touched. I had forgotten that I often misinterpret social rules. This is not a grand amnesia, in which everything before a certain date is erased, but a daily, ongoing forgetting, a refusal to join together the facts. I may know that I am not much of a hugger; I may know that I am baffled by social kissing; but I have allowed myself to believe that each instance is a one-off. I don't like being kissed by *this* person at *this* moment. I just don't feel like hugging *right now*. I have kept the faith that I am really just like everyone else, except perhaps sometimes, momentarily off-colour, and all the while, I have managed to stay magically unaware of the continuities behind each individual act of repulsion, blind to the fact that contact with other people is grindingly uncomfortable to me.

How can this be? It's as if there has been a conspiracy, an all-conquering desire to imagine myself as one sort of person, when I have always actually been another. I am a testament to the confabulatory powers of the human brain. I have made a whole, gleaming, normal person out of jagged shards of a broken one. That voice on the radio exploded me. Now, I am seeing all the contradictory fragments again. Now, I am piecing them back together to make an entirely different pot.

In the last straggly days before Christmas, I wrap presents, and dry-cure salmon, and wonder how I can construct the trampoline we've bought Bert while also keeping it hidden. And all the while, I wonder what I shall say about myself to my husband, now that I feel like I'm something else altogether. I wonder what I want him to say in return. My best-case scenario is, I think, surprised acceptance, preferably with a very short space of time between those two sentiments; as in, *Wow, I thought you were the most totally normal person I ever met, but I now recognise and welcome your new identity, and forgive you for every time you've been impossible to live with, ever.*

There's a worst-case scenario, too, one that preys on my mind. In this one, he simply sighs and clamps his teeth together, and doesn't say anything at all. But what he will be thinking – and he will refrain from telling me, because he no longer trusts my generalised unsteadiness – is that this is yet another outcropping of the exhausting, attention-guzzling instability that has come to define me since I got pregnant. He will say nothing, but he will be thinking that he is tired of this, that he is tired of me, and I will seem just a little bit more of a stranger than I already do.

My mother watches Bert for a day, and we go walking, just H and me, starting from where I left off in Shepherdswell. H, as I have mentioned before, doesn't really do long distances on foot, and today I'm planning twelve miles, which will take us neatly into Canterbury. He is incredulous that I would even attempt such a thing, and supposedly for fun. I am wondering whether it will be far enough.

The grim skies have gone, and today is unseasonably warm. We cross Shepherdswell's village green and pass behind some houses, before finding ourselves walking between paddocks where horses graze in their winter coats. A country fox crosses our path, her coat a dazzling red compared to the urban foxes we're used to. She's alert to us, pausing to assess the situation, and then darting off out of sight.

We are soon passing a series of villages that I recognise from the chant of the train announcer on the route from Canterbury to the coast: Snowdown, Aylesham, Adisham. It's a chain of familiar names but unfamiliar places. We get hungry around midday, and, finding ourselves nowhere near a pub, decide to divert over the main road to the village of Kingston, where the stalwart reviewers of Google, who unfathomably feel the urge to log their views on every meal, recommend the Black Robin. At this point, I badly misread the map, and rather than attempting to cross what is essentially a motorway, we are forced into a hunger-tantrum scramble along the steep – and surprisingly dense – shrubbery at the edge of the A2. Cars rush past below us, and I tear my running tights on blackthorn.

We eventually find a bridge to take us across the road, and agree with Google that the Black Robin is delightful, if unable to serve us any food due to its popularity. Lunch, then, is a selection of crisps and a packet of dry-roasted peanuts, while H slumps by the fire and wonders aloud if there's a location closer than Canterbury where my mother can pick us up. I'm feeling fine. I suppose I must have gained a bit in fitness after all.

I am unrelenting, though: there's no point sitting here, waiting for the dusk to arrive. I coach him through finishing his beer, and we set off again, through Bridge's broad, handsome main road, where H wonders if a late lunch is out of the question. 'You wouldn't get far on the South West Coast Path if you kept stopping to eat,' I tell him, and he glares at me. We pass under the A2, and find the North Downs Way again, which soon delivers us onto a hill above Canterbury. H falls silent. I recognise that state: every part of him must hurt by now, and his energy levels have deserted him. There's no way to go but onwards now, though, and we can see the cathedral in the far distance, glowing ever more brightly as dusk descends.

We arrive in the city centre to find the Christmas market in full swing, all fairy lights and mulled cider. The press of bodies around the stalls is absurd: hot and chaotic, too loud, too unpredictable. Other people seem to enjoy this, apparently – people who are not like me. We find a quiet cafe and sit with coffee and sandwiches, waiting until Bert arrives, wide-eyed because Santa is in the grotto down the street.

We walked all day, and I didn't say a word about the woman on the radio, and what I learned about myself when I heard her. The opportunity never seemed to arise; there was no moment that felt appropriate. What do you say, anyway? *Oh by the way, I'm autistic.* It just doesn't seem possible, after twenty years together.

I consider not telling him at all, knowing all the while that this won't work. I never have been able to leave a thought unspoken. The words – unformed, unsteady – lurk at the top of my throat, ready to spill out. I counsel myself that this urge to speak before I really know or understand is not to be trusted. I know he's already exhausted by my emotional high tides, but they always rush in anyway. This is the problem. This is my problem. I am unable to contain my thoughts as other people do. Everything always comes flooding out. I drown myself in words, and carry off all those around me, too.

I end up bursting my banks one night when we are lying side by side in bed, trying to touch. Or rather, I am trying to give in to touch, to enjoy it, to disengage with the minutiae of the bodily existence next to me. Sometimes I can pull this off; sometimes (and I accept that I am not usually sober when this occurs), I can manage not to remember that the body next to me is exhaling from the depths of sticky internal organs, and shedding an invisible dust of skin and hair, and emitting subtle odours of sweat and raw meat. Sometimes, touch doesn't tickle or burn or make me shudder. But not tonight. Tonight I have joined the dots, and I have remembered that I hate those things, and not just in this very moment, which will pass. Tonight, I have forgotten how to forget.

Tonight, H passes a hand around my waist and I have to move it away because his palm is too hot, and he leans in and kisses my ear, and I have to rub away the snaking imprint his lips leave behind. And I try to relax, to not let my body go rigid, to receive this touch in the spirit it's meant, but he's already sighed and given up, and has turned away. Aren't people on the autistic spectrum supposed to lack any empathy? Because I'm feeling for him now. I'm feeling the pain of longing to touch somebody who will only be touched under certain, very specific circumstances, which neither you nor they understand. I'm feeling the loneliness of committing to a life with someone who is about as affectionate as a wire coathanger. I begin to cry, quietly at first, but then I know that the words must come out. My voice is thick.

'I heard a radio programme last week,' I say, and try to explain the whole thing. It sounds stupid, out loud. It sounds like it can't possibly be true. 'It's about sensory overwhelm,' I say. 'It's about hearing and smelling and tasting everything all at once, and I can't filter anything out . . .'

He listens quietly, and I wonder if he has fallen asleep.

'What do you think?' I ask him. 'Do you think that might be me? Do you think that might be why everything's been so hard?'

He lets out a breath and says, 'Well . . . I suppose . . .'

and he's choosing his words so carefully that my stomach lurches. 'I suppose it does explain *how you are.*'

This is the worst thing of all, because he knows; he knew all along; he knew before I did. I have lived all my life thinking that I am just like everyone else, except that I get depressed and anxious sometimes, that I don't always understand the way that people react to me, that I need to make more of an effort than everyone else to get by. And while I've been busy thinking I'm one thing, he has known that I'm something altogether other, and he has quietly gone about trying to manage me without ever once being so cruel as to let me know that he was doing it.

'Oh God,' I say, 'are you my carer?'

And he laughs and says, 'No. No. I'm really not.' And then he thinks for a while and says, 'I don't know if you'd like me to give you a hug now?'

And I say, 'Yes.'

Canterbury to Chartham, January

I don't make any New Year's resolutions.

Being the sort of person who is in a constant state of resolution-making one way or another, I have little use for them. The last time I made one was about five years ago, when I vowed to stop talking people into things they didn't want to do. I had come to realise that this was a somewhat unappealing quality, rather than the glorious ability to triumph that I had previously believed it to be. In my imagination, I had been able to quell all objections through my sheer passion and reason; in reality, people were giving in to my all-encompassing, obsessive enthusiasms, and then dropping out when they were at a safe distance. Despite what the self-help guides will tell you, persistence isn't always a virtue. Sometimes, persistence is just shorthand for ignoring all feedback.

I wonder if I have enough persistence to start walking again. It seems to me that it has rained solidly since October. I could be wrong; there may have been interludes in which it was merely overcast. Either way, the ground in Kent – and I suspect in the West Country too – is waterlogged. My front garden is permanently under a thin veil of water which becomes a pond every time the skies open. Being an optimistic soul, I'm considering planting flag irises and water lilies, although I fear this would send out the wrong signals if we ever chose to sell.

All this weather has made walking an abortive experience over the last couple of weeks. I made an attempt on the North Downs Way between Canterbury and Chartham soon after Christmas, but H refused to go on after a mile, following an encounter with a relatively gentle slope that just happened to be ankle-deep in mud. Accusations were made of him being faint-hearted. He didn't appear to care whether or not these accusations were true. We ended up compromising on a pub lunch instead, provided I was allowed to pepper the conversation with battle-hardened anecdotes from the South West Coast Path in far more treacherous weather.

By the next weekend, I can think of nothing else but walking. The bounce from Christmas, with all its hours and hours of noise and social contact, into the New Year, and straight back into work has been too much for me. I'm rattling with sick nerves, the adrenaline rush of surviving, just smiling and surviving, until I can be alone. I need blasting fresh air, far horizons, the damp, green microclimate of woodland. I don't care whether or not I get wet in the process. Rain is the least of my worries.

I make a second attempt to reach Chartham, this time alone. In all fairness to H, I don't bother with the muddy slope a second time, but only because I've already done it once and have no need to cover old ground. I make it clear to him that I would have walked down that part of the path if I needed to; that the mud doesn't bother me in the least. This is becoming increasingly true, especially in my brand-new boots, which are identical to the old ones except they don't leak and they're not mouldy. In these, I feel invincible, if only to the bottoms of my shins.

He drops me off on a bridge that crosses the A2, and I sit on the rear bumper and get ready with the traffic zooming beneath me. Bert, who I suspect is heading for a nice, warm soft-play centre while H has a fry-up, taps on the window to wave goodbye. I tap back, twice, and remember my grandad's habit of knocking twice on the car's roof whenever we went home. As they drive away, my new boots making me feel stiff-legged on the tarmac, I stumble across the road and through an unpromising-looking metal gate, embedded in the sort of concrete barricade that might have stopped tanks in the Second World War.

I follow a path through coppiced chestnut woodland, the smooth, bronze trunks glowing gently against the grey sky. It's soft on the eye, a rare moment of visual warmth in the winter. From somewhere, there is the smell of smoke. I pass a bank on which the coppices have recently been cut, and then onto a path where those sheeny trunks make a cathedral around me.

After a while, I find myself in an orchard, its winter bareness revealing the careful diagonals in which the apple trees were planted. As I walk, the trees rearrange themselves into ranks of shifting diamonds. There are many different varieties in here, some tall and ancient-looking; others with hanging branches like weeping willows; others still which are mere saplings, tiny gestures of tree against their older, grander counterparts. A sign tells me this is No Man's Orchard, a community orchard planted in 1947 to preserve this unique Kentish ecosystem as farming began to change. It used to contain only Bramley apples; nowadays, it has cider apples too, and rare varieties like Flower of Kent and Kentish Fillbasket. All this wonderful diversity is invisible in the winter, but in a couple of months, it will begin again: buds, blossom, and then apples which will fall to reveal naked branches again. I have been walking through the most desolate part of the life cycle, and I am aching for the spring.

My primary school bordered an orchard just like this, where tiny pink-fleshed apples grew. Come autumn, they were piled up in boxes outside the secretary's office, and we could buy them for 2p at break time. Other kids – never me – used to climb over the rickety fence to steal them from the tree, leading to a heartfelt entreaty from our headmaster in assembly: *All right, everyone scrumps apples. But for heaven's sake, have the sense not to get caught.*

I didn't belong in that school. From where I was standing, there were groups of little girls playing together, all of whom had neat, thin bodies, perfect pony tails, and a striking interest in personal grooming, and there was me, alone, looking generally dishevelled and struggling to understand what they were talking about.

Everything I did seemed to offend them – perhaps there was something abrasive about the way I spoke, or maybe my bodily motion posed a threat to them – and they were offended en masse. I enjoyed a brief career as the playground circus freak, being, by the age of nine, already taller than my class teacher and at the wrong end of puberty for a sweet little girl. I would offer an array of lifts, carries and piggybacks to squealing children, and, if asked with enough enthusiasm, would flash them my burgeoning pubic hair, too. The problem was that this thrilling monsterishness was only tolerated until I dropped someone, or held them slightly wrong, and then tearful reports to the teachers would ensue, usually implying that my victim had not consented to their rough treatment. I realised early on that this may have looked like friendly contact, but that friendship was a one-way offer on the part of my peers, liable to be withdrawn at any moment, and very much at their convenience. I did everything I could to speak the same language as them, but I could see that it landed differently. I felt like a wild-eyed beast who speaks beautiful words, only to find them received as grunts and snarls. There was a translation error somewhere down the line.

I didn't even live in the right village. The kids at Shorne all played together in the village after school; I went home to the next village along, which might as well have been in the next county as far as I was concerned. The kids on my estate thought I was stuck up because I didn't go to their school. They slashed my bike tyres with their blunt little childhood penknives and shoved handfuls of stinging nettles down my back. I was, I learned, pretty much unlikeable to all parties, wherever I lived.

It was better to put on my roller skates and endlessly follow the fixed, cement track around my house: the front path, turning right into the tunnel between us and next-door, right again onto the patio, then turn around and do it all in reverse. It was soothing, the rumble of concrete under wheels, the watery echoes of the tunnel. I could go for hours, back and forth in my robotic 'c' shape, my stoppers hitting a pot plant at one end, and the garden fence at the other. Our neighbour said that I could skate into her garden too if I liked, and I thought about it and decided no. Better to just stick with the pattern I knew, on the nice, safe, flat path, where I wouldn't fall, and I wouldn't have to deal with the other children who never wanted to play the same games that I did.

It wasn't as if there was much else to do. Higham was nei-ther here nor there, sandwiched exactly between the River

Thames and the River Medway, with a Gravesend dialling code and a Medway postcode. I don't think any municipal authority was in a hurry to claim us. We were small without being picturesque, and prone to getting cut off in snowy winters. Our phone lines seemed unable to cope with the merest gasp of wind.

The village was remarkable only for being the site of Charles Dickens's house, Gads Hill Place. Even so, most mentions of Gads Hill tend to locate it in Rochester, eradicating Higham altogether. It's fair enough; Higham doesn't evoke anything much, even to locals. But it meant something to Dickens himself, I think; and not only easy access to London by coach. Dickens kept Rochester as a setting for his novels, but spent his mornings walking out across the marshes to the bleak outposts of Cliffe and Hoo.

Ours was the marsh country, down by the river. It certainly was, mine and his. I heard Dickens's name all my life, but never thought he was relevant to me until I was rush-reading *Great Expectations* on the night before my English GCSE (I had taken most of that year off sick), and I realised he was talking about all of my places. I thought no one else knew them, but here they were: the same bleak spaces I found if I wandered to the edge of the village in Higham, the same flat, grey marshes that I could see from my bedroom window when I was growing up in Chalk. On the marshes, the river was invisible, so the London-bound container ships seemed to sail through them without the aid of water. Every night, red lights speckled the power station chimneys across the Thames in Essex. I used to think they were lights in the sky, just floating there.

It is tempting to think that the marsh Dickens walked was an unspoiled, natural wonderland compared to mine, but I suspect it wasn't. It was already an industrial landscape,

littered with boatyards, forges like Joe Gargery's, abandoned forts from the Napoleonic Wars, and the prison hulks
struggling to contain the unruly. Walking at Cliffe, you find
yourself suddenly conscious of the two rivers that enclose
you, both of them teeming with boats going to London or
Tilbury. This landscape must have kept Dickens's profound
sense of humanity afloat: he escaped the bourgeois ease of
his country house to walk into a place where ordinary people
worked. This was a choice on his part. Had he walked in
the opposite direction, he would have immediately landed
in the quiet woodland of Shorne and Cobham, and then, a
little further, the leafy farmhouse wealth of Wealden Kent.
We know that he walked to these places too; but mostly,
and by habit, he chose the opposite direction. He chose the
marsh country.

I have been reading, trying to hunt myself down in blogs
and websites. It is an enervating, compulsive task. I already
understand that the very term 'Asperger syndrome' is no
longer neutral. It has been removed from the DSM V, the
most recent incarnation of the venerated Diagnostic and
Statistical Manual of the American Psychiatric Association.
That means that people who once would have been given
this label would now fall under the more generalised diagnosis of Autism Spectrum Disorder (ASD). Those who
continue to say they have Asperger syndrome – abbreviated
to AS – were perhaps diagnosed before the old categories
disappeared, but some are deliberately defying the new clinical order. They identify as Aspies; they do not want to be
thrown into a wider pool.

Reading some of the official guidelines on ASD leaves me
feeling like I'm trying to perform some kind of acrobatic
act of understanding, doubling over to see myself from

the outside. NHS Choices, for example, provides lists of symptoms for pre-school and school-age children, but only notes that those diagnosed in adulthood 'had features of the condition as a child, but enter adulthood without ever being diagnosed'. The website mentions language delay, difficulty with non-verbal communication, and repetitive activity; it notes that seventy per cent of children with ASD have an IQ under seventy. Nothing is said of the remaining thirty per cent.

This absence is vital to me. Descriptions of AS often note hyperlexia, an unusually enhanced ability to read and retain words, despite poor communication skills. This is where I recognise myself. I spent my childhood watching adults draw breath at my words, and my obsession with them. *She's swallowed a dictionary*: I heard that one over and over again. And I had. I often found the contents of novels impenetrable, the characters hard to fathom; but the thin pages of the *Concise Oxford English Dictionary*, 1976 Edition, were beguiling to me, full of sounds and meanings and information. I read it from cover to cover, over and over again; I lucky-dipped in it until the hardback cover peeled off. I am angry, still, when I come across a word I don't know.

When I spoke, they all reeled out of me, those words I'd imbibed, in one continuous ribbon. Over time, I realised that my fluency alarmed people. It was pleasurable to me, but for them it was a torrent gushing out, an inundation. I learned, eventually, to disrupt myself with pauses and pretend uncertainties, to back-fill inflections that didn't come naturally, to allow the estuarine vowels that I soaked up from those marshes to normalise me. I built a kind of dam to keep words in, constructed channels that let them flow away. Even now, I sometimes have to drive for an hour, talking to myself, to let them loose. Sometimes I sing to release them.

The only times my words fail me is when my mind melts. Otherwise, they're a spring tide that my sea wall struggles to retain. Communication difficulty, for me, was not born of an absence of words but of too many, too much breadth, and depth, and complexity. It is difficult to say what you mean through all those words. The message gets drowned.

The National Autistic Society's website has a page on Asperger syndrome, and it notes that this is still a 'useful profile for many diagnosticians and professionals' within the overarching category of ASD. I am back in more recognisable territory here, but the way they describe the features of AS leaves me feeling like a child again. They're not talking directly to me, but referring to people with AS as a distant 'they', perhaps to enlighten a doctor or concerned parent:

> Autistic people, including those with Asperger syndrome, have difficulties with interpreting both verbal and non-verbal language like gestures or tone of voice. Many have a very literal understanding of language, and think people always mean exactly what they say. They may find it difficult to use or understand:
> • facial expressions
> • tone of voice
> • jokes and sarcasm
> • vagueness
> • abstract concepts

These people, it goes on, have problems with social interaction:

> People with Asperger syndrome often have difficulty 'reading' other people – recognising or understanding

others' feelings and intentions – and expressing their own emotions. This can make it very hard for them to navigate the social world. They may:

- appear to be insensitive
- seek out time alone when overloaded by other people
- not seek comfort from other people
- appear to behave 'strangely' or in a way thought to be socially inappropriate.

They may find it hard to form friendships. Some may want to interact with other people and make friends, but may be unsure how to go about it.

We may also have 'repetitive behaviour and routines', the delicately phrased 'highly focused interests', and, last of all, 'sensory sensitivity'.

I recognise many of these things, but it's also a brutal read somehow, reminding me of a man I heard on the TV a few years ago. He tried to enlighten the presenter on how they might recognise someone with AS by giving the example of 'the guy who does sixty-five in the outside lane of the motorway, because he doesn't think anyone should go any faster'. It reminds me, too, of characters I've come across in books, people who make obsessive lists or who have laughably unsophisticated interpretations of any given social situation, when the true meaning is sledgehammer-obvious. I never saw myself in this, and I still don't, really; I can see some aspects of my own behaviour, but none of it seems to acknowledge the fact that I've moved on from being a bewildered eight-year-old girl. Nowadays, I might find complex social situations stressful and therefore exhausting, but can I read them? Sure I can. It's imperfect, but I get by.

It strikes me that these descriptions are totally external,

pitched at a paternalistic outsider who feels that a person in their care is a bit odd, and who might need a helpful list of observable behaviours in order to apply the correct label. The assumed subject is mute, unaware, incompetent. It feels as though the whole diagnostic thrust lies in placing a person on a neat, medical shelf rather than engaging with their experiences and difficulties.

On the other hand, I find blogs that make me sing with recognition. *Life on the Spectrum* is written by people with AS, and their approach is entirely different: what matters to them is how it feels to be an Aspie, rather than providing comfort to the people on the outside who have to deal with them. On the subject of diagnosis, they're pleasingly assertive about my right to decide whether I can relate to the set of telling features, rather than whether I fit the mould for outside observers: 'If you can strongly relate to the experiences of autistic people, and have similar stories of your own to tell, *then you are very likely autistic too*, and you should have confidence in that comparison,' they say, providing an experiential list of Asperger's symptoms. In these, finally, I find a series of mirrors in which I can see myself. Not all of them are true for me, but most are:

- People greet you by saying 'here comes trouble' and you don't know whether or not they're joking.
- You try to help someone, only to find your help wasn't wanted.
- You hear a lot about how 'you're only making things worse for yourself'.
- You don't understand what's so funny about teasing. You feel you're being mocked.
- You are exhausted by always pretending to be normal, but fearful the Real You will be rejected.

- You hope, with each new group of people you meet, that this time you'll get it right.
- People say you speak too quickly, but you know you have to get the words out before you forget them.
- You're the only person wanting the music turned down.
- You can cope with a party, but have to hide in the loo to recover every now and then.
- You see other people exchange 'a look' but don't know what it means.
- You like to hide away on your own, especially after spending time with other people.
- Other people think you're being intolerant, and you can't understand how they cope.
- You feel 'different' from most people, and feel that you don't 'fit in'.
- People think you're being rude and/or critical when you're not meaning to be.

The list has, perhaps, an anxious tone, a sense of bewilderment at how things can go so wrong with the best of intentions. There is dramatic irony lurking at the margins of the page, invisible to the person who wrote the list. This is exactly how it feels to be me: as though there is a subtext to my screenplay which only the audience can understand. They are grimacing and cringing at the irony of it all, and I'm left to play it out alone.

It seems, then, that AS is as much an identity as a diagnosis these days, a spark of common feeling among people who feel it's hard to find common feeling with anyone at all. I was hoping, I suppose, for a simple tick-list, a clear yes or no, but it's far more ambiguous than that, far more amorphous. This leaves me with an unsteady – and, frankly, unwanted – sense of responsibility towards my own diagnosis. I have never been much of a joiner. The question is, do I want to join this tribe?

I find that surprisingly easy to answer: here, finally, are the people like me. It's all I can do to stop myself running towards them with open arms. But there's a deeper question lurking underneath it all – a more uncomfortable one. I was happy with the label 'Asperger syndrome' because it carried the faintest taint of genius. It is the other word – the newer term – that makes me squirm: ASD.

Autism.

Is that really me? I will need to wear that one for a while, to see if it fits.

Even in misty January, the North Downs Way is profoundly green. I'm in the desirable part of the county here, far from the marsh; the hills roll and the houses are well kempt, lit up inside. It is so very different from the edgelands of Higham, Cliffe and Hoo; this is the centre of things, where people want to be. I pass through the village of Chartham Hatch, down a series of pavementless country lanes, bordered by more orchards. These ones contain the squat, efficient trees that farming turned to when it abandoned No Man's Orchard. The effect is the same. The land is announcing its own fecundity in ranks of apple trees. The bare, black winter branches do nothing to disrupt this impression.

Soon, I find myself somewhere I recognise, standing beside the main road, where cars rush past to Ashford. I know this place for the entirely unromantic reason that there is a garden centre a little further on, with a tiny soft-play centre that used to be just about right for Bert when he was first walking, and I was desperate for somewhere to be that wasn't home, enclosed.

I'm not convinced this is right. Did I expect to cross this road? I turn my map upside down, and squint. At the other side lies Chartham, a village I have only known in signpost form. *Posh Chatham*, goes the joke between H and I, mostly at our own expense. Like Dickens, we are definitely more Chatham than Chartham; more industrial grit than country charm. I have lost the ability to read my map entirely; the path seems to jump around, and I can no longer work out on which side of the page I ought to fall. I cross the road, wait at the signal box for a train to pass, and then walk down into the village, past a paper mill and a river lined with empty factory buildings. Perhaps it is more like Chatham than I expected.

And then, around a corner, is the village I was expecting to find, houses of white weatherboard and neat red Kentish brick. I am standing opposite a half-timbered pub called The Artichoke, its wooden frame aged to silvery grey. I use it to locate myself on the map, and find that I've wandered far off course somehow, missing a turning half a mile up the road. I could walk back to it, but I'm tired, and it's already lunchtime. It seems a long way to go. I text H and go in.

'Do you do coffee?' I say to the woman at the bar.

'Certainly,' she says. I always wonder what I look like, in my walking leggings and cagoule, coming in alone like this. I begin to scramble in my rucksack for my purse. It's not there.

'Wait,' I call after her. 'Don't make the coffee! I've left my purse at home!'

'Will you be all right?' she says.

'Yeah,' I say. 'Hopefully my husband will collect me soon.'

'I'll make you the coffee anyway.'

'No, no,' I say, 'it's fine.'

'Don't worry,' she says. 'It's only coffee.'

Always uncertain about kindnesses like this, I thank her more than I probably should, and wonder if I should make light conversation as I drink it. But she's already drifted off to the other side of the bar, so I sit at a table and try to make myself look tidy as I study my map. It's hard to imagine how I got so confused back at the junction.

After a while, H and Bert arrive, and I use his wallet to buy beer, apple juice and crisps, and pay for my coffee. 'To be honest,' says H, 'I've been constantly surprised you haven't got more lost before.'

'You have no faith!' I say, while wondering the same myself.

9

....

Whitstable to Seasalter, January

I am sitting in the back of our car next to Bert. My mother and H are in the front. Bert is playing on his tablet, which is aimed at keeping him quiet as we drive along.

He's swiping through his favourite new game. You're a fireman inspecting an apartment block, and every single room is on fire. It's not that the fire has spread; each room is alight for a different reason, and it always seems to have only just been kindled as you arrive at the window on your ladder. You can turn your hose on it, or use an axe on the fire for reasons I don't entirely understand, but whatever course of action you take, it seems that your very presence in the room makes more fires break out. Flames appear at the other side of the room, and black smoke begins to pour forth. From my limited experience of this game, the best strategy seems to be to simply close the door and go away, because you'll only make things worse. The only problem is, a fire will break out in the next room you go to, too. It's as though you emit some kind of destructive ray that ignites everything.

The whole experience is akin to one of those helpless nightmares, where you try to save yourself but your hands won't quite do your bidding. I find it stressful even being close to it; I can't comprehend why this is fun. Bert loves it. He wants to show me. Tap, tap, tap on my shoulder. Mummy, Mummy, Mummy. I get sick in the back of cars at the best of times, and I can't look at screens. I tell him this.

'Sorry, love, I can't look. I get carsick.'

'But look! It's afire!'

'I just can't. I'm sorry. I know it's rubbish.'

A pause. 'But look, Mummy.'

'Please, Bert. I just can't.'

'Why?'

'It's just how it is. I get sick in cars and looking at things makes it worse.'

And onwards. I'm already wound tight. We have just been to a shop where a man without a uniform flashed some kind of a card and asked to search my bag. Because of terrorism, he said.

I said, 'How do I know you're not the terrorist?'

Apparently I should have been able to recognise the card, because they're a national security company, and it's not like anyone with a half-decent home printer can produce one.

'It's for your own safety,' he says.

'Safety from what? Being asked by complete strangers to surrender my personal information before I spend money in their shop? Being harassed half to death while I'm going about my own business?'

The manager is called.

'We're just trying to keep you safe,' he says.

'Well how about issuing your security guards with uniforms, rather than having them wander up to people in jeans and a T-shirt, flash a non-specific card, and ask to see the contents of women's handbags?'

'It's a nationally recognised security firm,' he says.

'By whom? By people who work in security firms? The only national security firm I recognise is the police.'

The manager sighs. The security guard sighs. I can see my family out of the corner of my eye, visibly wondering whether they should intervene.

'So,' I say, 'are you going to insist on looking in my bag, and seeing the tampons and lip balms and keys? Or can I get on with my shopping?'

'We just do it for your safety,' he says again, but I suspect the whole shop can tell by now that his resolve is weakening.

'I don't believe that for one second.'

He grits his teeth and backs away. I'm not worth it. I'm too much trouble. I should really leave at this point and refuse to give him any of my hard-earned money. But I've driven an hour to get here, to this stupid big warehouse full of outdoor gear, and I'd be cutting my nose off to spite my face. I need the stuff in here. I need thermal underlayers and a jacket that doesn't take in water. I need proper, cushioned socks and a warm hoodie to throw on when I finish walking. I'm angry all the way around the shop, but it's cheap and the only way I can afford the things I need for February walking.

It doesn't help that Bert is wide-eyed with excitement at the vast expanses of the store. He runs around it like a wild animal, and keeps vanishing out of sight, leading to panicked chases around the stacks. By the time we're in the line to pay, my nerves are rattling. He grabs for a bottle of water by the till, and nearly knocks the whole shelf over. I have to count to get him to come back to my side, and it's lame because we both know I won't lose my place in the queue to make him sit in the car.

And then we eat lunch in Pizza Hut, which has loud

music in the background and a table of seven-year-old girls having a birthday party next to us. These places are not my natural habitat, but we have to come here because of Bert. Bert doesn't want to eat anything, or use the crayons. He wants to crawl under the table and smear dirty hands over the glass divide between us and the next customers. I just want to eat, and have a glass of wine. I'm hungry. I need something to numb me. I just want to feel on a level again.

So, by the time we get into the car on the way home, my head is already full. I wouldn't want to look at the tablet anyway, but really, really not now. The game makes a noise. Bert asks me to look. Up front, they're playing music. My mother begins to whistle. I hate whistling. Bert reaches over to get my attention: tap, tap, tap. Mummy, Mummy, Mummy.

We're going to a party this afternoon, a children's party. It will be in an echoing church hall, and the children will run about and scream, because that's what they do. That's what they're *entitled* to do. I cannot go. I have said that I'm going, but I cannot go. I have been hoping for a migraine, or a dose of the flu that's been going round. I even woke in the night and nearly convinced myself that I was sick, feverish. It wasn't true. It's no problem; H will take him, and my mother will probably go along too. She doesn't mind parties, or other people's children. I will simply have to not go, and say I'm not going. But it won't do. It's not enough to just not go. I do not have an acceptable excuse. What's more, the traffic is building, and it looks like we're going to be late. We are going to be late, and I'm going to be absent for no good reason.

Bert says, 'Mummy, look, he's using a chopping spade,' and I say, 'An axe,' and I realise the whiteness has already started, like a series of detonations across my brain that make my face numb and my vision cloud over. It's a mush-room cloud of searing blankness. It feels like someone has pushed a knitting needle through my skull – or maybe worse than that, maybe their whole hand is in there and is palpating the matter it finds inside, squeezing the sense out of whole regions of my mind. It's an electrical storm, streaks of lightning spiking across the cloud cover. I want to squeal, as though that would let the air escape. I want to sob. I fumble in my handbag for my earbuds, and play my recording of rain. It's white noise, to match the whiteness in my head. I push the heels of my hands into my eye sockets until everything pixelates. I press my head against the cold glass of the window.

I can hear H saying, 'Bertie, I think Mummy's sleeping,' but it's distant now. I am not here anymore. I am absent.

Once they have gone, I walk.

It's almost dark already, but I remember the walking I used to do, before everything was a project. I walk out of my front door, across the road, and down a street of Victorian terraces. I cross over Harbour Street, sombre now that the Christmas lights are down, but its windows already glow-ing with yellow light. Down between the shops, across Sea Street and past the Royal Native Oyster Stores, and then I am at the beach.

The floodgates are up, so I climb over the sea wall and land on the path the other side. Which way to go? Left or right? I choose left, as I have done many times before, heading along the coast towards the marshes at Seasalter. Whitstable sits at the very mouth of the estuary where the Thames and the Medway find the sea. We are separated from the rivers, though, by the Swale, a narrow strip of sea that divides the mainland from the Isle of Sheppey. This is why Whitstable never feels wild. It is sheltered, shingle-beached, flat-waved, and overlooked. It's a comfort in the winter.

Along this stretch of beach, you can look into the back gardens of the expensive houses of Island Wall and dream. We were fortunate to rent one of them when we first moved here; the owner over-wintered in Australia and let us have it for a peppercorn rent, just to keep the place occupied. How the rich live: a house like that, just left as spare for eight months of the year. The heating ran on such narrow copper pipes that we never really got warm, and the oven spewed out hot air from its rotted seal, but we couldn't believe our luck.

I never thought we would end up in Whitstable. I had always wanted to live by the sea, but I never believed I would dislodge H from his beloved Medway towns, to which we both felt the fierce loyalty that you find in people who have thrived in difficult places. It was a sleight of hand, really, but performed by the fates rather than me.

We had moved to a new house in Gillingham originally and, within days, my mind had started to show signs of one of its customary disintegrations. The new house was twice the size of our old terrace, and open on three sides to the elements. It was so loud. Voices echoed up from the train line below us, and cars screeched along the main road by the river. Our new bedroom was like a hall, the bed stranded against one wall and the rest of it open space. I would close my eyes and try to sleep, but from somewhere across town, amplified by the railway cutting, there would always be screaming.

'Did you hear that?' I would say to H, and we would both rush to the window and gaze out, but there was nothing to see, no direction to follow. It was just there, in the air, like a haunting. No point in even calling the police, because what would you say? *Someone is screaming in Gillingham.* We could all have guessed as much, without even hearing it.

'I don't like this house,' I said to H. 'It's too loud.'

We moved into the spare bedroom at the back of the house, where the walls were closer, and this was when I bought my recording of rain to play at night as I tried to sleep. Still, the other sounds overcame it; the neighbours arguing through the walls, the disorder that seemed to be lurking outside.

My hands began to shake. I started to leave the house with H every morning, and spend my day in the library, reading *Birds Britannica* over and over until I felt like one of the birds it contained, fast-hearted, flittish. I didn't want to go home. I couldn't go home. The thought of it made me sick with panic. I had made a wrong and very expensive decision, and there was nothing that could be done about it. Everybody came to visit, and said what a beautiful house it was. I couldn't seem to explain myself to them.

One day, from a phone booth outside the library, I called a helpline for people having panic attacks. A man with a kind voice answered and said, 'It's okay. You can get home and then you'll feel safe. Just take yourself home.'

And I said, 'I can't. I can't. Home is the problem.'

'You'll be safe at home,' he said, 'with people who love you.'

What do you do when you can't bear to be in your own home? There's nowhere to rest, nowhere to settle. And yes, I did have someone there who loved me, and they were bewildered. One night, someone outside slammed the boot of their car, and I wailed like a baby, inconsolable. Another day, I scalded my hand because H had picked up a picture frame with a spider clinging to it, and I had no words to tell him, just uncontrollable screaming.

'Just tell me what I need to do,' he kept saying to me. 'Just tell me what it is. Is it me? Is it the house? We can change it.'

To soothe ourselves, we drove to the sea at Whitstable in the evenings, staying out as late as we could before we drove back home and I tried to sleep again. Chips and vinegar, every night; it was about all I could digest. Eventually, he said to me, 'Come on, let's move here. We'll work it out.'

And we did. It was messy, and expensive, and we had to fend off an awful lot of baffled questions. But this was survival; it didn't matter. On the night we moved in, I remember taking a walk around the backstreets of the town, and hearing a party in somebody's garden. Just people having a barbecue: laughter, a friendly competition of voices. H turned to me and said, 'You're afraid of that, aren't you?' And I was. To me, it sounded like a riot breaking out.

But that night, I watched the empty beach from my bedroom window, with the window open to hear the faint shuffle of the sea on shingle. I had never seen a beach in darkness before; it was magical, a privilege I didn't think was mine. I woke in the middle of the night, and opened the curtains again, just to make sure it was still there.

Over the coming weeks, I learned that people land on the beach in all weathers and at all times of day. On Saturday nights, I watched drunken November skinny-dippers splash in the black water; on weekday afternoons, toddlers balanced along the sea wall at the bottom of our garden. I retrieved the odd dog from our patio and rushed out with Savlon and plasters for the cut knees of children I didn't know. I walked it every day, skipping over the groynes like hurdles, and wading out at low tide to find shards of old blue china and the skeletons of boats. I walked until I was too tired to feel anxious anymore. I became part of the beach, and it made me better.

Stalking that same path today, I realise how much I now take it for granted. It's flat along my stretch of coast, and I usually crave hills; but there's the curve of the shore and view out to Seasalter, the beach huts at West Beach, the fleeting views of Southend on a clear day. Flocks of sanderlings and turnstones pick over the shore, scattering as you approach them. The seabirds never leave us, black-headed gulls and herring gulls which float on unseen breezes over the sea. We even have a local cormorant, who dries his wings on a buoy just off the coast. I sometimes forget to be astonished that all of this is waiting a few footsteps from my front door.

Perhaps, also, I sometimes still forget that I'm at home, and safe.

10

....

Chartham to Chilham, January

By the end of January, I realise that there is a kind of a New Year's resolution lurking at the edges of my mind after all; a vague intention to sort out this autism business, somehow. I'm not sure what that might entail. I say to H, 'Should I go to the doctor, do you think?'

He says, 'I don't know; why?'

I say, 'I don't know really.'

It's not like I'm looking for a cure. I know there isn't one, and I know I wouldn't want one if there was. Imagine submitting yourself to an operation that changes all that you are, your way of relating to other people, your way of thinking, your way of perceiving the world. It's a horrifying thought, a hundred times more altering than a face transplant. I already know that I don't want a cure for being myself.

'I think I just want to know,' I say. 'I think I just want to make sure it's not some weird fantasy that I've got tangled up in.'

That's how it feels at the moment. It feels as though I'm using those powers of persuasion on myself, talking myself into the belief that I'm something else. It feels a lot like holding onto a dream after you wake up, in those baffled moments when the dream and your bedroom are both present at once, and your eyes are trying to make sense of two sets of shapes. Where am I? Who am I?

I keep thinking, *No, this is daft, I'm just the same me that I've always been*, and then realising that this is very much the point. Nobody is suggesting that I have 'caught' Asperger syndrome, perhaps in the quiet stacks of the university library where I'm researching my PhD. No. This is a process of reframing what I have always been.

'Perhaps they'll be able to help you cope better?' says H, and I say, 'Yes, maybe,' although I am doubtful.

I think that probably the best course of action is to leave it for a couple of months and read some more about it, and let the whole idea sit while I churn it over. But I book an appointment anyway. It's a bit like being pregnant, in the early weeks when everyone says you shouldn't even test, but you do, and you keep on testing until that pale pink line becomes darker, more decisive. It is simply not the kind of matter that you can leave to its own devices. I need, I think, to test it against someone else's judgement, a disinterested party.

I am walking, now, as a kind of compulsion. I keep my weekends free for it, giving noncommittal answers when friends suggest we should get together. In the new dawn of AS, I want to find out what not getting together feels like. I'm sick of people. I suspect people are making me sick. I want to be alone, in the January drear, with the voluminous space of the countryside around me, even if it is spiked with blackthorn and bare branches.

Bert has a friend over to play today, a friend from nursery.

I made arrangements myself with the other mother in the cloakroom, as the two boys pretended to put on their shoes. We have exchanged friendly texts, in which it has been made politely clear that she will not leave her child alone with us, but that she will stay. I know better than to take this personally; everybody stays these days. I suppose we all have to endlessly suspect each other of one perversion or another, as though the world is populated entirely by latent Jimmy Saviles, waiting to spring on our children. Those of us who lack this anxiety probably stay anyway, drinking tea and making awkward conversation, because we don't want to look like we don't care. And so we all take it in turns to invade each other's space while we could be doing something useful like tidying the house or having lunch with our partners, but we don't dare to argue because that would send out the signal that we have better things to do than constantly fawn over our children.

Anyway. In the days running up to the child's visit, it becomes clear to me that (a) I ought to be the one who entertains this mother, not H; and (b) that I have such a pronounced aversion to doing so that it's keeping me awake at night. How long do these playdates last? Two hours? Three? What on earth am I supposed to say to her in that time? A lifetime of being told I'm offhand and unfriendly forces to me to say, at this point, that she seems very nice. But that doesn't make enforced socialisation any more of an appetising prospect.

On Saturday morning, I cave in and ask H if he'll do the honours while I go walking.

'Of course,' he says. 'I never thought you'd stay anyway.'

'But I ought to,' I say. 'We all know I ought to.'

'Who says?'

'Everyone. Society. Mumsnet. I don't know. We're

supposed to have coffee and "natter" about . . . whatever women talk about. Our children, I should think.'

'Oh well,' says H. 'I'll manage.'

'Just don't tell her I'm walking. Tell her I'm working.'

'Why?'

'Walking's a leisure activity. I'm not supposed to avoid her for something like that.'

It doesn't feel like a leisure activity, though; it feels like survival. I drive myself back to Chartham, park by the level crossing, and cross back over the main road. I have to walk all the way back up to the top of the lane (and past a sign that warns of walkers in the road) before I find the turning I should have taken last week, discreetly tucked into a driveway, but nevertheless perfectly well signposted and obvious on the map.

I walk through farmland, under a railway bridge, and then past a set of sorry-looking caravans that probably host itinerant pickers in warmer seasons. I am back in an orchard, but this one is enormous, set on a slope and divided into fields. The trees here are chest-height and don't have branches so much as tangles of wiry twigs that wisp around them. They represent some kind of calculation, I suspect, that balances how many apples they can carry against how easily reached the fruit might be. I'm sure this calculation has something to do with the piles of bright red apples at the base of every trunk, even after all the leaves have gone. They glow against the low-sun gloom, an absurd, unwanted glut.

The map shows that I cut through the middle of this orchard to make my way into Old Wives Lees, but I cannot find a waymarked path. After stalking the edge of the field for a while, I decide just to walk between the lines of trees. The ground beneath my feet crunches with ice. I can see the general direction in which I need to go, but this off-roading panics me slightly anyway. What are the rules, I wonder, about trespassing on farmland? It suddenly occurs to me that the reason I feel so at home on the South West Coast Path is because it's almost impossible to get lost with the sea at your right. If nothing else, it is at least always clear which way is north. Here, far inland, I have no way of navigating. At this time of year, in the middle of the day, I have no idea whether the sun is even rising or setting.

There comes a point, I suppose, when every walker needs to buy a compass. But I'd choose getting lost like this any day over getting lost in the maze of small talk. Sometimes, getting lost is a pleasurable alternative.

I've never suffered from exam nerves because I can absorb huge amounts of information, and, if I'm honest, I enjoy spinning it to fit whatever question is on the paper, in my fastest handwriting, in a quiet room. Today, though, as I sit in the waiting room, I think I finally understand how other people must feel as they line up outside the school hall. This is the worst test of my life. I don't even know how to pass or fail it; I don't know whether I want to pass or fail. I'm wondering how you open up the conversation. You can't blurt, 'I think I have Asperger syndrome,' in the way that you would croak, 'I have a sore throat.' Or perhaps that is exactly what you ought to do. Perhaps you just say it straight.

I have failed to make a decision by the time my name is called. My GP is in the habit of coming to fetch you, rather than ringing a buzzer in his office. I'm always impressed by this; it shows, at the very least, a commitment to his own good health, but it's kind, too. I like him. Over the years I've been visiting him, I've developed the impression that he's a little bit of a data geek, and a precise thinker. He always states the evidence behind every decision he makes. This, as you may guess, wins my admiration. I want to impress him today. I realise I must fight this urge, and just be myself, straightforwardly. I have no idea how to do that.

I sit in his chair, shift, and sit again.

'So,' he says, 'how are you today?'

'Very well, thanks.'

'Great. What can I help you with?'

'I. I. I . . .' Where does this start? How far back? 'I've been finding life very difficult since I had my son.' A discreet glance at the screen. 'He's three and a half,' I say. 'I realise I've left it quite a while to say anything.'

Tears are here now. I didn't expect them so soon. My voice is clouded. 'Sorry,' I say.

'Take your time.'

'It's just that, well, I had mental-health problems when I was a teenager, and the treatment was . . . awful . . .'

His face collapses into a frown, but I think it's a sympathetic one. 'Oh,' he says. 'The way we care for teenage mental health is dreadful.'

I didn't expect this; I didn't expect sympathy for my own sense of dislocation. 'I think it's probably got better,' I say.

'I don't know,' he says, and I want to ask him what he sees, what he knows, what it feels like to know you're part of a system that doesn't always help.

'Well,' I say, 'I suppose it's put me off ever mentioning it again. I felt, for years after, like nobody heard me when I said something was wrong. Something like that gets put on your record, and it's the first thing anybody sees when you come in. That's why I didn't say anything when I had the baby. I was too afraid.'

My voice is a whisper. I don't know how to say this.

'So what about today?' he says.

'It's always been anxiety and depression, anxiety and depression. I don't think it's that anymore. I used to believe it, and now I don't. I'm anxious, yes, but I'm not depressed. I'm actually a very happy person. I know it doesn't look that way right now.'

A little smile. I'm proud of this. I like to think I can always help people along, even when I'm being difficult. But then, autistic people aren't supposed to have a sense of humour, or any empathy. I keep hearing that. What am I again?

'So what do you think it is?'

This feels like a trick. He might as well ask, *What have you been googling, then?* Doctors must get sick of this, their patients quoting search-engine results as though they can replace years of medical training and clinical experience, the sum total of which must surely lead to something more delicate and nuanced than anything I can glean from ten minutes on WebMD. I never google before I come to the doctor. Never. It's a point of honour, a mark of respect for their greater expertise.

But here I am, sitting at his desk on the say-so of a voice on a radio show and a gut instinct that I am one of those people. It isn't enough. I know it isn't enough, but I find that I've said it out loud.

'Asperger syndrome?' he says. A perplexed look. 'Can you talk me through why you think that?'

And I do. I talk about spending my days under assault from light and smell and noise, how people – how the chaos of people – sends me skittering for cover. I talk about how I can't bear to be touched, and how I can get physically sick, shivering, aching, from social contact.

'But,' he says, and it takes me a while to realise that it's a statement in itself, a general proclamation of objection. He's scrolling through my notes again, and I know he's hunting for something, some kind of marker or sign. He's a little excited, I think. This is different from the diagnostic mundane. It's a challenge. *I* am a challenge.

'Okay,' he says. 'Take me through this. I've been seeing you in here for years, and you have never once struck me as autistic. Quite the opposite, in fact.'

'I'm good at that,' I say, fighting back no small amount of pride. I had no idea he even remembered me from one dreary visit to the next. I always try to be as unobtrusive as possible; not to make a fuss. 'I learned how to act normal when I was a teenager. Bit by bit. I watched other people and worked it out.'

'But your eye contact is good.'

'I learned that, too. I still have to remind myself every time I talk to someone. I don't really like it, but I know that's what you have to do.'

Is this true? I can't tell. It's impossible to tell; the habits I created are so long-learned that I barely notice them anymore. Yet now I'm checking in, I can feel the urge to let my gaze slide off to the right of his head, and I can feel the electric tingle of his eyes on mine. I look at the ceiling.

'People with AS often say that they can't make friends. Is that true for you?'

'No,' I say. 'I can make friends. It's another thing I learned. They tend to drift off, though, and I don't understand why. I sometimes catch myself being boring, just talking at people and not noticing that they're not engaged. I don't mean to. Or I offend people; I say things that trample over their sensibilities, and it's not intentional, but not everyone can handle me. My life is littered with broken friendships. I'm embarrassed to say that, because I try so hard.'

'I'd say that too, though,' he says. 'About myself, I mean. We all fall out with people.'

'Yes,' I say. 'But I get the impression that I'm considered to be particularly difficult.'

But I do have friends; long-standing ones. Good ones. I can't admit to them here. If the diagnostic criteria is that I am repellent to people, then that's what I'm going for. It's partially true. I'm repellent to most people, most of the time. Other people, I think, adore me, if perhaps find me a bit of a strong flavour in large doses. I can't tell if what I'm saying is real, or just an improvisation I'm making on this spot; a truth for this moment. I don't know the answers to these questions. I'm confabulating. I want him to believe me.

'What about your childhood?' he says. 'What were you like as a child?'

What do you tell here? What parts are true? I don't remember much about being a child. It was a phase that I needed to pass through. It was concluded that I was a hyperactive child, and we avoided tartrazine. It didn't make much difference. I was capable of lashing out, at children and adults. My temper was legendary. I grew up as an only child of divorced parents, and people assumed, I think, that this was the cause. I was fiercely protected by my mother from the injuries of the outside world. Information leaked back to me anyway; invitations to parties that were skipped; comments from other parents. They hurt her more than they hurt me; I was oblivious. I didn't have close friends. I hung about with the other little girl that my mother took in after school, but she clearly hated me. My mother said it was a bit like having a sibling. At school, I sat with the quiet, nerdy boys at lunchtime, or, if they'd let me, worked through maths problems and science cards.

I did everything early, precociously: walking, speaking. I had to be held back from reading on the advice of a health visitor. It wasn't considered good, in those days, to just teach yourself to read. The moment I got into Reception class, I read, and then read everything on the shelves. I read every piece of information in the school, and wrote it, and made it into fractions and decimals and anything else that I could learn before I hit the limits of that place. I can only imagine what the internet would have given to a child like me. The limitless information; the astonishing networks of knowledge.

I was a dark little creature, afraid of everything. I spent years refusing to look at the sky in case I witnessed an alien invasion; I was equally afraid of the Bluebell Hill ghost, a be-draggled girl who would run out in front of your car on the road to Maidstone. All children have fears; I festered mine, obsessively. I got in trouble for writing poems about death. My mother was called in to school. There were thoughts that you simply weren't allowed to express as a little girl. I never understood this; still don't, now. We made sugar mice in Brownies and I made a vivisected one, all painted red eyes and stitched incisions. *You always have to go too far* was a phrase I encountered a lot. I didn't understand that, either. I just seemed to be interested in things that other people preferred to forget. All I knew was that I was so appallingly uncoordinated that I earned the nickname Clumsy Katie from my first teacher, and it stuck; and that I never seemed to make the netball team, even though I tried harder than all the other girls.

I don't tell him all of this, but I tell him some of it. There is too much to tell. He says, 'Huh,' and then, almost to himself, 'That's a classic case history of a child with Asperger's.' He shakes his head. It doesn't fit. It doesn't fit at all – what he sees before him, and what he's hearing. He's confused. I feel like order is breaking down. A defeated sigh.

'I mean, I see your husband in here sometimes. What does he think?'

'He thinks it's true. He thinks it all fits. He puts up with a lot behind the scenes, I think, and he's kind of . . . *relieved* . . . that it has a name.'

My doctor looks at me, looks at his screen, looks at his hands, and then does something extraordinary. He says, *Fuck.*

'*Fuck.* I never would have thought it.'

I don't think he says it to me. I think he says it to himself.

The sun is almost set by the time I finish my walk. I approach the lovely old village of Chilham from the rear of the church, crossing through the graveyard where Thomas Beckett was rumoured to have been buried. It was a major stopping point for the medieval Canterbury pilgrims, and as I round the front of the church, a man falls into step beside me and says, gently, 'Hail pilgrim! You've got a long walk to Guildford.'

I laugh. 'I'm stopping here,' I say, 'for today.'

He limps heavily beside me, his Labrador winding between us. 'You'll get there eventually, I shouldn't wonder.'

'I will,' I say. 'There or thereabouts.'

'Excellent,' he says, and nods, and diverts off down one of the graveyard paths. I am left, yet again, with a sense of wonder at the strange hospitalities of my own county; of these places that are becoming mine as I walk them.

Or perhaps I am becoming theirs.

PART TWO

Hartland

Imagine, for a moment, that land isn't divided up into areas, but into paths through.

So, you cannot put a fence around a piece of land and call it your own. You can only join the dots between significant places (a gate, a bus shelter, a tree). If this join-the-dots comes full circle (gate – bus shelter – tree – gate), then all you have is a circular path; the space inside the circle does not belong to you.

You have no more ownership over your back garden than over your journey to work. You cannot buy or sell land, because its only use is in providing scenery to pass through, and nobody has any interest in standing still. All that you possess is a way of travelling; a route. And each route is your own, unique sightline on the rest of the world. Many other paths will cross it, but only you can walk its full extent.

Now, imagine that you couldn't draw this path on a map, and not simply because maps don't exist. The depth, the weight of the information contained within your path is too great to be drawn. A line cannot contain it. A line would only convey the thinnest part of the information; the blank, formless geography.

Your path is more than that. Your path has peaks and valleys, yes, but it's also littered with things that you treasure. That stream is your stream; you took off your shoes and socks to wade through it as a child. That village is the place you drove to one day, when life was ripping at the seams, and you put your head on the steering wheel and cried. That junction box is the one you notice every time you crest the hill on your way home; you have come to think of it as a sign that says, *nearly there.* Your path is made of meaning. All of these things are encoded in it. Because they're too rich to be drawn, you must speak it. You don't tell everyone you meet, only those closest to you. You take them from place to place with your tongue and your teeth, chattering out the detail.

Unchecked, you would carelessly change the path every time you described it. Instead, you learn it, with all its diversions intact. You let it create a pattern for itself, a verse, a song. Now, you can sing this path to your friends, your lovers, your children, and as you sing it, you tell the story of all that you are. You transmit your creation myth. When you die, they are left with your song.

This isn't a utopia I've hallucinated at the low ebb of a long walk. Transpose it to Australia, and you have something approximating the Aboriginal understanding of territory. As Bruce Chatwin describes them in *The Songlines*, these paths memorialise the actions of the ancestors as they sang the Earth into existence. Australia is dotted with relics of the Dreamtime. They are sites of ritual significance, certainly, but they are also landmarks by which to navigate. The songlines link them together. By learning your song and singing it, you memorise a route that you have perhaps never even seen; and by walking the route that is encoded in your song, you assert a connection that flows through the generations to your clan ancestor's dreaming. This is all that you own: the whole of creation and nothing at all; a path that cuts through time.

Everybody has a song like this. A song that is a map, a compass; a song that sets you straight again. Learn it, and it will take you home.

That song, of course, is a very different matter on English terrain in February.

1

....

Appledore to Clovelly, February

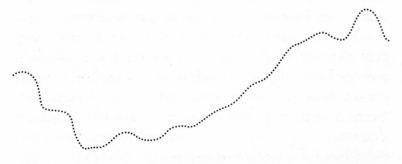

I have noticed that my South West Coast Path walks have become less of a leisure activity, and more of a gruelling contest against my own soul.

I'm not what you would call the traditional outdoorsy sort. I mean, I like the outdoors, but I really like the indoors, too. And I only really like the outdoors under certain conditions. That peak of autumn, when the air is crisp and the sky is a startling blue; or early spring, when you're grateful for the sudden outbursts of colour and light. Deep winter, frosty and dry. Summer, early in the morning. All of these are fine. I struggle to muster an interest in the outdoors when it's blazing hot or spitting rain into your face. My love is profoundly conditional.

I have been hearing about high winds and flooding in the South West all week, and that quickly becomes apparent on the ground as soon as I leave Appledore. Northam Burrows, the marshy western point of the Taw estuary, looked so picturesque from the road. Underfoot, though, it is one giant, deep puddle. A beautiful, crow-blown puddle, alive with terns, but also an impassable one. I wade into it for fifteen minutes before realising that it's impossible to trace its edge without risk of drowning, and so turn around and head back towards the road.

It's fine; I can just cut across towards Westward Ho! without even losing any time, but it's a disappointing start. Now I will have to track through streets of ugly, newish housing on concrete pavements. It is not a walk I particularly want to take. After only a few steps, a police car pulls up next to me and winds down its window. I stiffen. Am I trespassing, somehow? A WPC leans out and says, 'Sorry, I don't suppose you've seen a horse anywhere, have you?'

My mother taught me to always be helpful to the police. 'There's some over there,' I say, pointing at a field, where a brown mare and a grey Shetland pony are standing around looking entirely innocent.

'No,' she says, 'I mean an escaped one. She's white.'

'Oh,' I say, 'no. I don't think so.' Would I have remembered, even if I had? It's hard to say.

'Okay,' says the policewoman, 'thanks. If you see her . . . ring us, I suppose. Not 999.'

'No problem,' I say.

Perhaps Westward Ho! is more interesting than I initially thought. I press on through the suburban streets, waiting for beauty to grab me. I had been looking forward to this place: its swashbuckling exclamation mark implies maritime adventure and a certain colonial verve. I learned yesterday, however, that it got its name from the Charles Kingsley novel, rather than vice versa, and so I am now feeling deflated about the whole thing. Naming your village after a famous novel is an act of desperation, surely? I feel very far away from the wild Atlantic.

But then I round a corner and suddenly hear the tremendous roar of the sea. It's extraordinary how that happens; how the sound of the ocean can conceal itself and then simply appear, like a maritime peekaboo. Can sound not travel around bends? I'm sure it can, but then here it is: an incredible rush of white noise that makes me realise that I've been walking an estuary for a long time.

We are now at the seaside. There's a yellow shack selling ice-cream and people milling about on the wide, flat beach, walking dogs under the heavy skies. I'm searching for somewhere to buy a map, because I have stupidly left mine back in Kent, where it is no good to me whatsoever. It shouldn't be a problem; there's no urgent need of a map if you're just following the coastline, and there will surely be a post office or a corner shop selling Ordnance Survey maps in every town I come across. But there was nothing in Appledore, and there is even less here. I had expected something a little less desolate, if I'm honest, and this is the kind of place that takes a bad hit at low season. The glimpses of white-horsed waves between buildings keep me happy enough, but they are a little too distant for my liking.

Soon after leaving town, though, the ground begins to roll, and the familiar climb-and-descent starts again. Except today, the path is so wet that the slopes are like treadmills, gliding my feet back to their starting place at each step. My legs quickly become coated in thick, brick-red mud, making my trousers heavy and sticky. I'm gasping and spluttering with the effort of keeping upright.

At the top of one hill, I pause to watch a waterfall and then turn to see a descent so steep that I'm certain I won't ever get down it. The path has other ideas; as I am standing, wondering what to do, I begin to slide spontaneously towards the bottom. I have never been skiing, but I hope it's more enjoyable than this. My arms windmill about me as I attempt to grab on to anything that will steady me, but all that's on offer is gorse, brambles and barbed wire. I opt for the lesser of three evils and grasp at the gorse, leaving my palms a pincushion of thorns. Despite this, I still manage to fall on my backside (twice), and land at the bottom in what can only be described as ill humour.

These conditions are impossible. If I had a map, I would be able to work out an escape route, but without one, I have no choice but to get to the meeting place I agreed with H, a little place called Peppercombe where there appears to be a road running all the way down to the shore. The ability to leave the path is a rarity on this stretch of coast.

My mood does not improve when I reach a junction in the path and see a waymarker for Peppercombe: five miles. I had calculated my whole walk today to be about five miles in total, and I have surely already walked at least four. It's an hour before sunset, and it's already a grainy grey out here. I will end up scrambling through this mud in darkness. I try to download a map on my phone that could offer a route inland now, but it's no good; my tiny amount of signal barely supports the text I send to H, let alone enough data to render a map.

At this point the path displays some of the bloody-mindedness that I have slantingly admired in the past, but which now just seems cruel. I descend a slippery wooden staircase down into a tiny cove strewn with tangles of orange and blue nylon rope, only to climb again immediately afterwards, and then head downwards again. I clamber across the grey pebbles on shaking legs, mentally composing a series of letters to The Authorities: the first tackling the idiotic use of barbed wire alongside walking paths; the second bemoaning the cavalier arrogance of a path that has to dip down into *every fucking cove* when there's a perfectly good route around the top of the cliffs.

Just at that moment, I spot what looks like an exotic seed pod on the beach, a giant star anise the size of a hand, perhaps washed in from Zanzibar. I walk over and pick it up. On closer inspection, it's a vertebra, stained brown by the sea. I'm delighted. It must surely be from a whale. I slot it into my backpack and press on, thinking how pleased Bert will be to see it.

I try to let this sustain me, this fantasy of us both turning the vertebra in our hands and marvelling at its heft and rarity. But there's miles to go from here; more rise and fall, and much more mud. I am barely aware of it after a while, but only because my mind has shut down into exhausted blankness. I can just about go forward.

I finally arrive at Peppercombe in near-darkness, and find that H is not at the bottom of the lane as I had hoped. I'm furious with him; it's a further half-mile to reach the main road, all uphill. There's nothing to do but climb it, and at the top I find a locked gate, and Bert is running along to meet me. I'm too exhausted to speak. I try the gate dumbly, while H apologises and tells me about the day they've had, avoiding the squall in Dairy World, a theme park with cows and other things I can't take in. H is dairy intolerant. It's a wonder he hasn't come out in hives just from being there. I want to say this – this joke I have thought of – but my words won't come out in whole sentences. Everything is in fragments. I sit in the open boot and strip off my trousers in full view of passing cars. I don't care. At that moment, all I can think of are clean, dry leggings and the warm blast of the car heater.

As we drive off, H says, 'What did we see this morning, Bertie?'

Bert thinks for a while. 'A horse!'

'That's right! A white horse, just taking himself for a walk along the country lanes.'

I tell them about the policewoman who stopped me, and how strange it is that between us we had the solution to the whole thing, and this defrosts me.

We've made another throw of the dice at getting the accommodation right for this trip. Camping is now ruled out, particularly in this weather. I have realised that I need a hot bath after a long walk, anyway. Alongside my regime of popping a couple of ibuprofen immediately on my return, it makes a huge difference to how sore my legs are the next morning. I've also noticed that I get shivery soon after I finish a long walk, probably a combination of damp clothes and sheer exhaustion; a bath sets me straight. A bath sets an awful lot of things straight for me, I find, possibly because I can lock the bathroom door and be alone for an hour.

There's also the problem of what to do in the hours I'm not walking. In most hotels, there is just nowhere to *be* without spending extra money. Sometimes you want to pour a gin and tonic and just mooch around, without either being on public display or perching on the edge of a bed. Bert is not the kind of child who sits quietly in a corner with a book; he's a boisterous, bull-in-a-china-shop little boy who needs space to spread out his toys, and somewhere to run around. I have come to the conclusion that this all points only one way: the holiday camp.

I never really saw myself as the holiday camp sort of person, but then whoever did? Despite their new language of luxury spas and lodges rather than chalets, holiday camps are a compromise. They're relatively cheap, the housing is bulletproof, and they offer things for children to do. All the picturesque cottages in Christendom couldn't mitigate against the peace of mind that only comes from knowing that your child can't trash anything.

Our chalet is warm, the bed is comfortable (if a little small for two six-footers; H is immediately relegated to the spare bed in Bert's room), there's a proper sofa, and a proper bath. The kitchen is fully stocked with all that a kitchen needs, including a savagely sensitive smoke alarm that screams blue murder every time you make toast. There's even a barbecue outside the front door. The whole thing is a little more pine-clad than I would like my own house to be, but it's also completely fine.

Onsite, there is a duck pond, a playground (damp and slightly disappointing) and a swimming pool; a convenience store that sells crisps and branded wine; and a tavern where nobody minds kids running around and monopolising the pool table (although I do have to repeatedly tell Bert to stay away from the darts). There are moments in your life when you realise that all your silliest aspirations have died, and have been replaced by a set of more sensible concerns. I have found my spiritual home.

The only problem is that it's an hour's drive to the start of my walk, far over the border into Cornwall. I'm not sure I really clocked this information when I booked, but then I'm planning to really put some miles in this time. I have a lot to make up for; the hiatus over winter has put me far behind my initial aim to walk twenty-five miles per month. I've decided to catch up in one fell swoop, and cover eighty miles or so this week, walking every day. Everybody seems to suck in their breath when I tell them this, but then they don't have my kick-ass walking skills. I'm pretty sure that all I've endured so far has built me up towards some kind of mega-stamina. I just need a spate of decent weather.

I hadn't reckoned on the Atlantic Highway. The main road that runs parallel to the north coast of Cornwall turns out to wind slowly through a range of villages. It eventually breaks into a dual carriageway, but that only happens shortly before you cross into Devon and turn off into Hartland, where the roads are picturesquely narrow, obliging you to drop your speed to about twenty miles per hour. I hadn't considered how hard this would be for H. With no meaningful public transport options, he has to drive me to the beginning of my walk each morning, and pick me up at the end. That end-point is, of course, subject to revision, largely because I seem to be unable to set realistic goals. There's no point in him driving all the way back to our convenient, well-provisioned holiday park, and so he has to hang around nearby all day. It's cold, and intermittently rainy.

On my second day of walking, I wake up tense. The earlier we get going, the earlier I can finish walking, and then everyone can relax. Really, that means we need to leave the chalet by eight. That's ridiculously early for a holiday, I know, but if we dawdle and leave at, say, nine, I won't be anywhere by lunchtime. It's Valentine's Day. This is merely an inconvenient coincidence, but by my reckoning, I can make it along to the village of Clovelly by midday, and everything I've read tells me that it would be a picturesque site for a pub lunch. Thus, I can assuage my guilt and then carry on walking after lunch, finishing way into Hartland, and catching up some of my lost miles.

Bert has other ideas about the 8 a.m. start. He's never been one to rise and shine, and this morning he just wants to be left alone on the living-room floor with an upturned crate of Duplo. He refuses to eat breakfast, and growls at me when I start to pull off his pyjamas to get him dressed. I cajole, then count, then scold. H tries to help, and I snap at him. Just as we are about to finally get into the car, Bert decides that he's desperate for Marmite on toast after all. A sandwich won't do. I swear under my breath and harass the toaster with a dinner knife as it goes about its business at a leisurely pace. I accuse it of not actually being hot. I line up a sheet of tin foil in readiness, and load the knife with butter. Bert, sensing an opportunity, starts playing with the Duplo again.

We get into the car, and nearly as soon as we've left, H pulls over at a post office to see if he can find me a map. I'm not entirely supportive of this; it seems highly unlikely he'll find one here, and he's only slowing us down. But he emerges triumphantly clutching an OS Explorer 126, and we drive on to Peppercombe. Bert gets out of the car with me, and insists on following me down the steep gully that leads to the coast path. It's slick with rain, and I'm worried he'll fall, but it's pleasing to see him on my turf, his red coat shining against the moss and bracken. Perhaps the vertebra has piqued his interest: we washed it in the sink last night, and talked about how it would link together with other vertebrae to make a spine. A huge spine, like the 'humpback whale, immensely long' in our favourite, *The Snail and the Whale.* We are both excited at this thought.

Eventually, H realises just how far it is down to the beach (Me: *I know! I had to climb all the way back up here in the dark last night!*), and they turn around and head back to the car. I'm alone again.

It's still wet today, but this is undeniably a much more pleasant walk than yesterday. I climb up a valley and then the path levels and the weather clears. I pass through the kind of woodland that I'm beginning to see as a hallmark of the South West: outcropped with rock, dark, and evidently in a state of permanent dampness. The trees are carpeted in thick colonies of moss, and ferns of every kind jut and creep: lush bracken, rigid spikes of hart's tongue, delicate sprawls of maidenhair. I rarely glimpse the sea, but this is a different kind of calm, all deep greens and the scent of mulch underfoot.

The descents are still perilous, and the climbs still a slow process of striding and backsliding. At one point, I walk down a twisting, slippery path, my legs shaking with the effort of bracing them against the treacherous steps. By the time I get to the bottom, I am breathless and flustered, and I suddenly realise I'm in a village, the tiniest cluster of white houses and cobblestones set in a narrow valley. My map tells me it's Buck's Mills. A child is playing in the street, and a man is washing his car. They are calm, ordinary; I am wild and mud-splattered. I feel as though I have stumbled from one world into the next. We regard each other carefully, and I nod and cross the street to climb back into my otherness. I might as well have been a wolf.

The path now begins to skirt the woodland to the north, passing along the bottom of sloped fields which are so saturated that I often find myself wading. I am usually a stickler for the waymarked path, but in this instance I climb higher up the slope to walk across drier ground; surely no landowner would blame me. This makes it hard to spot the points where the path crosses the boundaries into the next piece of land, though, and at one point I find myself walking three sides of a field, utterly confused. From here, I can hear the traffic rushing past at Buck's Cross, and the temptation is great to walk up onto the road and call H from there. He and Bert won't be far away, and the struggle against the sodden soil is as tedious as it is tiring.

They're constantly on my mind today. I picture them killing time in some miserable soft-play centre, or a grim, out-of-season theme park, while I complete the next, mean-ingless section of my walk. It's not fair; I know it isn't. Bert hasn't had a chance to use the holiday camp's swimming pool yet, and I know he's desperate to. H doesn't even com-plain; he just unquestioningly facilitates. Tramping through a series of bland, drenched fields, I begin to question his motives. It feels as though any sane person would kick back, complain at the extent to which my project involves sacrifice on his part. It isn't fair that he has to drive me everywhere and pick me up. It isn't fair that he's spending a precious chunk of his annual leave drifting around the damp north-ern border between Devon and Cornwall, waiting for me to drag myself in.

I'm late again, of course. It's midday already, and I'm no-where near Clovelly. I text him to say that I'll be later than I thought; probably one o'clock*ish*.

No problem, he texts back.

Feed the boy, I reply. *Don't wait for me.*

Soon, the South West Coast Path merges with the Hobby Drive, a leisure roadway created for carriages in the early nineteenth century, covering the three miles running into Clovelly. This is a far more civilised path than I'm used to. The going is good underfoot, firm and flat, preferring to fold up into the Y-shaped valley that it showcases, rather than to climb down into each of the river cuttings in turn, as I'm certain the SWCP would have done, left to its own devices. The views down the high, undulating banks to the sea are told in glimpses through the bare trees.

Around the time the Hobby was built a notorious chap-book, *The History of John Gregg, and his Family of Robbers and Murderers*, described a family of cannibals, a few dozen in total, who lived in the caves at Clovelly and were reputed to have killed, pickled and eaten a thousand souls. The story is almost certainly a fiction that grew up to conceal a different nasty truth, warning people away from the caves where smuggling was rife. It may strike us as luridly unbelievable now, but it was written on the cusp of the world changing its mind about these wild, remote locations, rendering them sublime and awe-inspiring, rather than wind-battered and dangerous. As industrialisation took hold, the Romantic movement recast places like Clovelly in the light we now see them: as balm to the soul, rather than spaces where only the desperate live.

If we find Clovelly rather sedate in the present day, it's because we've entirely forgotten the visceral battles that are endured by anyone who works with the sea, and, in an age of the two-car family, we have lost all sense of what remoteness means. Eighteenth-century Clovelly was all but inaccessible to the outside world, and was found by only the committed traveller. It was part of the English Wild West, an unruly force of nature, red in tooth and claw. In the 1830s, just after the Hobby was finished, the artist Samuel Palmer came to draw the trees and the cliffs around Clovelly, admiring their untamed, coast-hardened forms. In his sketches and watercolours, we begin to see our own vision of the South West coast emerging: that balance of wild and knowable, remote and beautiful.

Carriages are no longer allowed on the Hobby, but there are plenty of walkers. I rarely pass anyone on the SWCP at this time of year, but here they all suddenly are, dawdling peacefully rather than marching with the intent I see in my fellow trail-followers. It's strange to think that most of these people must stop at the outer limits of the Hobby, and choose not to cross over onto the more rugged terrain. It's as though the Hobby is still defining what is civilised and what is wild.

Some signs of beastliness remain. I watch buzzards soaring and diving, and find the two separate wings of a kestrel at the side of the path, the soft blades of their feathers stripped away to reveal white spines. I nearly take them home for Bert, but decide to leave them there as a skeletal reminder of wilderness to those who would cling to the Hobby. I'm frustrated by this track. After two days of dragging my feet through mud and wondering whether I'll fall, I'm bored by the politeness I find here. The path goes out of its way to stay level, and I can't resist craving the uncertain climb down into the magnificent valley, the fierce scramble back up again. Time seems to be moving fast, and my progress is slow. The views are beautiful, but I don't feel as though I've earned them. I need some of the grunt-work to understand it.

I finally arrive in the car park at the top of the village at 2 p.m., and find H parked in a steamed-up car, with Bert asleep in the back.

'Sorry,' I say, 'I really thought I'd get here quicker than this.'

'Don't worry,' he says. 'Bert's worn himself out.'

'There's no point going down into the village now, is there?'

'No,' says H. 'Might as well just have a sandwich and you can carry on.'

I look at Bert in his car seat, and the guilt floods back. If I walk again now, it's hard to know when the next pickup will be, and then we're back to the holiday park in darkness again, and it'll be time for bed.

'Don't worry,' I say. 'I'll stop here for today.'

'Are you sure?' says H.

'Yes, I'm sure. I can't keep dragging you both around like this.'

*

After Bert's in bed, I pour a robust gin and tonic, and then another one. H finishes cleaning the kitchen, and sits down with me.

'I don't think I'll walk tomorrow,' I say. 'I think I'll take a day off. Spend some time with both of you.'

'No,' says H. 'Don't worry about that. We'll be fine.'

'It's too much,' I say. 'I never get the planning right, and we're driving for miles just to get to the start of the walk. It's not fair on Bert.'

'Bert's fine,' says H. 'He survives.'

'I don't want him to just survive.'

'That's not what I meant.'

'It's okay. I want to take some time off. I want some family time.'

H's face tenses.

'What?' I say.

'Nothing,' he says. 'Nothing. You're right. It'll be nice.'

'No, come on. Why don't you want me to come?'

H takes a breath and lets it out again, carefully. 'It's just that . . .' He thinks, shifts in his seat. 'It's just that everything changes when you're there. Me and Bert know what we're doing. We go somewhere and hang out. When you're there . . . everything bothers you.'

I try to arrange my face to receive this. This is feedback. This is information about my condition. This is the mirror on myself, the one I thought would be easier once I knew that I had AS. This is plain, simple *data*, and it should be received that way.

'You don't want me to come.' My voice is choked already. 'You actually don't want me to come.'

'I don't mean it like that, it's just . . .'

'I've been thinking that you're both missing me and

want me to be there, and you've actually been relieved that I'm occupying myself while you can go off and have fun. *So* you can go off and have fun. Because fun is impossible with me.'

'It's not impossible, it's just that you get frustrated and fed up, and you end up snapping at Bert, and it's just *easier* when you're not there.'

'I can't believe you don't want me there.'

'Stop saying that!' He's furious, and I don't understand why. *I'm* the one feeling the ground crumble under my feet here. *I'm* the one who's toxic. I begin to sob. They don't want me. I thought that I was getting my own personal space, but they were actually getting theirs. I have written myself out of our family, and they're relieved.

'Oh for Christ's sake,' says H.

'You don't want me!'

'I do want you.' His voice is like sandpaper.

'You don't love me.'

'Of course I fucking love you. If I didn't love you, why would I put up with . . . *this*.'

This is me right now, crumpled, incoherent, gasping for breath and flapping my forearms at the elbows like hyper-active windscreen wipers. My mind is white, a kind of sharp Arctic cold. I have no words. When I try to speak, there's only stuttering: I-I-I-I. C-c-c-c.

He's trying to talk to me now, to tell me it's all right, that we'll work something out, but he's angry. His voice is shouting out words that are supposed to be conciliatory, and he's touching me at the same time, patting at me with his big, electric hands, and it's like being jabbed with a live cable: boom! Boom! Boom!

I want to roll into a ball. I want to run away. I clasp my hands around my head and say, 'Stop! Stop!'

'You always do this!' he says. 'You always act like I'm going to beat you up! I can't keep taking this.'

I want to say, *I'm not! I'm not!* But there are no words now, only wasteland. I have to get away from the noise. I get up and run up the stairs into the bedroom. *My* bedroom, on my own. He doesn't come up after me. I don't want him to. I close the door and shift the chest of drawers in front of it, just in case. Then I start to pace the tight U of the space around the bed.

It's a small room, and it takes a long time to spend out the electricity.

At three in the morning, I move the drawers back into place, open the door, climb into his single bed, and cling to his back.

He turns, and kisses my head.

We sleep that way, knotted together.

2

....

Hartland Point to the Eden Project, via Tintagel, February

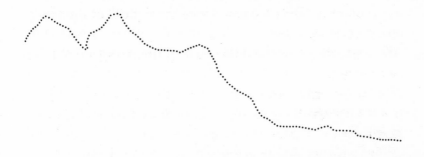

I feel sick the next morning. Bert, of course, wakes up at exactly the same time as he always does (7 a.m. on the dot, which I know is merciful by the standards of other children), and so we both get up with him, blinking and sighing and drinking the contents of the little metal teapot over and over again.

I say I won't walk today, and H says *no, come on, don't be silly*. I just want to be close to them both all day. I want them to want me. I want Bert to demand my attention, to be furious that I'll be absent again. But he's not that sort of child; he's laid-back, undemanding. Not for the first time, I wonder if he's like that because of me – because he's learned that there's no point in asking for anything much.

I say, 'What would you like to do today, Bert?'

'Soft play!' he says.

'Oh!' I say, faking laughter. 'You can go to soft play back

at home. How about something more interesting? How about something you can only do in Cornwall. We've never been to Cornwall before.'

'Soft play,' says Bert, not looking up from his train set.

'I think the soft play might be closed today,' I say, and Bert ignores me. He's stringing together yards of wooden track, with bridges and ramps and loops, and a level crossing for cars to pass through. It's all about the track for Bert, the process of engineering it and making the various ends join together. Once this is done, he'll run a couple of trains around it in a half-interested fashion, but there's no narrative for him, only structure.

I am trying very hard not to be fussy or demanding in any way today, so I go upstairs, take a shower, and get dressed in my walking leggings and fleece. I know I ought to be walking anyway, so I might as well get on with it. There's no point in forcing myself on two people who clearly don't want me around.

I don't rush them through breakfast, but eventually we find ourselves in the car anyway, driving up the Atlantic Highway towards Devon yet again. It's cold, but dry. I say I won't walk for long, and H says, 'See what you can do. We've come all the way down here.' He puts a hand on my leg, and squeezes it. He's showing me that he's meaning to be kind. He's showing me that I shouldn't be blown off course. I put my hand on top of his, and try not to feel the electricity. I'm miserable. Soon, he's wriggling his hand out from under mine to change gears, and I draw my knees up onto the dashboard to make myself into a ball.

We travel north up the coast, past Port Isaac, through the brilliantly named village of Box's Shop, and skirting Bude. I will walk, I suppose. I will walk, and try to learn not to be heartbroken. I will walk, and try to accept that my family find me too difficult to be with sometimes, but that they mean nothing by it. It's an act of self-acceptance: I am loved by people who are more than aware of my flaws. I should be grateful for it.

We are nearly at Clovelly when I see a sign for Hartland and say, 'Bert, there's a lighthouse at Hartland Point. I saw it on my map. Shall we go and see it?'

Bert says, 'Soft play.'

'What about your walk?' says H.

'I don't want to walk. I want to be with you two.'

'Really? Are you sure?'

'Yes,' I say. 'I want to work out how we can all be together. We have to start somewhere.'

'But what if you don't make your miles? Are you sure you won't regret it?'

'That ship has already sailed,' I say. It's true; after two days of walking, I'm already about fifteen miles behind target. It's only going to get worse. I turn to the back seat and say, 'Come on, Bert, let's go to a lighthouse!'

'I don't want to,' says Bert.

'Yay,' says H, rather suddenly. 'Lighthouse! Brilliant! Come on, Bert, it'll be great!'

'No,' says Bert.

'Well, we're going,' says H. 'With Mummy. We're going to have a day with Mummy! Won't that be brilliant?'

Bert sighs heavily. We drive through the narrowing roads towards Hartland Point. The land is as grey as the sky, drained of all its colour by the long winter. The GPS becomes baffled by the sheer remoteness after a while, and we end up following a series of signs that seem to endlessly tell us Hartland Point is a mile and a half away, whichever way we turn. Eventually, though, the horizon takes on that extra element of spaciousness that can only mean we're close to the sea, and there is a National Trust sign for parking on what appears to be a roadside verge. We are sceptical that this is where we ought to be, but obey it anyway. We lever Bert out of the car.

Walking up a lane, we pass the point where the South West Coast Path meets the open ground around Hartland Point, and find a surprising cluster of people gathered around a green tea hut. There is a thundering above, and I glance round to see a helicopter taking off, flying directly over our heads and out across the sea towards the island of Lundy. 'Changeover day,' says the man standing next to me, and I realise that all the people milling around have bags and suitcases with them, and are heading over to holiday on the three-mile wilderness in the Bristol Channel, famed for its puffins, seals and shearwaters.

The helicopter fades to a small dot over the island, and then it's back again, taking the last group of holidaymakers home and loading in the next lot. Bert is enthralled. We watch it go back and forth, against an increasingly blue sky. H buys tea from the hut, and I tread to the edge of the grass and admire the incredible zig-zags in the russet cliffs, as though the coast folded itself like a concertina at some point in its geological past. I photograph it, rust against periwinkle blue, and point out the pale heads of thrift, bobbing across the clifftop. It's everywhere on this path, and is becoming a favourite of mine, for its sheer, fragile tenacity. At this time of year it has dried to silvery husks, but come the summer, it will be pink and strong.

It turns out that we cannot go into the lighthouse, but we can follow the path out onto the rocks around it. The ground is uneven and the track is narrow; Bert rides on H's shoulders when we both become terrified he'll run off the edge of the headland in sheer enthusiasm.

This is the point where the coastline stops meandering vaguely westwards and turns abruptly south, as if rushing towards the Cornish border. I have been looking forward to it, from the shape it makes on the map, and it turns out I was right. After gazing out over the roof of the white lighthouse for a few moments, we double back on ourselves and follow the southern side of the path towards the helipad. A sea change has happened between the top of this tiny promontory and the bottom, and the waves have suddenly gathered an angry, crashing energy. They hurl themselves against the coastline, sending up explosions of white foam, then they retreat and hurl themselves again. We are now looking down over dark, striated rock, stretching far along the coast.

We get back in the car, and I say, 'Let's just drive around a bit.'

We used to do this a lot, in the days before Bert came along; just get in the car and follow the coast. We've skimmed the perimeter of Kent this way – at least as far as there are roads that allow it – and many other places, too. It's a soothing, meandering thing to do, a directionless, pointless intimacy that we lost when we acquired a passenger in an expensive car seat in the back, who gets bored on long journeys. There isn't a coastal road to follow here, but I can see on my Ordnance Survey map that the next point you can drive to the sea is Hartland Quay, so we head there.

Bert falls asleep on the way. We park up outside the hotel and perch on the bonnet of the Skoda to watch the sea, glancing nervously back to make sure he doesn't wake up. We are lower down here than at Hartland Point and, if anything, the waves have gathered even more angry energy. This was once known as the wreckers' coast, the sea as the sailors' graveyard, and it's easy to see why. The shoreline is spiked with rock, which the sea pounds against relentlessly, with such violence that gobbets of spume float towards us like blown bubble bath. Whenever the waves draw back, they reveal low ridges of rock, as if some vast ancient raked the whole thing over and it set there for good.

The sea is the ultimate white noise, somehow rhythmic and unpredictable at once. As it fills my ears I think, not for the first time, that I would be happy all the time if I lived beside a sea like this one. I am immediately calmed by it; I close my eyes and let it take me over. When I open them again, I see that H is doing the same thing. I reach over for his hand, and he smiles that tense, sorry kind of smile that two people share when they can't hide the compromises any longer. I prefer that, on balance, to the years when you have to pretend you think your partner is perfect, while secretly wondering whether one of their flaws will tip you over from love to not-love one day. I'm grateful for this phase, or at least grateful at right angles. He's with me, whatever I throw at him. He sees me clearly, and will stay anyway. I believe he'll always stay.

'I'm hungry,' I say, and we get in the car and back onto the Atlantic Highway. We stop off in Boscastle for lunch in a hotel, sitting beneath a painting whose accompanying card says it was donated by a stranger after the catastrophic floods of 2004. I recall seeing the high waters on the news, the people rowing down the high street, but I had forgotten until I was here; only the name had lodged. The village is folded into a valley at the confluence of two rivers, and I can picture the funnel it would make as a surge of rainwater rushed towards the sea. I wonder how many years it took for this place to dry out, after the high water had receded.

Sloshing with swollen tides myself, the painting immediately brings an assault of tears, which I swallow down for fear of seeming even more unstable. It would never have occurred to me to do such a thing myself, to imagine a person feeling things behind the facade of a hotel, and to think of a way that they might be comforted.

'Let's go to Tintagel,' I say.

Bert is charging dangerously between the tables, knocking into stools like a precarious game of human skittles. 'Now?' says H. 'Isn't it a bit late?'

'It's not far from here,' I say. 'Come on. I've always wanted to go.'

'I thought you wanted to walk there,' says H.

'For all I know, that might never happen.'

I want to show Bert Tintagel, this remote, mythical castle set out on a crag of rock. I want him to run around the ramparts and become imbued with a combined sense of history, folklore and the wild power of nature. Personally, I'm a little vague on the Arthurian legend behind it. If I'd known we were coming, I would have been more prepared. I know about the Knights of the Round Table and Merlin, Excalibur, Guinevere, and Launcelot; I know about the Lady of the Lake and the Sword in the Stone. I just have no idea how to piece them all together, and in what order. I now have to try to convey all of it to Bert in a way that will interest him.

'It's a castle where a king used to live,' I say. 'And there were knights and dragons, and he pulls a sword out of a stone, which is how he knew he was king – I think – and he had a round table so that all his knights had an equal say, and I think his chief knight was having an affair with his wife, or something. The queen. Is that right, H?'

'I dunno,' says H.

I can see that this has failed to even register on Bert's highly specific Geiger counter of interest.

I didn't realise how much our day had time-shifted; the first shades of dusk are drawing in as we park in Tintagel. I had hoped for something a little wilder. There's an attractive stone-built Old Post Office, owned, I note, by the National Trust, but once we're past that, the village is perhaps as depressing as I would have expected, had I stopped to think about it. There is an array of Arthurian-themed tat on offer, and a marked tendency towards fudge. It is hard not to suspect that American tourists come here on a regular basis, and they almost certainly spend more money than the British ones do.

The offerings become more sober as soon as we cross onto English Heritage territory and start to walk down the steep hill towards the castle. All is suddenly tasteful and restrained, from the grey-green doors of the cafe to the silk scarves and marmalade in the gift shop. This will tell you more about Britain, past and present, than any reproduction suit of armour. Here, we buy memberships to heritage organisations if we can afford to, and in practice we're paying to be shielded from the horrors of the commercial aesthetic. It's almost medieval, when you think about it: the rich are in this sanitised enclosure, where we can imagine that the world is elegant and tastefully luxurious; the poor are surging beyond the gates, effecting a goblin market of inaccurate historical reproductions and tooth-rotting confectionary. I am as in love with this arrangement as all the other passholders.

We climb the steps up to the castle, only to be told the main building is about to close, but that we're welcome to explore the part of the castle that's open to the general public. I am therefore denied my walk across the famous bridge that spans the mainland and the rock on which the castle stands, and I am also denied my hoped-for set of interpretation boards that would allow me to parse a better version of Arthurian myth as I explain it all to Bert.

Instead, we play hide-and-seek among the public ruins, and then trot onto the beach, where there is a cave that bores through the rock under the castle, and a waterfall that gushes down a cliff onto the sand. Here, as the sky grows dark, is my magic. We – all three of us – always end up gravitating towards the sea.

I don't walk the next day, either. We drive into Bodmin and take a vintage steam train out through the countryside and back again. I buy Bert a little train driver's cap and a flag from the gift shop, and we share a scone in the carriage. Then we drive up onto Bodmin Moor to see the woolly ponies and mounds of moss. We have lunch in a pub and make an unsuccessful attempt to wander around Camelford's shops, finding everything shut except a single charity shop, where we buy Bert a book on space exploration. We go back to our chalet, watch telly, and then go out to the camp's social club in the evening. It's too noisy for me, and the wine is awful, but Bert loves the children's entertainers, and the mini disco, and the Slush Puppies, and so we're almost content.

The next day, I don't even pretend to think about walking. My friend Beccy is joining me tonight to walk with me for the rest of the week, and so I tell H that I don't want to get stuck somewhere on the path and miss her arrival. I am wondering how I'll tell her that I don't want to walk anymore. I've given up. It's too hard for me, and for everyone else around me. We'll have to think of something else to do.

We go to the Eden Project while we're waiting for her to arrive. We first went just after it opened, on our only other holiday to Cornwall. It was an odd time to go; Britain was in the middle of a foot-and-mouth outbreak, and all the way down to our caravan at Hayle we witnessed tall, thin columns of smoke rising from farmland, and the ominous smell of barbecue as cattle carcasses were burned. We tried to walk the South West Coast Path that week, but found much of it cordoned off so that walkers couldn't pass through pasture and contaminate the livestock still further. We were left with little else to do but to drive from cove to cove, getting out of the car to wander on the beach before driving off again.

Amid all that, we visited the Eden Project. It was the talk of the town, a millennium project that people actually wanted. We drove across Cornwall and down into its quarry, and found a series of geodomes containing mainly bare soil. There was nothing there to see. It was desolate, pointless. We vowed never to return.

Today, though, the grey February weather has driven us back there. At least, we reason, it will be under cover. We see immediately that an astonishing change has taken place. The whole quarry is alive, and the domes are lush with plants. There are interactive automata, and enticing gift shops, and the overhead zoom of zip wires. Bert scuttles around the domes, and listens enthralled to a storyteller and a bug man, and would carry on listening if we didn't drag him away.

I am not at home here. There is a press of people; the dining hall is full of noise and people sit too close to me; the tropical zone is so hot and damp that I can't think straight. Everywhere is noisy. I can tell it's good; I can tell it's wonderful; but after a couple of hours I'm tired and disoriented, and I find myself agitated, asking, in delicate panic, if we shouldn't go home now, if it isn't time to move on. If Bert isn't getting tired, hungry, ratty.

'Go and have a cup of coffee,' says H. 'We'll play down here for a while.'

I obey. I take myself up to a quiet spot on the top floor of The Core, and drink an Americano on my own. I've failed, of course. I've not managed to enjoy myself even in this place, and I let the feeling become contagious, spreading, in my mind, to Bert. If it had just been the two of us here, I would have been in the car by now, and there would probably have been tears, his loud, mine silent. I remember the days when I was at home with him as a tiny baby and I would start getting him ready for bed at five o'clock, and then, as time went on, four. It didn't make any difference. H still came home at six thirty, and I would thrust Bert into his hands and accuse him of driving deliberately slowly to get here this late, of probably stopping off somewhere and not telling me, just so that he wouldn't have to take over. Bert would be suddenly giggly, beguiling, as if he hadn't griped at me all day until I was reduced to holding him in front of me at arm's length, saying, 'Why can't I make you happy? Why don't you ever stop?'

I don't suppose I was the first mother to wet my baby's head with tears, and I won't be the last. But I'm ashamed, still. Somehow, between us, we managed to love each other anyway. He seemed to arrive equipped to intercept the strange flows of my adoration, even when I couldn't interpret them myself.

After a very long time, H appears by my table, dragging a reluctant Bert behind him. He wants to play some more. 'It's getting dark,' says H. 'It's time to go home. We'll come back another day.' I give Bert the cookie and juice I've been saving for him, and ask him what he saw. Perhaps this is okay. Perhaps this is how it has to be.

Clovelly to Hartland Quay, February

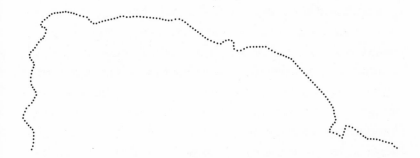

'At least show me where you would have walked,' says Beccy. We spread the map out on the pink carpet of our chalet, and I trace my finger along the coastline as I spill out my feelings.

I am failing, managing only ten miles a day at best. I'm not going to achieve anything like the mileage I'd planned for, and I've come all this way. There's no way I can walk the whole path before I'm forty. I might as well give up. I don't understand it. *Pensioners* do this. People double my age take a couple of months to walk the whole thing, hitting the path every single day. What the hell is wrong with me that I can't?

'You're not being realistic,' she says. 'It's the middle of winter. You've walked through terrible weather on a difficult bit of the path. Not many people could do more than you're doing.'

'I'm so slow,' I say.

'You're not slow; you're just not estimating your mileage

properly. Are you remembering the three miles per hour plus twenty minutes per contour line?'

I must admit, although I don't say it out loud, that in my memory three miles had become four. 'But all I do is cross contour lines. Nothing is flat.'

'Exactly.'

I huff, and keep my eyes on the map. The jagged coastline is as beguiling as it has always been to me, especially in the neat blues and rusts of the Ordnance Survey map, the path a string of green diamonds weaving through it. A couple of miles along from Clovelly, there will be a waterfall where a stream finds the sea, and, further still, a chance to get a close look at the radar station, a series of white dome dishes that you can see from the road, signposted only GCHQ. There are rocks that will jut out of the waves, and beaches and bays to gaze over. It doesn't look all that hard, but then it never does.

'Everyone's running around after me,' I say. 'I'm being indulged like a child. H is driving for miles to drop me off and pick me up, and then spending all day looking after Bert. I should be doing that too. I should be taking Bert for a day while *he* goes walking.'

'Does he want to do that?'

'No, he hates walking. You know that.'

'So that's fine then, isn't it? And I'll drive us there tomorrow.'

'He'll still have to pick us up.'

'He'll still have to pick us up. I get the impression he doesn't really mind.'

'I feel like this is my Asperger syndrome writ large. I feel like I've got obsessed with a set of metrics – I have to follow this path, in this time, with so many miles a month – and I didn't really think about how it would actually *be* to walk it.

I didn't think about what it would cost, or whether I'd be able to do it, or what it would be like for everyone else to facilitate me. I didn't realise how much H just gives in to me for a quiet life.'

Beccy and I bonded talking like this at university: we would sit side by side, playing two-player Tetris on my PC that H had built for me from component parts. We would both keep our eyes fixed on the screen, and manoeuvre the jelly-coloured shapes into place as we voiced all the dark parts of being a clever, difficult girl. We both washed up at Cambridge from Kentish council estates and grammar schools, and suffered a kind of amazement at how similar we were. We had grown up thinking we were the only one the world had ever made; at least, that's what our lives had made us feel so far. Our college put all the state-school kids in the same accommodation block, and there we both were, a kind of fairground mirror image of each other, one tall (me), the other tiny. We have always cut an odd figure together, with more than a foot between us, chattering away in our abrasive estuarine slang. We took no prisoners. It felt as though we had to face down half of Cambridge to survive it, and I just about clung on to the end, while she thrived.

She was the first person I texted when I realised I had Asperger's. *Bloody hell*, came the reply, *what am I then?*

She does herself down. Certainly, we both have the same, obsessive focus on the things that interest us, minds that love making connections between disparate ideas, and voices that love arguing about them, but after that we are different. Where I retreat in exhaustion from other people, Beccy goes on making more connections. At college, I found the braying student bar an actual terror, full of faces I never could recall and personalities that I didn't understand. Beccy just picked her way through them and found the people she liked. We both joined the choir and the football team together, but only one of us stuck with them. I needed time on my own in my room, usually with a bottle of red wine at my side. She just went on getting to know people, across the college, and the faculty, and the university. I skulked and went home as much as I could, and endured being told I was a quiet girl by my supervisors, lacking confidence perhaps.

She lays a finger on the map now and says, 'There'll be a hill fort. I love hill forts,' and that's it settled. We will walk tomorrow.

The next morning, we leave without the boys at 8 a.m., making arrangements with H to pick us up from Hartland Point at five. We brush icicles off the door handles of Beccy's little van, and drive up the Atlantic Highway with the wipers on full-pelt against sleet, singing 'Love Shack': *Headin' down the Atlantic Highway/Looking for the love getaway.* We are, both of us, best in the morning, but I would have been deterred by the weather without my friend's hardy presence beside me, almost daring me to chicken out.

By the time we reach the car park at the top of Clovelly, the sun has broken through, but it's still cold. We walk in the parkland of an old manor house, past pagodas and mannered woodland. We keep on high ground, and it's mostly dry underfoot. Soon, we take off our jumpers and walk in T-shirts because it's so warm. We stop at the hill fort for tea and peanut M&Ms, which are now my walking snack of choice, combining a sugar rush with what I assume to be the goodness of peanuts and the hyperactive flare of artificial colouring. We watch a pair of buzzards soaring overhead, and Beccy's archaeologist's eye reinterprets the land around me, showing me the defensive high ground and the accompanying ditch.

By eleven, we are crossing fields with the radar station at Hartland Point clearly in sight, and I am saying, 'We'll be there for lunchtime! I reckon we'll carry on around.'

'We'll see,' says Beccy, but at midday we are sitting on a picnic bench outside the green tea hut (now closed, this not being a changeover day), eating our sandwiches and letting our fingers travel southwards down the map. We estimate it's an hour further to Hartland Quay, and that we'll get even further than that, in this weather, with the path like this.

'Welcombe Mouth, I reckon,' says Beccy, and I agree, texting H to this effect, and cracking the first of many unsuitable jokes about this place name, with its delightful proximity to Lucky Hole.

For the second time this week, I notice how the waves gain energy as we round the corner from Hartland Point. They crash with unbelievable force against the dark rocks along the coast, and meanwhile, the path begins to rise and fall again. There are waterfalls at the top of every climb, fed by clear rivers that run through wild, bare clifftops where the winds harass your ears. The valleys are sheltered and lush, strangely quiet, and irrigated by trickling streams. The contrast is astonishing: the thunder of gale and falling water, and then the muffled quiet of grass and whispering bracken. We pass concealed cottages with sinuous roofs, weathered to echo the landscape around them, and, on a high ridge, see a cathedral of stone rising from the sea, the waters boiling around it. 'It's honestly like being in a fairy tale,' says Beccy. 'I feel like I'm walking through the Shire.'

The climbs seem worse than ever. The ground we're reaching isn't especially high, sometimes less than a hundred metres, but the slopes are steep, cut zig-zagging into the side of valleys, or as footholds in the banks. As we labour up them (and down again, which is often worse), we laugh about this ridiculous path with its iron will to stick to the coastline. After passing our second memorial bench, we decide that a more useful offering would be the occasional bridge and agree that, should either of us manage to make any meaningful money in our lifetime, we will leave such a stipulation in our will.

'Failing that,' says Beccy, 'you can build me a memorial bench, but only if you promise to ritually burn it afterwards.'

We don't really mind. Fighting our way up to those high ridges is worth it just to watch, breathless, a waterfall crash down into churning waves. It feels as though you ought to earn a view like this, rather than drive up to it in your car. I can't quite process the power or the splendour of it all. It's an embarrassment of riches, almost too magical to be real.

We walk, and stop, and photograph, and walk again, and climb slopes, and inch down banks. It is four o'clock by the time we reach Hartland Quay, and we can't account for the time it took us to move just a few inches down the map. It's as if we were absorbed into that faerie landscape, and time was absorbed there, too.

We won't make it to Welcombe Mouth today. It doesn't matter. We retire to a hotel bar at Hartland Quay, and order shandies and several bags of crisps.

'I ended up making exactly the same mistake as you,' says Beccy. 'I thought I could walk on for ever.'

'I'm not sure we factored in the contour lines again,' I say.

'Or stopping and looking. That's what takes the time. There's no point if you don't do that.'

I text H to tell him to collect us here, but there's no rush.

'Are you glad you walked after all?' says Beccy.

'You know I am,' I say.

4

....

Hartland Quay to Morwenstow, February

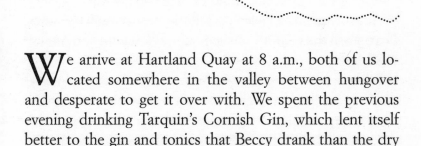

We arrive at Hartland Quay at 8 a.m., both of us located somewhere in the valley between hungover and desperate to get it over with. We spent the previous evening drinking Tarquin's Cornish Gin, which lent itself better to the gin and tonics that Beccy drank than the dry martinis I made for myself, served inelegantly in mock-cut-glass tumblers.

After the first couple, I mustered the courage to show Beccy my whale vertebra, knowing somehow that whatever I assumed it to be would be wrong. Archaeologists know their bones. Beccy turned it in her hands, stated, 'Bovid, first cervical,' and then sniffed it and said, 'Bronze Age.'

'Really?' I yelp. 'Bronze Age? Is it that old?' I hand it back to Bert and say, 'It's from a cow's spine, and it died a long, long time ago.'

'Bronze Age,' says Beccy, 'is really not that old.'

I do not doubt her ability to identify a bovid first cervical vertebra; after all, she spent our first year at university quick-liming small creatures in Tupperware in our communal fridge, just to get a look at their bones. I learned after some time that she was also boiling them first, in my set of Argos saucepans. Those who raised concerns about the hygiene of the whole process – and I, for one, didn't have the nerve – were treated to a stare of such contempt that we all just got used to avoiding the plastic tubs on the bottom shelf of the fridge, and trying not to think too hard about the pink goop that sloshed about inside them. In time, I think we all came to agree with Beccy's view that our resident law student's endless porridge-making actually resulted in far more disgusting remains.

'But how can you smell the Bronze Age?' I ask.

An amused stare. 'I can't smell the Bronze Age, you idiot. I can smell the peat it's washed out of. Why did you think it was brown?'

I do not have an answer for this. I only know that I regret toasting the Bronze Age bone with another martini. The wind is squalling at Hartland Quay. It's cold, and there's the kind of rain in the air that sand-blasts your cheeks. We walk up onto the path and immediately see signs warning of a cliff fall. It is even wilder here than it was yesterday. The climbs are steeper, the descents more knee-clenchingly painful, and the wind is not our friend. After a mile I have earache, and Beccy lends me her snood, which I fashion into an entirely unstylish hat by pulling the drawstring taut. To think, I undertook my first walk in lipstick. I have surrendered all dignity now, let alone the notion of personal style.

It's beautiful, even in the rain. The high ground is even more bare and other-worldly; the valleys are so deep and quiet that you could imagine undiscovered civilisations sheltering there, away from human view. Really, a unicorn wouldn't be out of place. Everywhere we go, we are followed by ravens, vast black birds who emit a brittle grunt where their song should be. There are kestrels, too, their feathers the deep rust of the soil.

We cross a field, and Beccy points out a lark, a tiny bird that seems to have cast itself into the open space above us, and is now flapping frantically to stay aloft. I have never known what a lark sounds like before, but now I begin to spot them every few paces, their call sounding to me more like a ZX Spectrum loading than Ralph Vaughan Williams's weaving violin in *The Lark Ascending*. I suppose Vaughan Williams had a different frame of reference from me.

But then again, perhaps it was not so different: the first bars of *The Lark Ascending* came into the composer's mind when he was on holiday in Margate at the outbreak of the First World War. He began to jot down the musical notes right away, as he paced along the coast, most likely eyeing the early military exercises out at sea. A young Scout thought he was writing enemy code and placed him under citizen's arrest.

I have lived close to Margate all my life, close enough to be unable to resist trying to visualise exactly where Vaughan Williams was walking as those first few notes swam into his head. Many of the accounts of this moment have him pacing along a cliff, and that puts us closer to Broadstairs by my reckoning, a little further along the coast. It certainly isn't along the low, paved Margate sea-front, where T. S. Eliot sat in a shelter a few years later in 1921, while recovering from an attack of nerves, and wrote part of *The Waste Land*.

On Margate Sands.
I can connect
Nothing with nothing.

Strange to think that both of these men drew inspiration from the same sea, one of them perhaps thinking of the men going off to war, the other witnessing what they brought back. The sea is a place we retreat to when our nerves need to be settled; it contains the memory of our wild, whole selves. There is a theory that Eliot's Margate Sands is not in fact the one in Kent, but an ersatz echo of it, a temporary beach constructed on the Thames one summer. It would, I suppose, make sense within the poem's hall of mirrors; a fake Margate Sands triggering the memory of the real one. Nothing with nothing.

The nothingness of the sea is what I came here for. It is empty, wide, rhythmic; it's the ultimate antidote to the brash noise of people. Certainly, the sea is loud too, but it's the sort of sound that has no meaning or sense, and therefore asks nothing of you. I spend my whole life turning down the TV, or asking H to nudge down the volume on his music, or asking Bert to mute his tablet as he plays a game. My own devices are eternally silent, and free, too, of vibrations or notifications. Mine is a fragile peace with the everyday world; I can live with it for as long as it doesn't demand too much of me. Every scrap of noise – and I mean visual noise too, and the noise made by chaos and movement – drains me. Half an hour in a crowd or a noisy bar and I'm hollowed out entirely. But the noise of the sea is different; it nourishes me. It allows me to reset.

The wind worsens as we carry on around the coast. We find ourselves bent double against it as we cut diagonally across one clifftop field, the rain scouring our faces. I am craving tea now, and a spell sitting down in a warm room, just so that my hair can dry. I have noticed there is a National Trust symbol on my map at Welcombe Mouth, and Beccy and I develop a shared fantasy that there must, therefore, be a tea room, because really it would be such a good idea. When we get there, inching down the valley, there is inevitably nothing, except a few cars.

'Shall we stop anyway?' I say, and Beccy says, 'No point walking all this way to eat our sandwiches in a car park.' This leaves me something close to outraged: can't she see I'm tired? Must this be an endurance test? I drag my feet up the opposite slope of the valley, and wonder when this tyranny will end and I will be allowed to have my lunch.

At the top of the valley we come across a tiny, stone-built hut with a sign gaffer-taped to the door, saying *RONALD DUNCAN'S HUT IS OPEN.*

'Do you think we're allowed in?' I say.

Beccy shrugs and opens the door. Inside is a handsome, bare room, with a pair of windows looking out over the sea, and another one looking west. Underneath them is a writing desk, and on top of it an empty milk bottle full of water, and a glass. An information board on the wall tells us that we're to make ourselves at home, and lays out the life of the local farmer and writer, who died in 1983 and left instructions for his hut to stay open for other admirers of this astonishing stretch of coast to rest and contemplate. The view today is of a grey sea and squalls of rain, but it's definitely better encountered from the inside looking out, with our ears still ringing from the wind.

We unwrap our sandwiches on the desk, and lay out our map, too, to study how far we've come: three, perhaps four miles from Hartland Quay over an entire morning. It doesn't seem possible to travel so slowly; we are not dawdling by any stretch of the imagination. It's wet and uncomfortable and hard and frustrating, and we don't dare get too near the edges of any cliffs to take a look at the view. The ideal situation would be to see if we could get away with spending the rest of the day in Ronald Duncan's hut, and perhaps subsequently arrange some kind of air-lift home. We get through our sandwiches far too quickly, take an elaborate interest in the information boards, and then look at each other and silently agree that we might as well get on with it.

As it turns out, it's worth pressing on; the next valley has a little bridge over a stream, and there, on the other side, is a sign that says:

CORNWALL
KERNOW

I have walked the entire northern seaboard of Devon, a hundred miles of it. I have got from Exmoor, bronzed by autumn, through white sands at Croyde, and grey estuaries at Bideford and Barnstaple; I have left behind the south coast of Wales and the little island of Lundy. I have felt the soil change beneath my feet as I have walked westward, and the sea change beside me. I have grown stronger, slimmer, more restless to use up my stray energy. I have learned to crave the whisper of wind through leaves and the roar of the sea. I take a photo of myself grinning beside the sign, my wet hair plastered to my forehead under Beccy's repurposed snood, my glasses beaded with rain.

As we walk on, the winds become higher and the rain more relentless. A little way south of Welcombe, we reach a place where the cliff has fallen into the sea, and we are diverted into a field. There is the smell of a freshly dug garden, and a timber-yard-fresh South West Coast Path fence keeping us a few metres away from the raw edge. Here, in the Wild West, the sea is reclaiming England in big, vicious bites. A little further still, and we find sudden dips in the soil where the ground beneath our feet is disintegrating.

'If I die,' says Beccy, 'just roll me off a cliff into the sea.'

'I suspect that's what will have killed you in the first place.'

'True,' says Beccy.

'Anyway, they'll think I've murdered you. It wouldn't look good.'

'*I couldn't help myself,*' says Beccy. '*She kept making me walk up hills in the rain!*'

'It *is* bloody awful,' I say. 'You can say all you like about having the right clothing, but I'm properly dressed and this sucks.'

'You know your problem?' says Beccy. 'You take the weather personally.'

And she's right, I do. I have a running, secret theory that, ever since I've started this walk, some malevolent power or other has arranged for the wettest winter on record, and for the especially cold, damp patches to coincide with the brief moments I get to walk. That's not the only thing I take personally either: I take the climbs personally, and the descents. I take it personally that this path refuses to ever make it easy for me; that it always has to take me to the raw, ragged edge of coping, just as it clings to the raw, ragged edge of the coast. I take it personally that it takes three hours to walk four miles, and that we never once seem to pass a cafe that's open. I have no doubt that all of these things are what makes me so obsessed with the South West Coast Path in the first place, but I also resent it with a fury that's hard to fathom. I feel like it's trying to teach me a lesson, and I am never a willing pupil.

As we approach a deep valley that leads to Morwenstow, we agree that this is where we should stop for the day. We immediately break into a dispute over exactly which path we will take into the village; Beccy wants to descend the valley and climb it again; I want to avoid this by cutting into the village from the north.

'But there's a medieval well,' says Beccy.

'I don't care about the well,' I say. 'Half the time, these things are marked on the map, and there's nothing to see.'

'There's a waterfall, too,' she says. 'You like those.'

'I'm sick of waterfalls.'

'No you're not.'

'Okay, but I'm not as impressed by them as I once was. There are too many along here. They ought to try to maintain their mystique a bit more.'

'You'll only have to do the valley the next time you come.'

'No I won't,' I say, pointing to a path at the south of Morwenstow, which takes me straight back onto the high ground. 'I can skip it altogether for once.'

Eventually, we compromise and agree that I'll descend the valley – because surely my legs will allow that, but take a lower path into Morwenstow that avoids a further climb. We turn inland and follow the stream along an eccentrically maintained path that eventually climbs up into the village. We pass the rectory on a path teeming with star-flowered alliums, their garlicky scent filling the air, and it's here that I see my first snowdrops of the year, too, peeping out between them.

Morwenstow gets its name from Saint Morwenna, the daughter of a Welsh king who came to Cornwall and lived in a hermitage on Henna Cliff. She reputedly built a church there with her own hands, and a holy spring gushed forth from where she stopped for a rest one day. Her hardy devotion and goodness made her a local saint, but it seems that, at some point in history, she was seen as not enough on her own. The church is now dedicated to St Morwenna *and* St John the Baptist. Here is my first taste of Cornwall: a place that has its own, undomesticated saints.

The churchyard is set on a slope, and we are greeted by a weathered Celtic cross, worn smooth by time. Further along, we find a ship's figurehead springing out of the grass, a woman with a sword and a cap, painted thick with white gloss paint. Both were planted there by another wild Cornish saint, Robert Stephen Hawker, the famous vicar of Morwenstow who was preferred to the parish in 1829. Despite growing up locally near Bude, he was shocked by the conditions he found in Morwenstow: in this isolated parish, workers subsisted on starvation wages, children baited drunks as they once would bears, and wives were sometimes sold at market to the highest bidder. Hawker wrote to friends about unwed dissenter mothers committing infanticide, and children dying of exposure after being driven out of the house to collect firewood. In Morwenstow, poverty led to wretched morals. As Piers Brendon notes in his excellent biography of Hawker, the lives of the local working class were enough to drive anyone to commit atrocities: 'they lived almost exclusively on bread, potatoes and tea. This had to sustain the men for long hours of hard labour which in many cases literally killed them.'

Although he sympathised with the conditions that led to it, Hawker was particularly appalled by wrecking, the practice of raiding goods from ships that foundered on the rocks nearby. He spoke of his 'nervous terror' at what he would find in the sea after a shipwreck, when the Bristol Channel would be 'peopled with corpses', some mutilated beyond all recognition. Unlike some of his neighbouring churchmen, who were wont to simply leave human remains in the sea in the hope that they would float away with the next tide, Hawker believed it was his duty to recover them and give them a proper burial.

Given his sense of humanity towards the lost sailors, it's

perhaps unsurprising that Hawker sought to break the association between shipwrecks and unexpected bounty in the minds of his parishioners. Early in his pastoral career, he had asked a parishioner what should be done about the body of a drowned sailor, washed up on the shore. 'Sarch 'is pockets,' came the reply. By the time the *Caledonia* was wrecked in 1842, Hawker had developed a more comprehensive response of his own. A team of local men was rallied to carry every single body up to the top of the cliff ('our dead', as Hawker called them), and all were interred in the churchyard in a series of ceremonies, with the ship's figurehead planted over the grave of the captain.

Hawker's reputation today rests mostly on his eccentric dress, opium-eating, occasionally bizarre scriptural interpretations (he famously excommunicated the church cat for mousing on a Sunday), and his literary work as a poet and folklorist, which betrayed an eye for the Cornish eccentrics who came before him. Here in the churchyard, though, it's clear that this wild mind could see things that others were missing. He bore witness to the connection between the degradations of rural poverty and the cruel behaviour it engendered, and stood against both. Eccentricity (meaning, literally, 'not conforming to the centre') is a gift, and the sea invites it.

We leave the churchyard in favour of Morwenstow's lovely pub, the Bush Inn. Inside, there's a fire burning, and a group of farmers at the bar, talking about immigration and arguments they've had on Facebook. We are back, thoroughly, in the twenty-first century. We order hot Belgian waffles and a pot of tea, and wait for H to pick us up again.

5

Chilham to Chartham, February

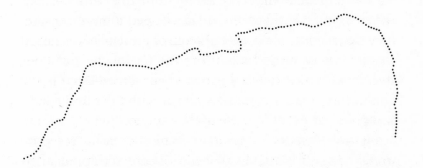

The land is starting to recover itself after winter. As I follow the North Downs Way out of Chilham, the trees are still bare, but the grass is scattered with snowdrops and narcissi. There are catkins on the branches of trees, and the sun is, I believe, trying to shine.

I feel guilty about walking today, so soon after our holiday in Cornwall. But I've got a project on the go, and I have to follow it. As soon as I saw on my map that the next part of the NDW skirts the King's Wood in Challock, I fell in love with the idea of walking the whole extent of this ancient wood, and therefore edging slightly closer to stringing my own county together in a line that makes sense to me.

As ever, nobody minds much. Until recently, I looked after Bert at home on Wednesdays, and H took him on Saturdays while I worked. Now, I work on Wednesdays and walk on Saturdays. It's yet another part of my maternal deficit, but since I've been walking, I have finally got a glimpse of how I might cope again. My working week leaves me drained beyond all sense, and the only way I can reset is to walk it off on Saturday morning, ensuring that the rest of the weekend is relatively harmonious.

If that seems like a high price to pay, then I suppose it is, but we need the money, and, as H says, when I'm not working I only make trouble. My beehive of a brain will buzz on either way. On my own, in a quiet house, that can quickly turn destructive. I can be paranoid, hyperactive, maudlin, obsessive. I am prone to endlessly rearranging the furniture and cooking vast batches of food that nobody can eat. I pounce on H the second he walks through the front door, and pour out the million things that are rattling around my head, and then get frustrated if he can't match my pace straight away. Even taking my exhaustion into account, we are both happier when I'm working.

I can't help wondering if I'd have got past the interview had I said I had AS, though. I worry about this. I worry about the slight shift in perception that the label will bring about. I worry that, despite what they see in front of them, and despite everything I demonstrably manage, the idea of me being autistic will worm around people's minds, and that, rather than making them question what they thought they knew about people like me, they will instead try to find ways to fit their prejudices around me. From now on, I'm afraid that every time I fail, or falter, or lose my composure, people will shrug and say, *Well, what did you expect?*

But then, I still don't feel certain I'm even allowed to call myself an Aspie. My GP agreed with my analysis of the situation, but this merely opened the gate to a referral. 'There's a specialist clinic in London for cases like yours,' he said. 'But it's got a long waiting list. You may as well take a standardised test – the clinic will only use the same criteria anyway. They're all on the internet. I'm sure I won't need to tell you that it's sensible to triangulate your results by taking more than one.'

I'm not sure what a long waiting list means in this context; it's not like there's an urgency in any realistic sense. I have heard a rumour that eighteen months is common; all I know is that, two months on, I haven't had so much as a letter. And even when I get there, what would it possibly do for me? My GP said he knows an occupational therapist who specialises in adults with AS; 'In fact, I think they'd love the chance to work with you.' But then, honestly, I think I cope pretty well. At the same time, perhaps I could cope better, and I don't even know what that might feel like.

As for the tests, I have avoided them so far. They seem so blunt, so final, so absolute. I am worried that I will fail them, or that I will be so invested in getting the diagnosis that I'm convinced is right for me that I'll throw the results. I suspect I'm a borderline case. After all, I've gone undetected so far. What happens if my expression of AS is too delicate to be picked up by the test, and I am left somehow stranded, being no longer able to explain myself? Because, whatever I am, this has been a comfort for the last couple of months. Knowing that I might have AS – believing it, the more I read – has made me feel like I might not be so bad after all.

The climb onto the downs at Chilham is dry underfoot, thanks to the chalk that lurks just beneath the soil, peeking through in the middle of the path. The water just runs off this ground; there's one major benefit of Kent over Devon. I pass a field that is so strewn with chalk that it looks as though snow has fallen; further on, the foundations for a house have been dug out, revealing a dazzling white chalk-pit.

As the land around me becomes steadily more wooded, I see that the bluebells have already put up their leaves this year, fresh green spikes amid the litter of last autumn's fall. After a mile or so, a wooden sign marks the beginning of the King's Wood, and I am again surrounded by straight bronze poles of beech. The path is busy here: there are runners and people walking dogs, and families strolling together.

I should do more of this with Bert: become less obsessed with racking up miles and more amenable to meandering. I pass a deer leap, a ridge that allowed deer into the adjacent Godmersham Park so that they could be hunted, but didn't allow them to retreat into the forest. I remember walking in this wood years ago, when suddenly a pack of roe deer – about a dozen of them – came thundering past, and disappeared into the trees. It strikes me that the difference between letting Bert run around here or at a soft-play centre lies in the sheer depth of information that's contained in a wood. There's history and memory and the biology of an entire life cycle all encoded in one space. There is no information at soft play; nothing other than flat, shining plastic. Outside, there is birdsong and the minute shifting of branches; there is tree bark and there are beetles; there is the odd glimpse of squirrel or rabbit. There are facts to be discussed and dreams to be had, and shared. Life – real life – has a texture, and an electric charge.

A little further on, I stop to read a sign that identifies this spot as the first glimpse that pilgrims would have had of Canterbury Cathedral, coming down from London. I squint into the distance, and there it is, a tiny speck amid the wintry haze. The sign was erected by a group of modern-day pilgrims, who walk the route from St Martin-in-the-Fields in Trafalgar Square to Canterbury Cathedral every year, to raise money for the homeless charity Connection at St Martin's. Seventy-four miles over four days. I didn't think people walked that far anymore. I'm pretty certain I couldn't.

Soon after I leave the King's Wood behind, I come to the village of Boughton Aluph, and here I find the first, tentative outbursts of blackthorn blossom, stark white against the drear. And then I come to a crossroads, and there's a signpost showing how the North Downs Way splits here: to the right, Dover, 25 miles; to the left, Farnham, 98 miles.

I stand there for a moment, eyeing the sign. I hadn't really thought about this. It is tempting to loop back to Dover and call it a job. Farnham is far away from where I live, and sounds impossible to walk to. But then, isn't impossibility the point, sometimes? Shouldn't we all ask ourselves to do impossible things, just once in a while? I touch the sign with my gloved hand, and take the right turn towards Farnham.

I have already taken a sly look at the HR form I would need to complete if I were certain of my diagnosis; AS would be termed a 'neurological impairment' in the official language of my records. I do not feel neurologically impaired. A bit awkward, maybe; a bit clumsy; a bit prone to being stressed by things that really ought not to stress anybody (I completed an expenses claim last week that involved multiple receipts, and found myself upset that all the bits of paper involved were different sizes). But impaired? No.

If I take the tests and they come back negative, I can just quietly move on and say no more about it. Sure, I will have to come to terms with the idea that I'm hopeless at most aspects of normal life, but then I already knew that. At the bottom of it all, the urge to take this test reasserts my commonality with other humans; that quest for self-knowledge is just as strong with me as with everyone else. I need to know what I am.

I browse the possible tests online. Each of them comes from a different theory of the cause of ASD, and this alarms me. If the basis of the condition isn't stable, and the tests all interrogate different attributes, how on earth can we assume that we're testing the same thing? If one test tries to get at the components of Extreme Male Brain theory, and another tests Neanderthal Autism Theory (noted as 'controversial' by the *Life on the Spectrum* blog, largely, it appears, because it's based on a complete absence of understanding of either Neanderthal behaviour or biology), then what on earth am I to conclude if one says I have autistic traits and another says I don't?

I need to approach this systematically. I decide that I will take three tests, whatever happens, and store the results to think about tomorrow. It puts a firebreak (a deer leap?) between the act of testing and the act of understanding.

I start with the Asperger's Quotient (AQ) test, which is based on Simon Baron-Cohen's Extreme Male Brain theory. I am not certain that I want to be found to have an Extreme Male Brain, not least because I'm not entirely convinced that we can comfortably attribute a stable set of character traits to male or female bodies.

Nevertheless, I take the test. It consists of fifty simple questions, which are answered using a Likert scale of Strongly Disagree, Slightly Disagree, Slightly Agree, Strongly Agree. There is no neutral middle option that might allow me to simply have no view on a subject, as I might for questions such as 'I find myself more strongly drawn to people than to things' – the correct answer being, 'Depends on the people; depends on the things.' Similarly, the question 'I would rather go to the theatre than a museum' elicits nothing from me but a series of qualifications: it depends on whether it's a loud museum or a quiet one; it depends how closely the exhibits are packed together; it depends how many people are visiting that day. It depends on whether the seats in the theatre are comfortable and not itchy; whether the people sitting beside me are fidgeting, talking, sniffing, wearing strong perfume, or emitting some form of malodour. It depends on whether the play is entertaining, or whether it expects me to sit through endless emotional nuance and no drama. It depends on whether there are flashing lights and loud sound effects. I like museums; I like the theatre; I have, in fact, devoted most of my career to art galleries and cultural events. But there's plenty I avoid. I have developed the skills, knowledge and understanding to manage my tastes.

Anyone with any basic understanding of AS could give the right answers and get whatever result they wanted. There is a small amount of scale-reversing going on, but only enough to trick a particularly dim-witted respondent. The problem, for people like me, is that it's hard to know what to answer when you've spent so long trying to construct an acceptable personality that you're not sure what your real self looks like anymore. For example, I *do* 'know how to tell if someone listening to me is getting bored', but that's the result of years of getting it horribly wrong, and a blanket policy of watchfulness every time I speak, trying to pick up the tiniest hints of waning interest. I do not want to be stopped again, mid-flow, and be told that my companion is drowning in information.

I suppose, on the other hand, the fact that I can put these coping strategies in place at all is a sign that my AS isn't exactly all-encompassing. I complete the test, trying to answer from my real self, but allowing my coping self to intervene. I don't 'enjoy social chit chat' one little bit; but, equally, I am quite 'good at social chit chat', because I have some strategies that I can drop into place if I need to, and I'm certainly no worse than anyone else anymore. The whole experience leaves me wanting to discuss the questions with some friendly researcher. They are too blunt on their own.

Nevertheless, I answer them all and press *Calculate Score*. Despite all my careful qualifications and hand-wringing honesty, the number that comes back is 43. I check it against the scale:

0–11 low result – indicating no tendency at all towards autistic traits

11–21 is the average result that people get

22–25 shows autistic tendencies slightly above the population average

26–31 gives a borderline indication of an autism spectrum disorder. It is also possible to have Aspergers or mild autism within this range

32–50 indicates a strong likelihood of Asperger syndrome or autism.

I am a little taken aback. More than a little. I was expecting 'autistic tendencies slightly above the population average' or 'borderline indication of an autism spectrum disorder'. I was not expecting 'strong likelihood'. I am, after all, coping. I have a husband and a job, and a social life. I decide that this test was too easy to over-interpret, and take another.

The Ritvo Autism Asperger Diagnostic Scale is noted as both 'reliable' and 'valid' by *Life on the Spectrum*. I plough through its seventy questions, being more careful this time to ensure I'm not exaggerating the effects of my condition in any way. I far prefer this test. Its questions vary more than the AQ, and although it still uses a Likert scale, the options I have make far more sense to me. I can answer, 'True now and when I was young'; 'True only now'; 'True only when I was younger than 16'; and 'Never true'. Here is a test that might acknowledge my ability to change.

In practice, though, I still find it difficult, because there's no nuance. Sure, 'I only like to think and talk about a few things that interest me', but there's room for manoeuvre. I want to be able to tick, 'Now and when I was young; slightly agree'. I supposed I've never been comfortable in the same category as everyone else. Even so, my score comes back as 170. It takes me a while to understand the values, but again, I'm startled. The average score for a neurotypical person is around 85. The average score for a man diagnosed with ASD is 148.4; for a woman, 164.5 (this is not because female autism is more severe, but rather, I suspect, because women hide the effects of ASD better and therefore only more severe cases come to medical attention). I am far into that territory.

Reluctantly, I also take the Rdos Aspie Quiz, which is based on the Neanderthal Autism Theory, but which still, apparently, is thought to produce valid results. What the hell. This is even longer, weighing in at 121 questions, some of which are distinctly odd.

'Do you have an urge to jump over things?' it asks; 'Do you have trouble reading clocks?' 'Do you have an urge to peel flakes off yourself and/or others?' Oh come on; everybody does that.

At the end, I'm presented with a diagram that maps my various competencies (talent, communication, perception, relationship, social) against autistic and neurotypical traits. The graph is skewed strongly towards the right-hand side, and that, of course, is the autistic half. It awards me a 'neurodiverse score' of 132 out of 200, and a 'neurotypical score' of 62 out of 200.

'You are very likely neurodiverse (Aspie)' it says.

6

The White Cliffs of Dover, March

It is Mother's Day. As a seasoned critic of forced levity, it will come as no surprise to know that this is possibly one of my least favourite days in the calendar, coming hot on the heels of Hallowe'en and New Year's Eve. I always found it toxic as a daughter, loaded with the expectation of impossible-to-gauge emotional flourishes and expensive rituals that panicked me as an only child of a single parent. I vowed that, when I became a mother myself, I would continue to despise it. And, bar the first one, which was a novelty that bought me a pub lunch and a couple of glasses of wine, I have stayed true to my word. It's a sticky, sentimental swamp in which I have no desire to engulf Bert.

I'm pretty sure that H feels the same. But this year, he appears to have decided that the time has come to do it properly. A gift – a surprise gift – has been hinted at, and apparently I will love it. I doubt this. I hate surprises. Surprises don't give me enough time to find a response. Last Mother's Day, he aced it and bought me a case of dry white wine, which I worked through dutifully over the coming weeks. Twelve bottles of white wine is not the kind of thing you refer to as a surprise; it's more like a benevolent grocery shop. A surprise will, I fear, entail activity.

The afternoon before, H's phone rings, and he huddles in the garden for a while, deep in conversation.

'I'm afraid,' he says on his return, 'that tomorrow's surprise has been postponed. The weather forecast says high winds. I've rebooked it, but I couldn't get in for a few weeks. I'm so sorry.'

'High winds?' I say. I can't imagine what he might have booked me that could be curtailed by high winds. I hope to God it has nothing to do with flying. Aeroplanes and I have entered an uneasy truce over the last decade, based on my willingness to acknowledge that they tend to stay in the sky, no matter how odd the noises they emit. I am increasingly comforted by the rule that I will only start panicking if the flight attendants start to panic, and I have not yet seen this happen. A friend of mine once did; the plane went through a particularly bad patch of turbulence and the attendants started screaming and crying. Unsurprisingly, this had a deleterious effect on the passengers, who responded in kind. Then the turbulent patch passed, the cabin crew straightened their hats, refilled the spilled coffee pots, and everything went back to normal. The strangest part of the story is that, shortly after, my friend became an air hostess herself.

'Do you want me to tell you what it is?' says H. 'You'll like it.'

'No,' I say. 'It's fine. I'll wait.'

Mother's Day morning arrives. I wake, as usual, before everyone else, and go downstairs to read. An hour later, H emerges, carrying a mussed-up Bert.

'You should have had a lie-in,' he says.

'I didn't want a lie-in.'

I am already anxious; my throat is tight with it. Bert is a little bit grouchy. He clings to H and refuses to sit on my lap.

'Come on, Bertie,' says H, 'it's Mummy's special day.'

'Don't worry,' I say, 'it's just another day.'

'Shall we give Mummy the special present you made her?'

Bert is cheered by this. H goes into the cupboard and fetches out a card made of pink sugar paper, with a red bow Sellotaped on the front and, on the back, a felt-pen drawing of a person with stick legs (no arms), and an egg-shaped belly like a matryoshka doll. Inside the vast cavern of her abdomen is a pair of linked circles. 'That,' says Bert proudly, 'is me when I was in your tummy.'

I love it. I really do. Inside, he has written *ALBERT* in unsteady capitals, copied, I suppose, from H's hand. Bert has already sniffed the prospect of school, and he's desperate to get there. He can recite his alphabet and copy letters, but he never remembers how to write whole words. He must have written his own name a dozen times now, but still, every time, he asks, 'How do I do it?'

'What does it start with?' I always say, and it's met with a blank shrug. The information doesn't stick. At his age, I can remember devoting hours to pretending to write, filling pages with loops of mock-cursive. I always was full of words wanting to come out. The books I have left from my pre-school years are all emblazoned with *katie* in red biro; I suspect I did a job lot one day. I was a sickly child, all nose-bleeds and tonsils and blocked ears. But my mother always said I was bright, and that made up for it. She did all she could to quell my spontaneous outbursts of reading, 'But you were so frustrated,' she says, 'always so frustrated.'

She is an absorbent soul, my mother, who tends to soak up other people's misdemeanours rather than react. What

she means is that I was difficult. I was permanently uncomfortable, hysterically so. I can't imagine I much liked to be
touched. I was repelled by intimacy, obsessively secretive.
I could feel an adult's woollen skirt through two layers of
my own clothing, and so writhed on people's laps like a
little snake. Washing powder brought me out in blisters. I
found the seams of clothing so unbearable that my grandma
took to hand-stitching silk ribbon over every single one
of them.

One of my earliest memories is kicking one of my
mother's friends, hard, in the shins, and laughing. It was
decided that I was a hyperactive child but still, *very bright*.
That was my mother's mantra; I think it probably helped
her to survive through all of it. Very bright, despite being
beyond anyone's control. A handful. Can't stop moving.
Can't stop. She lost friends over me, when their little girls
didn't invite me to their birthday parties. Very bright,
though. Frustrated. Just not like the other children. Into
my teens, she used to mournfully tell me how popular
she'd been at school; how everyone cheered when she
was voted Head Girl. That trait didn't pass to the next
generation.

She would nudge me, gently, into normal things. *If I were
you*, I remember her saying of a friend's boyfriend, *I'd have
a crush on him.* I dutifully pretended I was in love, but I
could see that she knew I was over-acting, which was probably worse. It's pretty hard to develop crushes on people
when you can't really remember faces, anyway. Most of my
crushes were just based on names I knew from the boys'
school opposite. There was nothing real about them. I just
conjured names and produced an ardour to fit them. Despite that, I was the first girl in my class to kiss a boy, and
probably the first to have sex, too. There was cachet in both

of them, I could tell. No matter how unpleasant I found it, it seemed like a good way to trumpet my normalcy.

H has mobilised onto breakfast.

'What would you like?' he says. 'Pancakes? Bacon? Dippy egg?'

I feel sick. 'I think I'll just have some toast,' I say.

'Dippy egg,' says Bert.

H sighs and cooks a dippy egg for Bert, toast for me, and, I notice, toast for himself. 'Why didn't you have an egg?' I say.

'You weren't having one, so I felt bad,' he says.

Bert empties his egg over the plate, just so that he can smash the shell. 'Bertie!' says H. 'This is supposed to be Mummy's special day!'

Bert responds by getting down from his chair and crawling under the table.

'BERT,' says H, 'you should be on your extra special best behaviour today.'

'No, Bert,' I say, 'you don't have to be extra good. You just have to be a normal level of good. Let's just all behave normally, shall we?'

H glares at me, so I say, 'Well if it's really my special day, then I'm going to go and read a book in the front room, and then we'll go for a walk a bit later.'

There were a couple of days, after I emailed him my AS test results with a paragraph of careful interpretation, that he treated me gently, sighing patiently at any outbursts of temper and checking whether I was okay whenever I fell silent. I thought, *This is my future now.* This is how everyone will treat me: carefully. Kindly. Like I'm an object too fragile for normal congress. But it soon passed. He didn't have the patience for it. He wasn't in the habit. We have spent twenty years together, being ratty and over-reacting and pushing our luck and forgetting each other's feelings, and this is really the only way we know how to operate. I'm proud of it: the ability to snap, and to snap back. We are resilient, both singly and combined. The day that H starts treating me like a delicate flower is the day I'll know it's over. Three days after I took the tests, I was almost glad when I asked him to turn his music down because it was driving me mad, and he said, 'No, you go into the other room and then it won't bother you.'

Today, he lets me read for ten minutes before standing next to my chair and saying, 'Come on then, where do you want to walk?'

As he knows very well, it would be unlike me not to have a preference. I have walked the White Cliffs of Dover before, a long time ago, and its historical significance aside, it's a remarkable coastal landscape for Kent, craggy and steep. The full route from Fox Hill Down to the South Foreland lighthouse and back again is probably too far for Bert to walk under his own steam, but he'll be able to make a go of it, at least. Plus, I have a new bit of kit: a cloth backpack to carry him in when he gets tired. We chose the pattern between us: Day of the Dead skulls on a grey background. We are both partial to a skull, Bert and I.

I spent Bert's entire babyhood resisting the entreaties of every earth mother around me to 'wear' Bert, and so the irony isn't lost on me that I've bought a carrier at about the moment when everyone else is setting their burgeoning toddlers down on the ground. But there it is: our rate of physical contact has dropped far enough that I'm not hor-rified by it anymore. In actual fact, I'm quite keen on the idea. It reminds me of my new-found sturdiness, and opens

171

up the prospect of walking without anyone whining at me.

H is behaving normally again once we arrive at the National Trust centre at the beginning of the walk. Bert watches a crow pick through the grass verge, and we have an intensely felt debate about whether it's all right to call it a blackbird. I really feel that it is not. Bert begs to differ.

At first, we are walking with a wall of chalk to our left, its face yellowed and chipped into a rugged chequerboard. Bert attempts to scale it, and gets surprisingly far. Soon, the land opens up, and we can range over the grassy clifftops, the sea turquoise with suspended chalk beneath us. The path rises and falls, and sometimes undulates so dramatically that it's easy to imagine the whole lot disintegrating into the sea. We pass fissures in the ground that look right down onto the shore, with the startling blue water foaming below.

The sea in Kent is always a gentler affair than in the South West. In Whitstable, I'm surprised if I see a wave at all, but even further round the coast, sheltered in the English Channel, it's well tempered. There are waves, but they never crash and drag in the same way as the ones around Hartland, and they're generally brown with Channel mud, rather than the clear water you find on rockier shores. The chalk is a welcome intervention, giving Dover a Caribbean tinge. I like to swim just around the corner at one of the bays that cluster around Broadstairs (though not Broadstairs Sands itself, which is always full of people): at Botany Bay and Joss Bay, there is flat sand through which rasps of chalk-bed protrude, and high chalk monoliths, orphaned from the surrounding cliffs by the action of the sea, for shade.

I have been visiting those beaches all my life, and only now do I understand that this is just an outcrop of a chalk ridge that runs down the length of Kent, much of which I have now walked. It's also the reason why my grandad used to dig up chunks of chalk from the back garden so that I could draw on the patio; and the reason that our village was called Chalk in the first place. I somehow got this far without ever connecting it all together, or realising that it was any different from anywhere else. Doesn't everyone endlessly dig up chalk in their garden? I always thought so until now.

The fields around the cliffs are full of larks this morning, and this time, I recognise them. They flutter in the air, trilling their mechanical song, and I say, 'Lark,' as if this is entirely ordinary knowledge to me. To my surprise, Bert makes it all the way to the lighthouse on foot, and we pile around a table in the tea shop with coffee and cake. Bert mines the buttercream out of his, leaving two cliffs of chocolate sponge standing side by side on his plate.

We begin to walk back, but now Bert is tired and cold, and so I rig up the child carrier and we fold him into it. He complains it hurts his legs, and then his shoulders, and we fuss around, pulling at straps and shifting his weight until he's comfortable enough to start complaining about the wind in his ears instead. So I take off my scarf, and wrap it over the back of his head, and soon I feel him fall fast asleep on my back.

I think he will wake when we get back to the visitor centre, but he doesn't, even when I go into the gift shop and buy him a children's book of birds, so that he will be able to tell the difference between a crow and a blackbird the next time he sees one. Then, I find a seat in the noisy cafe and take him onto my lap, knowing it won't be long before he stops falling asleep on me altogether, and savouring the slump of him in my arms.

A woman comes over to admire him, his little mouth pinched into a pout as he leans against me. 'Happy Mother's

Day, eh, love? Mine are too old to come and see me today. I might get a phone call later, if I'm lucky.' She pats me on the shoulder and Bert stirs, sits up, rubs his eyes and says, 'Jacket be-tato.'

Before we go, he ticks off 'Crow' in his birds book, and as we drive home, he keeps tapping his finger on the window and saying, 'What's that one? What's that one? Find it in my book.'

Back at home, we light the fire, and I decide I'm allowed to make prosecco cocktails at three in the afternoon, seeing as it's my special day and all. Bert builds a train track that sprawls over the whole living-room floor, weaving in and out of chair legs and across doorways.

H boots up his laptop and taps away at the keys, his brow ridged as it always is when he's concentrating. It makes him look furious, outraged at the rumble of the keys or the flicker of the screen.

'Is you staring at your laptop part of my special day?' I ask.

He looks up. 'Give me a minute,' he says, 'and you'll have my full attention.' The angry face returns for a while. He clicks the mouse pad over and over again. Then, he tips his head to one side and looks at me, and shuts the lid.

'I just took the same AS test as you,' he says.

'And?'

'And I'm borderline, but honestly much less than I expected. Given that I'm a computer programmer who likes science fiction, and colour-codes his record collection.'

'God,' I say. 'I never would have thought that *I* was the autistic one in our relationship.'

He tries, briefly, to look offended. 'Me neither, to be honest.'

'Come on then,' I say, 'tell me what this surprise is.' I am braced, by now, for parascending, or whatever cold, dangerous thing people do around the steeper slopes of the downs these days. The last time he gifted me an adrenaline rush was a joint surfing lesson for my thirtieth birthday, in one of those chalky bays at the tip of Kent. This was something of an ambition of mine, something I had always seen myself doing, some day. In practice, it turned out that my ability to catch a wave was significantly thwarted by the fact that I got sea-sick just watching the board float next to me. There was no way I could actually get onto the damned thing for fear losing my composure altogether. I waited most of the lesson out from the beach, with a polystyrene cup of tea and a KitKat, and watched H. What he lacked in flexibility he made up for in enthusiasm, and soon he was exhibiting a talent for lying prone on his board while the sea zipped him to shore. After a particularly vicious current crashed him onto a protruding chalk-bed, though, he joined me on the beach; we later learned that he had broken a toe and two ribs. Really, we are not made for thrill-seeking, either of us.

'Are you sure you want to know?' says H.

'Yes,' I say, 'come on.'

He pulls from his pocket a folded sheet of paper, which, like all the other sheets of paper he keeps in his pockets, is worn to softness. I unfold it, and squint past the weathered-in creases to read it.

'Oh!' I say. 'Oh! That's actually really great.'

'You sound surprised.'

'I am. In a nice way. That's . . . that's such a good idea.' A couple of weeks from now, I am going to spend an afternoon flying falcons.

'Can you imagine,' he says, 'if it had actually been today?

Can you imagine what a brilliant surprise it would have been. It wasn't even windy, in the end.'

I kiss him on the cheek. 'I suppose you can't risk your hawks blowing away,' I say.

'I suppose not,' he says.

....

Morwenstow to Widemouth Bay, March

I was only here a month ago, but in that time spring has broken out. The slopes are still covered in the deep terracotta of dead bracken, but there are also new outbreaks of green leaf, clumps of primroses, and tiny, delicate violets shivering in the undergrowth. The hedgerows that surround my path are scattered in white flowers: a blackthorn winter, the blossom gracing jagged twigs like snow.

The coastline is gradually changing, too. Just outside Morwenstow, there are still the extraordinary geometric rocks, the deep valleys and high, bald moors on top. The ground is still sodden and the sea still roars into every crevasse. But a change is coming at Bude. The cliffs will become friendlier, my walk more leisurely. I will be sorry to leave beautiful Hartland behind, for all its gut-wrenching crenellations. But there are a few more agonies in store for me before I go; a few more leg-bracing descents and a few more aching climbs. There is also the GCHQ sonar array at Harscott, a field of enormous white dishes, pointing in all directions, surrounded by high wire fences and cracked roads. I photograph them guiltily, half expecting someone to appear from nowhere and confiscate my phone, or a drone to fly overhead, barking orders. But I am left unmolested by the military authorities. There is surprisingly little to see here.

I manage about four miles this morning and, although I won't be winning an Iron Man challenge any time soon, I'm pleased to note that for once I manage to correctly estimate the time this will take: two hours. It's pathetically slow, but I'm used to it. I have found my pace, finally accepting my own speed and endurance. I am certain that others could walk faster, for longer, but that knowledge gets me nowhere at all. I meet H and Bert for lunch in Sandymouth, my half-way point. The rain has almost cleared by the time I come over the brow of the hill towards the beach, and there I see my first swallows of the year. They're a favourite of mine, with their bat-like flappy grace, their compact dives, the occasional red cut-throat flash when they get close enough. They always seem to me to enjoy flight for its own sake, to explore all the dimensions of the air.

Bert is walking towards me as I get down to beach level, and I point out the swallows to him. He asks if he can climb to the top of the cliff with me, and I'm delighted to oblige. I help him up the steep steps and they don't seem so bad if that's all you're doing, just getting to the top and not walking onwards. We watch the swallows, and then go back down again and I try to interest him in eating lunch, but his mind is already flitting around like those birds. He wants to build a sandcastle, to kick a ball, to play frisbee. It is wise, for all of us, that I press on.

It's a far gentler walk to Widemouth Bay, along low cliffs where ewes guard their new, matchstick-legged lambs. At Bude, there are smooth, pastel pebbles, sand dunes and a sea-bathing pool. I am back, finally, at the seaside.

*

The author Jean Rhys moved to Bude in 1955. She nicknamed it Bude the Obscure, and complained about the summer tourists who endlessly knocked on her door, assuming that the whole town was open for business. She threatened to nail a sign to her front door that said: *No matches, No cigarettes, No sandwiches, No water. Don't know where anybody lives. Don't know anything. Now BUGGER OFF.* Only her husband stopped her from seeing it through.

But then, by the time she washed up in Bude, Rhys had a track record burning through places and people, leaving her constantly on the run. After coming to England from Dominica at seventeen to go to school, she lived all over Europe with her first husband, before an affair with Ford Maddox Ford ended their marriage. When she left, she left her six-year-old daughter behind in France. She married again in 1934, and although she lived in London with her husband Leslie, he often paid for her to go elsewhere: to the seaside to dry out after she started to drink two bottles of wine a day; to Paris in 1937 when she felt she could no longer write in her study. Here, she appears to have had some kind of breakdown, and ended up in a clinic in Versailles. Back home again, she refused to get out of bed, writing in her notebook, 'I'm drunk mostly all the time.'

When the Second World War came in 1939, Jean was nearly fifty. She had published four novels and a collection of short stories, and although she was admired in the literary world, she had yet to capture the popular imagination. She saw nothing in common with the other writers of the time, and so drifted away from the scene. Her husband, who had typed many of her previous manuscripts, became too engaged in war work to support her; she worried constantly about her daughter, now seventeen and living in occupied Holland. She had to move out of the RAF base in Norfolk where Leslie was stationed; she had embarrassed herself somehow, stepped over some boundary or other. She ended up living alone in a rural cottage in another Norfolk village. She could hear the villagers talking about her through the walls. In 1941, she was fined for being drunk and disorderly in Holt, shouting, 'I am West Indian, and I hate the English. They are a bloody mean and dirty lot.'

There were other incidents: Leslie felt he had to leave the RAF because of Jean's conduct, and wouldn't let his own daughter have contact with her. At the end of the war, Leslie and Jean went on holiday to a cottage on Dartmoor, where Leslie died suddenly. The neighbours reported hearing a screaming row the night before. Jean gave several conflicting accounts of the circumstances of his death. At the very least, she exacerbated the stress that led to it; other people suspected darker truths.

Ever the survivor, she married again, this time to a relative of Leslie's, Max Hamer. Max was a solicitor, and they moved to a large house in Beckenham in Kent, which they planned to renovate, turn into flats, and rent out the top floors. But there were problems, as there always were. The builders ripped them off; Max lost his job at a law firm and made a series of questionable investments instead. Jean began to fall out with the neighbours. When the next-door neighbour's dog killed Jean's beloved cat, Mr Wu, she threw a brick through the window. She was remanded on bail for thirteen days. The next year, she got into a row with her tenant when he held a party in his flat; she ended up slapping his face, hurling abuse at his wife and their guests, and then throwing a punch. She slapped and bit the constable who came to arrest her, and called him a 'dirty gestapo'.

She was fined four pounds in court, and then got into another altercation with the same tenant on returning home.

This time, she was referred for psychiatric examination. The psychiatrist diagnosed her as a 'hysteric'. In court, Jean said she felt he had been 'very fair', but then lost control of herself and embarked on a tirade that only served to underline the severity of her condition in the eyes of the judge. She spent a week in Holloway, on the psychiatric wing. She was glad of it; it shut everyone else out. She later referred to herself as an 'old Hollowayian'.

It didn't stop her fighting. She couldn't get control of it. She went to the police station in 1950 to report being struck by a neighbour. But she was very drunk, and panicked. She ended up shouting that England was run by 'rotten, stinking Jews', and she carried on shouting after she was thrown out of the police station. They had to arrest her. She was fined a pound in court, but three days later the argument broke out again, and she was charged with three assaults. This time, the court gave her three weeks to leave Beckenham. It didn't matter by then, anyway: Max was awaiting trial for some misdemeanours of his own: larceny and gaining money under false pretences.

While Max served two years in prison, Jean found a strange peace. She moved to Maidstone to be near him and lived above a pub, which had the curious effect of stopping her drinking. She started writing the story she had yearned to tell about the first Mrs Rochester, the madwoman in the attic in *Jane Eyre*. It had been a long time since she had been able to write. When Max was released, they moved to the cottage in Bude, where she admired the kitchen but fought against the cold. She wrote to her granddaughter about wreckers, railed against the local sheep who ate her spring flowers, and craved trees instead of sand and rocks.

It is tempting to say 'and so on' at this point, and note the cycle of cantankerousness, drunkenness and rage that saw Jean through to her death in 1979, aged eighty-eight. But here's the thing: in Bude, she finally settled down seriously to writing *The Wide Sargasso Sea*, at that point called *The Revenant* or *Creole*. She signed a publishing contract in 1957, and delivered the book nine years later, the day after Max died.

The novel was immediately acknowledged as a work of considerable significance and genius, and, of course, now finds its way onto school syllabuses and lists of favourite, life-changing books. Perhaps it is the psychological realism of a woman driven to madness by an inhospitable world around her, which could only be told by a woman who herself fought hard against the necessity of an attic and the custody of a Grace Poole. Literary success made Jean no less difficult, coming so late in her life, when she was fast approaching her eighties, but she made the most of it, drinking whisky in London night clubs, wearing a pink wig that protected her from the shyness she had always felt around people. There was sympathy for Jean now, but friends continued to peel away from her, right to the end of her life. Yet people continued to adhere to her too; to find her electric and extraordinary. Friends, to Jean, were like a fuel that stoked her fire, and she burned them up accordingly.

We will never know, now, what made the world chafe so horribly against Jean – whether it was the trauma of her early years, or something deeper-seated, that would never let her settle. None of us has the right to speculate. But she was a difficult woman who found the world difficult, who found the city too crowded and the country too quiet. She found solace in walking from Bude to Widemouth Bay, even if the fields were so damp and cow-infested that she wished they would all get washed into the sea. This is a kind of balance that I recognise.

*

I start the next day at Widemouth Bay, with the sand from yesterday's walk still in my boots. I leave Bert playing on the beach, scrambling over the low rocks while H positions himself to catch any falls. By the time I've walked the first half a mile, I've stopped to shake out my boots six times. It just won't seem to budge. It's drizzly this morning, and I'm stressed by the prospect of the walk ahead, which seems to be an endless succession of up-and-down. I'm sick of up-and-down. I thought I'd finally left it behind, but it's back again. I'm soon climbing up a tarmac road, feeling harassed by the passing minibuses full of surfers. I don't seem to have enough breath today. I hate gradual climbs. I'd far rather haul myself up somewhere steep and get it over with. By the time I reach the top, it's so grey and drizzly that I can't see anything. Soon, I'm climbing again, and again. The larks – now that I can identify them so freely – annoy me.

I am making my way along the bank near Dizzard, hoping that at least I can rush through this and have a good lunch, when I see a man and a dog come towards me. I rarely meet other people on the path, and I resent it when I do; it's a huge effort to drag my mind back from its quiet perambulations and speak. I fix my eyes to the ground and prepare myself to fake the briefest greeting I can, but the man stops and puts his hands on his hips and says, 'I don't think it will turn out too bad after all.' His dog – an alert border collie – comes and sniffs at my boots, and I scratch his head.

'You think?' I say. 'It's been nothing but drizzle so far.'

'Oh well, the May blossom will set and go again before we see properly good weather,' he says, standing easy. 'I meant it ain't bad for April in Cornwall.' He has a face worn into crinkles and the kind of broad West Country accent I thought only existed in period dramas.

'I can't really grumble,' I say. 'I've walked through far worse this winter.'

He works on the farm at the top of the hill, and has done all his life. I tell him I'm walking the whole South West Coast Path, and he says he did that once too, with his wife, back in 1974. He waited until the summer, though; he says he knew better than to try it over winter. I share a rueful laugh.

'I walk here every day,' he says. 'I watch the year changing.'

His hand scans over the coast as he talks me through the year, and I can see everything shift around me, past the May blossom and into high summer, when his dog will chase the swallows. 'The damned fool,' he says, and pats her. She is snuffing around our feet, grubbing up wild garlic bulbs.

In the autumn, he says, it will all turn bronze, and I realise that this will be the point where I started, and in a few months' time I will know the whole life cycle of this coast, and I will be able to predict it, too. Under his gaze, this cycle is all there is; all the rest of time seems to merge into one layer. He points to rocks beneath us and remembers rescuing people from a wrecked yacht down there ('didn't know what they were doing, poor souls') and then nearly drowning there himself as a boy, and staggering halfway up the cliff but having to stop for a sleep before he made it home. The door to his father's house came from a ship-wreck; lord only knows how the old man dragged it all the way up to the top, heavy thing that it was. The low trees to the east, which I'll walk through in just a moment, are a rare species of dwarf oak, a whole little forest of them, but you'd never know they were anything special to look at them. The bluebells will be just coming out in the wood beyond.

When I finally say, 'I'd better go; I need to get to Crackington Haven for lunchtime,' he says kindly, 'I doubt you'll make it in time, my dear.'

'Oh well,' I say. 'I'll keep walking until I get there.'

'Right you are,' he says. 'Good to talk to yer. Most walkers just carry on past and stare at their maps. All I get is a grunt.' I try to look appalled, and hope he doesn't realise that half an hour ago, I tried to do the same.

I'm reminded again of my Grandad Jim, who I think sometimes found the confines of the house too quiet, and used to head out into the village just to talk to people. He would stand at the bus stop and help women off with their pushchairs, or lurk around the till at the village store, packing bags. My other grandad, who owned the shop for a while before I was born, once told me that he first thought Jim was some sort of a beggar, forcing his labour upon the shop in an effort to make money. There were, I suspect, words exchanged, and Jim left him in no doubt that he didn't want paying; he had packed bags before the shop was taken over, and would carry on doing so. The arrangement continued through the next decades; in the 1980s, Mr Patel took over and soon Jim was disappearing for hours on end, coming home after afternoons being fed tea and samosas by Mrs Patel. 'She never even lets me do the washing-up!' he used to exclaim, tucking Tupperwares of unfamiliar Indian snacks into the fridge for later.

I suppose the Patels thought he was lonely; perhaps he was. My grandma kept a quiet house, which I always found serene, but maybe it was more than he could bear. The quiet routines that they kept together, of cooking and washing, of tending the garden and taking the bus into town on a Friday, were never broken. Once they were done, Grandma would sit down in her green chair, with her legs stretched out in front of her, hands folded in her lap, and a book resting on her knees. She had read her way through entire libraries, hundreds and hundreds of books over a lifetime.

Sometimes she would finish a book and then say, 'I think I might have already read that one,' but really I think it didn't matter to her. The point of the exercise was to cast her eyes over the words and be peaceful. She read Catherine Cookson and Stephen King, P.D. James and Virginia Andrews. I don't think she ever saw it as her business to pass judgement on any one of them, but she sifted them instead: historical romance to my aunt, crime to my mother. To me, she passed on *The Shining*, and *The Famished Road*, and *The Unbearable Lightness of Being*.

It was only after she died that I realised things hadn't always been so calm and certain. Grandad tried to put a brave face on it by saying that he'd never have to eat vegetables again and that he'd have chips with every meal, but it wasn't hard to see through it. It was dreadful to see him so alone. My aunt and uncle moved to Spain, and he decided to go with them, leaving behind his beloved village where he had shepherded the residents for his entire adult life. Just before he went, he came for dinner, and I made him spaghetti bolognaise, no salad. At the end of the meal, he leaned over the table and said, 'I worked away for years you know, up at Watford. Left your gran at home, looking after everything. It took her doctor to call me and tell me she couldn't do it alone. *You've got to come back and help her*, he said. *She can't be on her own*. And I did.' His voice breaks a little, something I've become painfully used to seeing these last few years. 'I did. And you might do it too, one day.'

Today, passing the huddled oak trees and crossing into the woods where, sure enough, the first few bluebells are showing, I think how similar we are, my gran and me. I inherited her need to eat through words, and her habit of asking for darkness and silence. I inherited her talent for worry, her suspicion of too much levity, although not her catchphrase, *Laughter always ends in tears.* Perhaps I just haven't got there yet. Perhaps I will grow into it as I get older.

It is nearly lunchtime now, and exhaustion has set in. It is slippery underfoot and my muscles are tired from bracing against the path as it swivels and slopes. I'm back to counting my steps in groups of a hundred, and checking the map over and over again to register how little progress I'm making. I'm furious at the path for being so difficult, and at myself for being so weak. I text H to warn him of the inevitable delay, and then, when even this looks impossible, I ask him to pick me up earlier, avoiding the double headland at Pencannow Point, which I estimate will add another hour onto my route. I can't do it.

Instead, I embark on a steep descent through gorse and then a clamber up an equally steep, muddy bank, upon which I fall, repeatedly, coating my knees in dirt. I shout, out loud, 'Fuck this fucking mud!' and scramble up further, emerging at the top by St Gennys church, where H is waiting patiently in the car. He turns off his music when I get in, and drives me to Crackington Haven, where he buys me lunch and a deep, cold glass of wine in the Coombe Barton Inn.

I haven't got many words left, but I'm glad he comes back to help me, over and over again.

Widemouth Bay to Mawgan Porth, March

I have been dreading High Cliff. At 223 metres, it's the highest point on the SWCP in Cornwall, and I'm sick of hills.

Still, I have my friend Emma with me, and she's climbed Mount Kilimanjaro, so I'm planning to just fall into pace behind her, and let her superior fitness and mental control get us both up there. Provided, of course, there is no sinister livestock blocking our route.

We agree to take it step by step, and start to ascend through a series of fields. The ground slopes only gently, and soon I find myself dispensing advice that I didn't know I had in me: climbing, I say, is a matter of rhythm. You take shallow steps, keep time, and imagine you're floating. Before we know it, we're at the top, eating M&Ms on a bench and catching our breath. We look at the map: in my anxiety about this climb, I have failed to notice that there are five valleys ahead of us, and Rusey Cliff next door is 222 metres high.

'Come on, then,' I say. 'Let's get on with it.' There are blue skies and calm winds, and the edge of Cornwall crinkles into the sea beneath us. I feel like I'm invincible, but

I also feel like I have the measure of this now. I know how to walk this path. I have the right equipment and I know where to put my feet. I know how to think about it.

The ravens are out in force today, nesting in the sides of the cliffs. On this stretch of coast, there are deep inlets where the sea floods in, and we watch kestrels darting between the sheer faces of rock, testing the crevices and holes. Everything is coming to life again. The path is busier too; it's Easter already, the beginning of holiday season. We reach Boscastle at lunchtime, following the perfect natural fold of its harbour down onto the quayside, where we eat chips in a packed cafe, and then set off again towards Tintagel.

'Already?' says Emma.

'No point hanging around,' I say.

There are more steep climbs to follow, most of them on deep, slippery staircases cut into the valleys. By mid-afternoon, it's clear that Emma is exhausted, and yet I am not. 'When did you get this fast?' she keeps saying, and I honestly don't know. In actual fact, I've always been a fast walker; it's just that suddenly I have the fitness to keep being fast over a whole day. There is power in my legs and air in my lungs. It feels so straightforward now the weather is clear. It's almost too easy.

When I started the walk, descending into Tintagel was one of the moments I pictured, approaching the ancient castle with the roar of the sea in my ears. I have cheated, of course, and already been there, and in the event I'm glad I did, because it's hard to glimpse the castle until you're right upon it, and in any case, Bert and Emma's two boys spot us at the top of the cliff, and come running up to meet us, and we're entirely distracted by admiring the maracas they've made with plastic bottles and stolen shingle from the English Heritage cafe, and by trying to foil their dangerous plan to roll back down the cliff-face to where H is waiting, exasperated.

I walk with H the next day, while Emma looks after our gaggle of boys. It no longer upsets me that I am not left taking a turn looking after all three of them together. I am, quite simply, not cut out for such things.

Reading the map the night before, I realise that neither is H cut out for the walk between Tintagel and Port Isaac. It looks beautiful, but there are simply too many rivers making their way to the sea on that stretch, corrugating the coastline in a way that will be agonising for him. I hate the idea of deliberately skipping a bit of the SWCP, and potentially a good bit, too. I am tempted to tell him to drop me off at Tintagel and meet me for lunch at Port Isaac.

But that's not fair, and I know it. We have the rare gift of a day together, alone, and I can't use it to turn him into my chauffeur. I will have to bend. I never meant this to be a simple process of following a route from one place to another; I meant it to make things better. I decide, instead, that we will walk from Port Isaac to Polzeath, and I will make up the missed stretch of coast another time – perhaps later in the week. It doesn't hurt as much as I thought it would.

We park above Port Isaac and walk down into the village. H immediately wants to stop to get something to eat. I refuse; we'll never get started. 'I have a cereal bar in my bag,' I say.

'Maybe someone will do a bacon sandwich,' he says.

'This wouldn't have happened with Emma.'

'For fuck's sake,' he says, 'don't start already.'

We bicker over where the path starts, and we dawdle up a hill onto the clifftops.

'Small steps,' I call from twenty metres ahead; 'imagine you're floating upwards.'

H ignores me. I get to a kissing gate and wait for him to catch up. 'Now we're on the flat,' I say, 'take bigger steps to stretch out your thigh muscles.'

'I know how to walk,' he says.

We begin a process of stopping every quarter of a mile while H relaces his shoes, or catches his breath, or pretends to admire the view. He does not know how to walk. He talks obsessively about the prospect of a cup of tea, as if the SWCP is lined with tea vans. I have a flask in my backpack, but he doesn't want it. He's convinced there will be a cafe in Port Quinn, and will not believe me when I tell him that there's rarely tea anywhere.

'We'll see,' he says.

There is no cafe in Port Quinn. It's a tiny, pretty village in a narrow bay, and that's about it. We pause at the side of the road, and he finally consents to a drink from my flask and a cereal bar. I calculate that we've only managed 1.5 miles per hour across unchallenging terrain.

'You have to go faster than this,' I say. 'It's ridiculous.'

We set off again, in silence. There are old mine shafts on the top of the next cliff, and it takes all I've got to let him pause to look at them. It feels like a waste of time. I've seen it all before. It's a terrible thing to say, but after a couple of hundred miles of beauty, it's become uniform. I keep trying to look closer, to feel my heart lift again, to tell myself I'm taking it for granted, but it's all just miles to me. I want to get to Newquay by the end of this week, because then I can see my way around to St Ives, and then Penzance, and then to the Lizard Peninsular. These places, magnificent as I'm sure they are, stand in my way of getting to South Devon, my South West Coast Path mothership. Until I'm there again, it's all just detail.

As we pass Trevan Point, the weather suddenly changes.

First the sky goes black, and then the temperature falls. Soon, a wind is blasting us nearly horizontal and then it begins to rain. We have just walked down into a dip by a rock when it starts, and I crouch down for shelter, calling to H, 'Stay here until it passes; it'll be over quickly. It's not worth the risk of walking along the cliff in this.'

'It's fine,' he says, and staggers up to the top of the ridge, where I see the wind nearly take him off his feet. For a few seconds I think he'll fall, but then he turns and hunches down next to me.

'I have learned *some* things,' I say. 'It's worth listening to me every now and again.'

'Yeah,' he says, 'I know.'

'I'm sorry,' I say. 'I'm not a great walking partner.'

The rain switches off like a tap, and we get up, climbing back up onto the top of the ridge where the wind is still strong but bearable. And then it starts to hail. People often mean sleet when they say hail; but this is the real deal, a bombardment of ice-stones the size of cat litter. We shield our faces with our hands, and bend double to stagger through it. By the time it's over, I'm soaked to the skin, despite my cagoule. We are at the foot of Pentire Point.

'Right,' I say, 'I'm going to suggest we cut across to Polzeath. I've had enough of this.'

'You can't do that!' says H. 'We've got to see it through.'

'No,' I say. 'It's lunchtime, we're tired and wet, and if we have another bout of that hail we might end up falling off a cliff. You have to know when to give up.'

We follow a zig-zag of footpaths across to Slipper Point, and I remember how much I like inland views, too. It's nice to know that the sea isn't far away, surrounding us discreetly. When we get to the beach, we stagger along with the sand blowing in our faces, and find Surfside, a cafe with a picture window that serves lobster rolls and negronis. The sun breaks out, warming our faces through the glass and drying our clothes, and soon we can see the boys beneath us, running through the streams that cross the beach with their shoes and socks still on, and I say, 'Do you think Emma can manage without us for another ten minutes?' We have fought our way to this peace, and I don't want to leave it behind.

I walk with Emma the next day. We consider starting from Polzeath, but that would mean walking a mile along an estuary and then catching a ferry from Rock to Padstow.

'It's pointless,' I say. 'We can park at Padstow and look at Rock from the other side of the River Camel.'

'Blimey,' says Emma. 'You've changed. Six months ago you'd have made us start on the exact spot you stopped the day before.'

'Yeah,' I say, 'well.'

Padstow is already heaving at 10 a.m. on a Thursday. It was probably once a quaint harbour; it is now something resembling a theme park for the middle classes. There are coffee shops and fancy bakeries, and restaurants bearing the names of famous chefs (and not just Rick Stein anymore; others have joined in, soaking up the legions of gastro-tourists); there are gift shops and galleries and clothes shops that promise surfer chic or smart-casual nautique. There is an awful lot of bunting. But, unlike my beloved Whitstable, which has all of these things, it's hard to imagine the place having a life outside tourism; it's overrun with the sort of businesses that exist solely to appeal to outsiders. It just makes me want to go home.

We buy a coffee each, which I then spend the next mile regretting as it sloshes over my hand and makes my sleeves smell of stale milk. We walk through a busy park and then up to Stepper Point, past the famous Doom Bar, a bank of sand at the mouth of the Camel which makes navigation to Padstow a dangerous affair. Local legend has it that it was put there as a curse by a dying mermaid, shot by the sailor Tom Yeo after she tried to prevent him from hunting seals with his crossbow. She swore Padstow Harbour would be useless ever after. Little did she realise that Padstow's future prosperity could arrive from the other direction.

We turn at Stepper Point and are by the sea again, and it's deep blue, and beautiful, and windy, but somehow it feels less wild than the sea that accompanied me just a few days ago. The cliffs are lower, perhaps; the small harbour villages more frequent. We stop for lunch at Harlyn, and I show Emma a path that cuts off Trevose Head altogether, taking us straight to the surfing cove Treyarnon Bay.

'Are you sure?' says Emma. 'You're missing about three miles of coastline there.'

'Exactly,' I say. 'It'll save loads of time.'

'There might be seals out there.'

'I've seen seals,' I say.

'Up to you. Your walk.'

I steer us through Harlyn, along residential roads and beside a golf course. It's not an attractive route, but it works; we're soon back by the coast, on the lovely, steep-sided beach at Treyarnon. From there, the path becomes a little wilder again. There are meadows set aside for migratory birds to breed, and the damp tang of new soil due to extensive cliff falls. I'm just counting off the inlets on my map, seeing how fast we can make progress across this relatively flat ground. Soon we are at Porthcothan, and I wonder if we can skip the long walk inland around the cove by cutting across the beach. But it's impossible; the tide is in. We stop for coffee and a cake, surrounded by other walkers in bright waterproofs. I unfold the map again.

'Do you think we'll make it as far as Newquay today?' I say.

'It'll be tight,' says Emma. 'We could probably do it if you really want to.'

'I'm not bothered about Newquay.'

'You're not bothered about any of it today!'

'No,' I say. 'I'm not much, am I?'

'You're bored,' says Emma. 'You've had too much sea.'

'It all looks the same after a while,' I say. 'I've walked through so many places this week, and I don't even remember the names, let alone what they look like.'

'So slow down a bit.'

'I can't. It's so expensive to keep coming down here. H wants to go on holiday somewhere else for a change. I've got to pack it all in while I get the chance.'

'Maybe you should take a break for a while.'

'If I take a break, I won't ever start again. I just want to get round to South Devon. That's the bit I wanted to walk in the first place.'

'So why don't you just do that?'

'I said I'd walk the whole thing. People will think I'm a quitter.'

'You *are* a quitter,' says Emma. 'Always have been. It's one of your endearing qualities. You know when to give up.'

'Like when I leave the last mouthful of dinner,' I say.

'I'll never understand that. Never.' We look down at the table, where I have left one-eighth of a flapjack.

'I just didn't want the last bit,' I say. I consider eating it now, to make a point, but I can't face it. 'Problem is, I don't care about Cornwall. I mean, it's fine. It's nice. But my heart doesn't cry out for it. I crave Devon if I'm away from it for too long. I'll never feel that about here.'

'Look,' says Emma. 'It's your walk. You've got to do what you want with it. It's no one else's business what you do.'

We meet H and the three boys in Mawgan Porth, where the tide is in so far that we have to take off our boots and wade through the sea. Just around the corner is the long beach at Watergate Bay, and then there's Newquay, the gateway to the true South West, the end of the world before America.

I could get a bit further tonight, if I really cared. I could finish my fish and chips, and press on. I could go out walking again tomorrow, and cover the stretch between Tintagel and Port Isaac; or I could march on past Newquay, and see the dune systems at Holywell and Penhale Sands, the ancient landscape at St Agnes Head.

But I will not, and not simply because I'm bored. I have had my time in the wilderness; I have been alone. Somewhere along the last hundred miles, I completed a cycle of thought and now I'm ready to return to society. I am a poor recluse. I could not match the hermitudes of St Morwenna or the Reverend Hawker. I could not match the bitter eccentricities of Jean Rhys. I could not even match the solitudes of my own grandmother. I want to learn to be with my family again – or perhaps, for the first time. I want to stop passing through places.

I want to learn to stay.

PART THREE

Outer Hope

Today, just like every other day, I will sit down to meditate. It's a habit I picked up ten years ago, when I had to leave the house in Gillingham. I swore to myself that I would never get into this state again without having a tool to haul myself back out. I spotted the course on a card in the library, while I was in hiding from my own house, and thought, *What the hell*. It just happened to fall on the weekend of the move – bad timing, but that couldn't be helped. As H unpacked boxes, I drove over to a yoga studio in Canterbury in search of peace.

I learned Transcendental Meditation. If it was good enough for Stevie Wonder, it's good enough for me. At the time, the TM movement was not officially providing classes in Britain in protest at the War on Terror. The man who taught me had formed a breakaway group, which suited me just fine, not least because it was far cheaper than the real thing. He reassured me that I didn't have to take on any spiritual beliefs; that the technique was enough in itself.

I had expected to land in an earnest group of novices, but once I'm in the room, I see that everyone looks a bit like me: tired, quiet, world-worn. The introductory speech alights on addiction, depression, anxiety, eating disorders, and there are murmurs of recognition. Apart from that, we're not invited to say much. 'I don't need to know what your problems are,' says the teacher. 'It works just the same.' I am relieved. There's nothing I want to tell him, or anyone else here. By all outward appearances, the rest of the group feel the same.

On Friday night, we are taken through a ritual in which we're given an apple, a carnation, a clean handkerchief and a secret mantra, which we should disclose to nobody. The symbolism of these things are immediately lost on me. Afterwards, we mill around outside, smoking and avoiding each other's gaze, before going home for the night to our bewildered families who probably think we've joined a cult.

I don't know what I was expecting from meditation: a psychedelic experience, maybe, like the trip sequences in sixties movies. It wasn't like that at all. It was fidgety, twitchy, uncomfortable at first; it made me sea-sick. But there was peace there, straight away, even though it was a fragile one. I sat, repeated my mantra in my head, and tried not to hate myself when my mind wandered. This was all part of it: going astray and gently coming back again, over and over. Somehow, if you can manage this for twenty minutes, your mind eventually surrenders and drifts away. Your breathing becomes shallow. Everything goes quiet, even if for a few precious moments. Coming out the other side, you feel slightly better.

In the week after the course, I must have called my teacher half a dozen times. Whenever I closed my eyes, I could hear a distinct crunching sound, like the march of a million tiny feet parading through my body. My neck felt like it stretched to six feet long, so that my head was floating somewhere near the ceiling. I kept thinking I was choking. The answer was always the same: *Notice the feeling, and return to your mantra*. I'd never realised how much time I spent running away from what my senses were reporting.

I, who never stick with anything, stuck with it. Twenty

minutes, twice a day. Being a person with a peripatetic job and few routines, I had to improvise. I meditated in my car and in pubs. I attracted the attention of a security guard by meditating on the bench of a shopping centre. I learned to time my meditations to the train stops between Whitstable and London Victoria. They steadied me before the onslaught of meetings and phone calls, and helped me to come down from emergency functioning when I got home at the end of the day. In them, I found new perspectives that I couldn't access before, new depths of empathy. My mind would replay the day's events, and I would be able to perceive, the second or third time around, the reactions of those around me. I'm almost ashamed to say it, but I finally saw other people in three dimensions. I knew it before, but this was the moment it finally sunk in.

I stuck with meditation because I was desperate, but also because it brought so many good things. Within a month, people were saying how much I'd changed. I was calmer, less inclined to rage; I was able to focus. For the first time in my working life, colleagues started telling me I was good at my job. It's an odd experience, to be perceived to have reformed. Inside, I felt like I had continued to be myself, if a lot less afraid.

After three years, I began to get twitchy about practising TM. Even if the organisation didn't demand that I believed anything, I knew the teachers believed that there was a spiritual realm beyond this one, and it was hard to shake the feeling that I would never succeed in their eyes without perceiving it. There would always be a block that they were patiently waiting for me to clear. I'm not much of a joiner anyway, but I was particularly suspicious of this group. The demand to keep my mantra secret, lest it lose its power, was surely the business of superstition. 'It's how they make their money,' said a friend who had learned TM and given up. 'They've made you believe in magic.'

I went to see a new meditation teacher who said, 'Tell me your mantra, then. That'll be the end of it.' Despite myself, I hesitated. But I told him, and he showed me how I could unpick every rule that I'd been taught, throwing whatever delighted me into my meditations. He taught me that the simplest things could draw me in: sipping a glass of water; gazing at the shape of a city skyline; inhaling the first hit of morning air. He said, 'I can see you like rolling your hands together. You should do that at the beginning of your practice to help you relax. You shouldn't try to be still.'

More troubling for me, he also told me that I had an enormous aura; that it filled the room. 'You can sense when anyone crosses it, can't you?' he said. 'It's queenly. People should ask your permission to enter it. You have a right to their respect.'

The talk of auras – and of energies, flows, secret mantras and all the other accoutrements of the spiritual industries – sit badly with me. They're too imprecise, too contingent on belief itself to have their effects. There is too little structure propping them up. I can't observe them objectively, record them, show them to somebody else. But he was one of the few people to have ever perceived the range of little movements I need to make, and to honour them; to sense the extent of my need for personal space. He could detect the minute flinch as he got too close, which – and we tested this – was about four metres away. He may have been using a different language, but he was paying attention.

It's an uncomfortable truth for a materialist like me, but through this man's eyes, I found the kindest account of myself I have ever been offered. Not prickly or awkward or difficult; not over-sensitive or afraid of intimacy. Instead,

queenly. Instead, having a sense of personal space that re-
quired respect. It's funny, isn't it, to flip that on its head?
Imagine if the responsibility didn't fall to people like me
– people with AS, *women* – to modify our reactions to the
intrusions of other people. Imagine if, instead, it was considered a basic politeness to observe other people's responses
to our social overtures, and adjust accordingly. Imagine if
we accepted that there are a whole range of personalities out
there, and that one size does not fit all.

I am telling you this because, long before I had a name
for what I am, I had found a way of coping. It's imperfect;
it doesn't solve everything; but it makes everything better.
Before I learned to meditate, my diagnosis would have surprised no one but me. Ten years on, the opposite is true:
I now cope well enough to pass, but I know, instinctively,
that the world lands on me differently from other people. I
sometimes wonder if I'd have found meditation if I already
knew that I had AS; or if I would have seen myself as incor-
rigible, stuck just as I was for ever.

But this is the smallest thing that meditation has given
me, really. It has left me with a sense, not of God, but of a
current that flows through all things. Everything is strung
together like fairy lights. If that electricity sometimes over-
powers me, then it also often lights my way, and joins me to
the rest of the world. In bed at night, I can reach my foot out
of the covers to lay it on the cat and feel the subtle tingle of
her charge. I can sniff the air at sunrise, and become electri-
fied by the new day. I can press my cheek against Bert's and
light up like Regent Street at Christmas.

If meditation converts the world's electric current to
something manageable, then so does walking. Sometimes
you need to do more than just sit down. I now see that,
when I set out on the South West Coast Path, I needed to

get exhausted beyond all thought. I needed to be alone, silent, hungry, distracted by the exactitudes of maps and waymarkers, of avoiding brambles, of second-guessing the weather.

When I walk, a space opens up, and I can finally perceive the fine texture of my own life. It's like dropping through a trapdoor into another world: my world. The Maori have recently developed a new set of words to adapt their lexicon for the twenty-first century. Autism is 'takiwatanga', meaning 'in your own time and space'. I find something in this definition that I've been craving all my life – the restless urge to live in the time and space that I was born to perceive, rather than to fit badly into the one that suits everyone else.

My own time and space. Like the child of displaced parents, I yearn for this place, without ever having known it myself. It's always been there in my peripheral vision, a lost continent, long neglected, waiting there for me. Home.

The question is, can I find my way back there so late?

1

......

Whitstable to Canterbury, May

I have started to come out. I have started, falteringly, to
tell friends that I have – no I might have – be – no I *am*
– autistic. Maybe. I'm still waiting to hear back about an appointment with the consultant. Nothing seems very certain.

As I feel my way through the process, I find my language
changing. My initial instinct was to hide behind the cosy
term 'Aspie', with its unthreatening, child-like inflections.
But it just doesn't sound like me, or like something I would
say. Cuteness never did sit well in my mouth. I am too old
for 'Aspie'. It's partly because I've come into this game at
a time when Asperger syndrome would be something of
an atavistic diagnosis. But I am suspicious, too, of my own
instinct to grasp for a label that attempts to diminish the
blow of what I am, and what I have been through to get
here. I started off feeling like 'autism' threw me into a vast,
unknowable stew. It asserts the complexity and individu-
ality of what I experience. It forces outsiders to ask how
I experience *my* autism, rather than to assume that they
already know.

It's a gut-wrenching process to deliberately unpick a
lifetime's commitment to passing myself off as being just

like everyone else. I don't know what to say, and when, and to whom. The new knowledge that I'm poor at taking the social temperature makes this even worse. Understanding, mechanically, that your judgement is bad does nothing to improve your judgement; it just makes you self-conscious. It suddenly seems better to keep quiet, to avoid people entirely. I can't be boring or *intense* or Marmitey if I'm not there.

I think, on balance, that my good friends won't be too thrown by the news. But, like everyone else, I rely on having a mix of people around me, from the nearest and dearest whom I'd trust with my life, to the distant acquaintances who I think are funny and cool, and whom I will perhaps see for coffee once a year, or even less. It's those people I worry about, the ones I know already, and the ones I have yet to meet. What will they think, now, about going for a drink with an autistic person? It will, I fear, become a substantially less tantalising prospect. They will be waiting for me to be boring, to hook, dead-eyed, onto a conversational topic and refuse to let go. They will be waiting for me to be cold, or humourless, or unfeeling. Or worse, perhaps they will now spend time with me to bolster their own sense of charity, to signal their own impressive commitment to diversity. 'I had tea with Katherine last week,' they will announce; 'you know, the autistic one. She's ever so lovely, bless her. I mean, obviously,' and here they will drop their voice to show their extreme sensitivity to the situation, 'she struggles in so many ways.'

I wonder if I should bother coming out at all. After all, I've got this far without making any excuses, and I'm not short of company. Certainly, there have been many friends who have fallen by the wayside over the years, but isn't that true of everybody? I know that I'm brash and opinionated, that I talk too fast. I know that I have no patience for small talk; that, as my mother always tells me, I don't suffer fools gladly. She doesn't mean that as a compliment; it's an expression of exasperation that I heard throughout my teens, when it seemed like I'd never attach to anyone. 'Why should I make an effort with the other kids?' I would say. 'We've got nothing in common.'

I went through this all over again when Bert was a baby and I attempted to fit in with the other mothers of infants, only to discover that they were engaged in an endless process of slimming, feeling guilty about falling off the wagon of their ridiculously self-denying diets, and systematically naming all the things they considered to be 'lovely', 'nice', or 'really nice'. I find it hard to believe that people can content themselves with insubstantial things when there's so much wonder in the world.

I think I may be constitutionally unable to prioritise fitting in over saying what I think. I have no interest in milling about in little groups of people who all have the same views; to me, it becomes so close and precious that it starts to feel a lot like physical contact. My brain may be unable to store the contents of today's diary (or, indeed, what time my weekly yoga class starts, or how much it costs to take part), but it is a receptacle for a dazzling array of facts and statistics and views. I don't seem to have the same ability as others to filter. Even when I'm in a room of people with whom I broadly agree, I can't resist appalling them by playing devil's advocate, or compulsively pointing out the complexity of the situation. I find the alternative entirely uninteresting. Why should I be the one who changes?

One of the features of autism is supposed to be the inability to read the feelings of others. In many ways, I think I have the opposite problem: I over-read other people's feelings to the point that they choke me. But then, perhaps this is because I've learned to pay close attention. As a child, other people's emotions seemed to come out of nowhere. There would suddenly be crying or hysterical laughter, and I would flounder, wondering how on earth we got *here*. I was equally poor at signalling back my own emotions to myself. I remember a class discussion in Year 8, when another pupil started talking about my infamous temper tantrums, and how amazing they were, and everyone else laughed along and threw in their own examples of a time I'd gone into complete meltdown. And me, laughing along too, because it seemed, really, like an unusual incidence of positive attention as far as I was concerned, but thinking, *I have no idea what we're referring to*.

And then the teacher – who I suppose must have been bored that afternoon, and looking for a way to stretch out the class with minimum effort – said, 'Come on then, Katherine, let's see what one of these fits looks like.'

I stood up, gamely, and straightened my shirt, and didn't know what I ought to do next. My classmates clapped. I was red-faced already. All that came to mind was Rumpelstiltskin jumping up and down in fury when he found that his tricks had been turned back on him, and pounding the floor until he fell right through. My best hope, I decided, was to mimic this, and so I did. I growled and I stamped and I clenched my fists, hammering my feet into the floor until the walls shook. When I came to a halt, I expected there to be silence, but instead there was laughter, howls of recognition. I watched them, bewildered, as my pulse settled. Was this acceptance? I found it hard to tell.

A year later, I ticked 'Tries hard to please others' on the Careers Guidance questionnaire we were given, and found, again, that same response: laughter. *You? Really?* Even the teacher joined in. *Of all the people . . . I thought you just liked being different.*

There was a party, at fourteen, when I suddenly saw coloured lines strung between everyone in the room, and I realised it was a kind of code. There were green lines for spite, and red for anger; yellow marked a sense of superiority; blue was amicable. I watched the guests for a while, and I could see, decorating the air in front of me, everything that everyone thought about each other. I thought I was the only one ever to perceive it, and I told the whole room about it, explaining who had a crush, and who hated whom. My new-found skills of perception clearly didn't stretch to understanding what was better left unstated. The party host later told me that she couldn't risk inviting me to anything else, because all her friends thought I was weird.

I now see this through completely different eyes. It was the beginning of something for me; the first stirring of recognition for the feelings of others. I had studied them long and hard, and was finally learning to read them. Perhaps because I couldn't interpret the findings through more usual routes – couldn't feel along with those people – I saw it in a different way instead, as a diagram. It is almost as though, exasperated, my brain had to find a format that I could read. It's easy to forget that people don't stay in their raw form for ever; we learn. It's as true for me as it is for anyone else.

I'm worried that my walking has disintegrated altogether. I can't even fathom how I'm going to get to Cornwall next, and when. I keep looking at it on a map, its big, blunt form staring numbly back at me. It will take hours to get there, and I don't particularly care about it. It's just a means to an end, before I can get back to Devon, and stage a triumphant return to my favourite bit of the path. It's pathetic. Cornwall is a perfectly good place. But it's not mine. It's someone else's dream.

Meanwhile, I'm not walking locally either. The next stretch of the North Downs Way is beginning to feel like a long way away, and the thought of it renders me strangely motionless. It just doesn't do, all this running away, all these difficult journeys to escape from real life. It doesn't get me anywhere closer to coping with the mundane. I need to find a way to manage everyday life, rather than storing up the horrors until they spill over, and I have to run away.

But then one morning, it occurs to me that I could walk to work, from Whitstable all the way over to the centre of Canterbury. I usually drive; it takes about twenty minutes at best, but it's often nearer to forty when you factor in the traffic caused by two schools, two universities and a city centre. I check Google Maps: following the Crab and Winkle Way, it's just over seven miles. Nothing, really. A mere stroll; a couple of hours' walking. I can't believe I haven't thought of it before.

I pause at the front door, wearing trainers and a rucksack. I'm not due in until midday, but it still seems somehow transgressive to be walking there, taking all that extra time when being busy is such a status symbol. But I'll be teaching until eight tonight, and there's no rule that says I have to build a twelve-hour day around it, just because my timetable shifts across the week. I twist the front-door key off my keyring, leaving my bulky pair of car keys in the tray by the door.

The spring has broken into warmth. There are blue skies above me, and the fields at South Street are already turning yellow with rapeseed. The Crab and Winkle Way mostly follows an old train line – the first passenger railway in the world, no less – that cuts through Clowes wood and finally emerges on the outskirts of Canterbury. It's a broad, busy path, always full of dog-walkers and cyclists. Before Bert came along (and while H could still be persuaded onto a bicycle), we sometimes rode along it to the cinema, pedalling back home through the thrillingly black woods late at night. H thought it was a dreadful thing to do, and would much rather have driven. I, who am romantic at heart and fond of a glass of wine with my film, felt the pitchy journey home was more than worth it.

Within an hour, I'm deep into the woods, and there's no point in turning back anymore. Soon, I'm walking through pine trees, and then farmland with enormous crates of apples stacked up around me. No one else is walking far here; only me. I feel like I've asserted another tiny piece of ownership: over the route, over my own life and its habits. It's satisfyingly tiring. By the time I meet St Stephen's Hill, with its steep descent into the city and cathedral views, my legs are tingling and my knees are hot. I pick up speed, almost skipping downhill. When I reach my work, I'm disappointed to find it quiet, because I want to tell everybody that I walked here, that it's possible, that I carved out the time. I am joyfully, pristinely tired, just enough to merit a cold carton of Ribena and a baguette from the canteen. I feel as though I have conquered something that nobody knew was even there to be conquered. There is far more satisfaction in this than in completing a path that thousands of others have conquered. This is mine. This is my own little songline.

The first friends I come out to are as confused as they are enlightened. I think that's partly because they don't know what to say. Do you express surprise or satisfaction? Do they congratulate or commiserate? I'm not sure myself, until the first person – someone I don't know very well – says, 'Oh,

I'm so sorry to hear that,' and I'm furious. I can't think what business of theirs it is to feel sorry for me. We should not, I feel, commiserate with other people for mere difference.

Overall, though, the bulk of the work lies in explaining what ASD *is*. Everyone has the same inaccurate notion that I ought to be something entirely other than what I am: humourless, mechanical, with the slight edge of a sneer in everything I say. Male, probably. I find myself explaining over and over again that the important thing is not the minor inconveniences experienced by those dealing with autistic people; it's the way that it's experienced from the inside. I find I don't mind this. I'm asserting something about myself that I've never been able to assert before. I am unlearning my habit of passing, and I'm telling people how often I feel overwhelmed, how far close to the edge I'm pushed by ordinary events.

Mostly, they understand. In fact, they relate. Everyone knows how it feels, to some extent. What's startling, though, is that, once they've taken in my news, nearly everybody tells me the same story about myself: *Oh*, they say, *that explains why you disappear.*

H is the first one to say it. He chews over the facts for a week or so after my first announcement, and then says, 'Do you know what? Every single time we've ever been to a gig, you've either vanished or needed to go home. Every single time.'

This is important to H. Music is his thing. I met him when I was eighteen, and he was running a monthly club night which – a rare thing in Chatham – was attracting approving notices in *Mixmag* and, bizarrely, the *Sun*. I used to go after the pub, and then immediately fall asleep on the pile of coats at the side of the room. It seemed perfectly reasonable to me, particularly given how drunk I needed to get to cope with the noise. After a few months together, he would drive me home between sets, when I would start to feel stranded in a sea of rattling sound. I liked the music. I never understood why I'd suddenly feel so tired when I was there, almost by coincidence.

Eventually, I found I was much happier running the door, totting up the money, organising the cloakroom, making sure the band were happy. It was quieter out in the lobby, and I could keep myself busy. I would tag along with him to other people's gigs too, usually clinging to the edges of the room to avoid the press on the dancefloor. Sometimes I'd dance, and enjoy it, but usually that entailed a hideous hangover the day afterwards. It takes a hefty blow of intoxication to break down my personal barriers enough to manage it. Most often, I would seek out a quiet toilet cubicle, and lock the door, and read the graffiti on the walls. Smartphones have improved my life no end in this respect. There's always something to immerse yourself in when the outside world is too hot and too noisy.

I've always loved the line on Björk's 'There's More to Life Than This':

Come on girl
Let's sneak out of this party
It's getting boring
There's more to life than this.

Given the enervating disco track behind those lyrics, I don't blame her. But there's a moment in the song when a door opens and closes and suddenly the music sounds far away, and you can hear the delighted shiver in Björk's voice as she sings. I decided long ago that this was really a song about escaping to the toilets. It captures the experience exactly:

the cool, echoing quiet; the music droning on behind the door just to emphasise the fact you've escaped. Thinking about it, I've passed some of my happiest moments like this.

But this is only retrospective wisdom. Until a couple of months ago, I'd have told you that I love parties; that I'm a social animal. I wouldn't have been lying exactly. I have spent my whole adult life believing that I love parties, and then making myself sick with anxiety in the run-up to them. Never once did I recognise this as a pattern, but apparently all my friends did. I struggle to join up the two versions of myself: the one I believed in, and that one that existed for everyone else.

And then, one Saturday, I find myself in the midst of one of my vanishings. It's the first time I have ever noticed it happening; the first time I am able to connect the urge to disappear with the experience of being autistic. We have taken Bert to the Science Museum. Bert loves the Science Museum. It has rockets and engines and interactive displays of light and geometry; it has water pumps and a climbing frame in the basement. It also has artificially dark rooms and a continuous press of people. It reminds me of the question in the AQ test: would I rather go to a theatre or a museum? All things being equal, my answer is an empty museum. But they are never empty anymore, not the kinds of museum that you go to with a child.

We are in a dark room full of children and their parents, and things happening everywhere, and sudden flashes of light, and noises I can't place. Bert is playing with a ball that rolls around and around a shiny bowl, before spinning, finally, around a hole in the bottom, rather like the striped charity collection boxes that encourage children to beg their parents for coins. Other kids keep throwing in balls that bump into Bert's one, and disrupt its smooth orbit. He's getting frustrated. So am I. It's so loud in here, and the visual chaos. The visual chaos of the yellow balls banging into each other. The charge of Bert's anger next to me. It's too much.

I leave him with H and go to the toilets, and think, *Here I am, vanishing.* I feel sick, desperate, on the edge of tears. It's such a little thing, really; some noise; a few people. There's no menace in it. The hand-dryer is going on and off next to my cubicle. They have got worse in recent years. I wish we could all revert to nice, quiet towels again. I can't stay here.

I walk back into the exhibition hall and scan the crowd. H, at six feet four, is usually easy to spot, but it's loud and hot, and everything is moving, and so there might as well be a thick fog in the room. My attention is being pulled in so many different directions. I can't see them. *All right*, I say to myself. *They're here. Concentrate.* I steady myself, because I realise I'm swaying, just a little, in my anxiety. I look systematically through the room. I can't make them out. I just can't, and I never can. I've always struggled to recognise faces, but when there are so many of them at once, they might as well all be blank masks. *I am not recognising my own son*, I think, and try to swallow the shame of it. I have been through this before, every night when I collected Bert from nursery, and had to try to pick him out from twenty blonde-haired little boys, and usually couldn't do it. I always wonder how long I got away with saying, 'Oh there you are, right under my nose!' before the nursery assistants cottoned on. I wonder what they thought of me.

I wonder how long I have been standing still in the middle of this room, alone, staring all about me. I must move, before somebody notices. I stalk towards the middle of the room, the thick centre of the action. My face: my face is wrong now, I can feel it. It has fallen into its mask, when the muscles seem to set into slackness and I can't corral it into a human expression. I blink, and try to regain control of it, but there's too much going on around me. I cannot see them. If I could see them, I could tell them I am going.

But then I notice that it's not just that I am not seeing them; I am now seeing myself, everywhere. Walking towards me; cutting across my path; standing, absorbed, by a brightly lit gallery case: here I am. Just a fleeting drift of recognition, an *is that?*, the same sensation you get when catching your reflection in a shop window. Suddenly, I am in a hall of mirrors, except the reflections are not me, and do not, in fact, on closer inspection, look at all like me. I mistake myself for pregnant women, for men with beards. My overloaded brain is entirely indiscriminate in its systematic labour:

A face!
My face?
No.
A face!
My face?
No.
A face!
My face?

I can't breathe. All the bodies around me seem like numb, senseless things, just moving without feeling. I am operating faster than them. I need to be away. I push out between them, out into the sudden cold white space of a corridor where a screen is showing the same promotional film, looped over and over. I stand in front of it, and hope that anyone passing will believe I'm watching it as I close my eyes, and let my attention sink inwards to the briefest meditation I can afford. There's a prickly black fog in the middle of my forehead, or that's how it feels. As it begins to clear, I send a text to H, and wait for the slightly baffled, slightly angry faces to appear, wondering why I vanished.

It's not such a tragedy. No harm is done. But it's a revelation to have watched it happening, consciously, perhaps for the first time ever. Fifteen minutes later, I can't work out what all the fuss was about. It feels as though I have two different selves; a desperate, animal self that emerges in chaos, and a calm, wise human who squints to recognise her twin.

But isn't that the nature of ASD? It's a semaphore through a fairground mirror, where the signals get warped and mangled so that they're sickening. A call-and-response that comes back disharmonious. A Chinese whisper between the speakers of two different languages. It's an endless miscommunication between the world and me; between me and the world.

For me, there are habits to be unlearned, and new ones to be acquired. I'm left with a strange sense of trying to understand something that's invisible to me. I feel like I'm investigating a set of absences in my life, and trying to see them through the lens of other people's half-remembered, half-perceived responses. It's full of loss. It's the end of my life story, the comforting, consistent one I've told myself so far. I'm unpicking it. I have to reset the seams again.

2

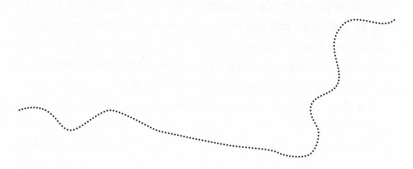

Whitstable to Thornden Wood, May

The day has arrived to fly my Mother's Day hawks. I wonder, slightly, what H is trying to set me up for here. Only last week, he drew my attention to an article about therapy dogs for people with ASD. 'Apparently they'd help you to communicate with the outside world,' he says. He's mocking me; I hate dogs. Or actually, I don't hate them; it's just that we have a mutual suspicion of each other. They're over-eager, and make your hands smell disgusting for hours after touching them. And even when I do try to pet them a little (if, for example, there is copious running water and Carex in my line of sight), I get the angle of approach wrong and we all get confused. I have no idea what people see in them. I have a feeling – albeit an oblique one – that H is suggesting I might access the services of a therapy merlin instead.

To be fair, he also knows how much I love birds. This is not obvious from the outside; I am not given to spending my weekend on RSPB reserves, gazing out of hides with a pair of binoculars. That's all a little too static for me. No, I enjoy random encounters with birds: the sparrow flitting from tree to tree in the garden; the starlings bathing in puddles on the beach. I'm fond of ordinary birds; birds you can build a relationship with. I was brought up with Mr and Mrs Blackbird in my grandparents' back garden, and with the thrush that my grandma slowly trained to eat sultanas out of her hand. Those are the birds that matter to me, the ones that animate everyday life. I don't want to have to go looking for them. I want them to find me.

Look around you, any time you're outside: the air is full of birds. There's nothing exotic about them. Here in Whitstable, we have herring gulls nesting on the roof and there are always black-headed gulls riding the air above the beach, as if they're suspended on hidden strings. There's the occasional wagtail, or blue tit, or chaffinch. Nothing special, really. But the world seethes with them, and we barely even notice. We might remark on a kestrel hovering at the side of the motorway, or a buzzard soaring over farmland, but if that buzzard turns out to be a crow, we're disappointed.

We shouldn't be. Birds – ordinary birds – give the world its full three dimensions. Without them, the air is a flat surface, an absence of matter. Birds populate that space, explore it. They fill it with song. They mark the dawn and the dusk for us, the first heat of spring and the last gasp of autumn. In return, we're busy forgetting them.

It has struck me over the last year that this is a loss we're suffering as an entire society, a quiet recession of knowledge. We are losing the ability to name ordinary things. We have forgotten to notice birdsong, to the extent that we no longer hear it; and now, on the rare occasions we tune in to it, we can no longer identify the bird it comes from. We can no longer pick out the individual flowers in the tangle of greenery at the side of the road. We can no longer separate out the different trees in the wood. We are fascinated by exotic animals on Attenborough documentaries or prowling in compounds at the zoo; we can detail the life cycle of a penguin but know little about the robin or the wren. We seem to judge these domestic creatures too mundane to merit our detailed attention. They are too quiet; too brown. We have too many other opportunities elsewhere.

While we're looking the other way, our British birds are in decline. A 2015 report from the Department for Environment, Food and Rural Affairs shows a widespread decline in UK bird populations since 1970, brought on by changes in farming methods, habitat loss and shifting seasons. These are your greenfinches, wagtails and buntings; partridges, linnets and doves. The thrushes and blackbirds that my grandma used to feed are disappearing, as well as the starlings that she used to shoo away because of the greedy squabble they raised. The birds we used to glimpse rarely are now rarer still. Tawny owls and lesser-spotted woodpeckers; herons and kingfishers. All of them vanishing, and without most of us noticing at all.

This comes at a time when we're more conscious than ever of conservation, and of showing respect for animals in their natural habitats. When I was a child, there used to be a stack of boxes in the top of my mother's wardrobe containing the blown-out eggs of dozens of bird species, all nestled on a bed of cotton wool. 'I'm not sure it's even legal to have them anymore,' I remember her telling me. 'I really ought to throw them out.' The terrible truth is that, when my dad was building this collection as a boy, he was also building a relationship with an array of birds, and learning the detail of them. I am, of course, not suggesting that egg collecting is in any way a good idea. But we live in an age when we routinely warn children away from interaction with wild spaces – don't disturb the rocks in rock pools; don't take insects away from their natural habitats; don't pick wild flowers – and that's without our fear of letting them explore anywhere on their own. I am beginning to wonder whether a few more beetles in boxes, or sticklebacks in jam jars, or wild flowers pressed between the pages of books, wouldn't rebuild our detailed relationship with our own wildlife. Too much careful respect has become complete separation.

Keeping birds of prey is a good example of this. It rubs against our current desire to keep our animals in as natural a state as possible. We prefer to see our raptors flying free. I agree with the sentiment, but I think there's room for both. We can learn something of their wildness even in domestication.

I am introduced to the falconer, and he talks to me for a while about how the birds are cared for, the careful process of weighing, observing and recording that keeps the birds just hungry enough to come back to you, without starving them altogether. It strikes me as nerve-wrackingly precise, with the ever-present risk of losing your bird. It's a far cry from the pouch of Felix and bowl of biscuits I put down for my cats each morning.

Then we meet the raptors themselves. I wear a thick leather gauntlet and am allowed to receive bird after bird on my fist. There's a tiny American kestrel who weighs almost nothing; a buzzard with fierce black eyes who has such a startling gaze that I never want to let him go.

I'm allowed to fly a barn owl on a long leash, or créance, tempting her back with nuggets of chopped raw chick. That low, intent swoop she makes is magical. I'm invisible to her, irrelevant; a mere prop for offering meat. She exists in a slightly other dimension from me, one that's more spacious, more minutely adjusted.

Once she's back in her box, I get the best prize of them all: a walk in the woods with a Harris hawk, a highly social raptor that can be trusted to fly back to a human companion, even when they're a near-stranger, as I am. Harris hawks have been used to clear pigeons from Trafalgar Square and scare away gulls at London City Airport. They are magnificent birds. Mine hunches malevolently on my arm, ruffling out her chocolatey feathers. We walk out into a patch of woodland where there's still a sparse scattering of bluebells. I'm loath to admit it, but I really do find the Harris's presence therapeutic. She exudes a kind of calm, proud alertness; she's with me, but is self-contained at the same time. By supporting her poised weight on my hand, I feel as though I absorb a little of her composure.

I'm shown how to throw out my arm to send her flapping into the air to land on a nearby branch and survey the scene. At my signal, she returns again. We walk further, and off she flies. This time, I can't spot her. I scan the trees, but she's well hidden. 'Don't worry,' says the falconer, 'just stick out your arm and she'll come back.' And she does. A glide out of nowhere, and again the reassuring presence on my wrist. I want to bury my face in her feathers, but I suspect this would be too great an impingement on her dignity. She flies off, and returns.

And then, to our left, there is a rustle in a clump of nettles and she takes off without warning and darts above them, angling herself this way and that to get a better view. A rabbit. It has certainly clocked her; although we can't see it, we can track its path through the hawk's reaction, as she zig-zags to catch it. Then she dives, disappearing into the undergrowth for a few, heart-stopping seconds before flying back up again with empty talons.

I throw out my arm and she lands, scratching sulkily. 'Bad luck, Harry,' I say, and give her a little scrap of meat to soothe her wounded pride.

I walk again from my front door. It's hard to believe I haven't done this until recently – headed inland instead of endlessly skirting the flat, concrete paths that edge the coast. This time, I take a map and no plan. I follow the Crab and Winkle Way for a mile or so, and then strike off across those rapeseed fields I noticed last week. I find a stream that I drive across every single day without ever knowing it's there. How can it be that I carefully pay tribute to every last rivulet in Exmoor, but arrogantly ignore my own, local gods?

This part of the county is absolutely cross-hatched with footpaths. I choose one that takes me – somewhat anxiously – through the centre of Chestfield Golf Course. It's marked on the Ordnance Survey, but I'm really not sure I'm allowed to be here. Won't my heavy-soled boots ruin their grass? I brace myself to be shouted at, or questioned by some offi-cious middle-aged man, but all I get are friendly smiles and waves from everyone I pass. It's almost disappointing; I was thinking of waving my Ramblers Association membership card and asserting my right to roam.

It soon becomes evident that the route I planned to follow back out of the golf course is adjacent to a putting green, around which stands a group of men in sleeveless V-necks and sun hats. I edge around the longer grass, and make the merest nod of greeting while avoiding eye contact. My path appears to take me into a small copse, although it's really not obvious where I'm supposed to enter it. There's no signpost. Not wishing to invite the attention of the golfers, I try to look competent and stroll towards the trees as if I know what I'm doing. It works, for a while. There is a path of sorts into the thicket, but after a few metres I'm bent double under the overgrowth of branches, and a few steps beyond that, the path is blocked entirely by a profusion of bald blackthorn, covered in thick lichen. This has been there for some time.

I stare at my map, think half-heartedly about trying to beat it back with a stick, and then look at the map again. I bet those bastards on the putting green are just *waiting* for me to come out again. Well, I won't do it. I will find a way through. I am a walker, for God's sake; and this is very clearly a public right of way.

I back up a little, and look around me for alternative routes through; someone surely must have made a desire path around this. There's nothing. I wonder if perhaps I can just wait it out here for an hour or so, and pretend that I've been somewhere and come back again. But I suspect, bitterly, that the golfers can see my yellow jacket beaming through the trees. I will have to go back.

In all fairness to them, they don't patronise me at all, but they do wave their arms around a lot and say, 'It's that way!'

'Oh,' I say, 'thanks,' as if I'm at all grateful. I would prefer to get lost in privacy. I skirt the putting green again, and dive back into the thicket. This is little better. In fact, after about thirty seconds, it's clear that this path is just as blocked as the previous one. The blackthorn is rampant, and intertwined with fresh spring nettles. I'm not going back a second time, though. I wrap my scarf around my face, get down on my hands and knees, and crawl. It's scratchy and wet, and it's unclear how far back the copse extends, but despite all these things, it's preferable to repeated social contact with a group of strangers in sports casual.

I used to think I liked contact with people. I used to think it stimulated me, revved me up, kept me sane. I now realise how crucial it is for me to be alone on a regular basis. I'm coming to see that I was drawn to people in the way that addicts are drawn to their poison. I find social contact abrasive, and that over-stimulates me, creating an adrenal charge that gets misread as pleasure. The comedown afterwards is diabolical. I've always told myself that my social life is a sign that I'm coping, but it's actually the reverse. It's a sign that I'm not looking after myself. It's a sign that I don't acknowledge what I need. I need to find a better way to live than this. I need to find a way to be straightforward with the world.

I emerge, with twigs in my hair, in Crow Park, a huge meadow on what counts as high ground in Whitstable. It's surrounded by big, old trees and is bisected by a stream that has burst its banks after months of damp weather. The ground is covered in mysterious bumps which hint at centuries of use. It feels like no other soul has been there in years. True to its name, it's full of crows, strutting importantly in their ancestral home and picking at the grass. I watch them for a while, and then climb over a stile and cross a road into Thornden Wood, passing extraordinarily ordered ranks of pine trees before finding myself in the more familiar territory of oak and beech wood.

There are white wood anemones and sparse bluebells, and a stream that cuts deeply into the earth. I am not sure if I lose my path here, or if there simply isn't one to speak of. I walk uphill through the trees, becoming increasingly disoriented until I hear traffic and realise I must be close to Gipsy Corner. I locate the path again, only to find it submerged a few strides later. The woodland floor is flooded all the way alongside the road. At first, it's hard to even understand what I'm looking at; the black mulch made by centuries of accumulated leaves creates a perfect mirror from the deep, still pools of water, reflecting the tangle of trees and the sky above me. For a few moments, it seems infinite, and I have to throw a stick into it just to reassure myself that it's all an illusion. The water ripples, and then calms into perfect flatness again.

I have to cross it, somehow. Taking hold of a pair of tree trunks, I begin to balance along the raised ridges of their roots, carefully choosing the places where the water is shallow. If I were doing this properly, I suspect I should take off my boots and wade, but the black water is eerie and suggestive of leeches. Or at least gnats and the odd water boatman. So instead, I balance on tiptoe across fallen trunks and splash across roots until I can scramble up the bank to the side of the road.

On the way home, I divert again and again, taking whichever paths offer themselves along the way. The whole adventure takes, in total, about two hours, perhaps three. It's hard to gauge how far I walked because I'm not entirely sure I can locate my meanderings on the map; I reckon on eight miles, or ten. My legs feel like it was ten, but then that's because they were uncertain for so much of it, and I forgot to take a rest in the middle. But I have adventured, and I am back in time for lunch in my own kitchen.

When I took up walking, I accidentally found another way to meditate. The gifts are the same. My brain alights on the problems that walking throws up – finding my route, managing aching legs, hunger, thirst – and while my conscious self is otherwise occupied, other processes grind on quietly beneath. For the first few hours of a long walk, I'm brimming with new ideas and insights. After that, everything falls blissfully quiet, and I am empty. In that wide-open space, mountains can move. Without walking, I don't think

I would ever have realised what I am. I had never made room to realise it before.

When I walk, I feel as though I acquire the compactness of one of those hawks, the same sense of focused sufficiency. I am lean like them; strong and continent. I am able to draw my wings around myself, and to stare past the fussy surface of this world.

3

....

London to Canterbury, May

I am standing under the portico of St Martin-in-the-Fields church on Trafalgar Square, trying to find the right level of blending into the background without appearing rude and standoffish. Everyone else is in high spirits, and I suppose I must be, too. I queue to register, hand in my health questionnaire, and check in my bag of clean clothes. They will come back to me this evening, when I'll be in sore need of them. Then, I descend into the crypt for tea and tentative discussions about exactly how fast I might walk. Quite fast, I think, given that I'm used to this sort of thing.

You may remember, way back at the beginning of the year, that I was walking through the Kings Wood near Chilham when I stopped to read an information board about an annual pilgrimage from London to Canterbury. Well, it preyed on my mind. Seventy-five miles in four days, over moderate terrain. It seemed, frankly, like the kind of thing I ought to be able to manage.

I asked H what he thought.

'Well,' he said, 'if you want to do it, you should do it.'

'I do want to do it. I think.'

'But I'll say one thing: you should come home every night.'

The pilgrims go whole-hog and sleep in church halls along the route, in varying levels of comfort. There aren't always showers. It seems to me that this is a vital part of the experience, the communal roughing it. I'll be a traitor if I go home.

'You won't cope,' he says. 'You'll be miserable. You hate roughing it.'

I shrug. If everyone else manages it, then I don't see why I shouldn't be able to.

'Look,' he says, 'the walking's not going to be the worst thing for you. But you'll be walking in a group. People will be chatting. There will be at least one person you find annoying; maybe more. You're going to be exhausted by the end of the day. You'll need your personal space.'

'But aren't I supposed to be learning to cope better?'

He sighs.

'Look, it's up to you. I'm just saying that I wouldn't do it myself.'

I think on it, and he's right. This is not learning to cope better; it's just doing what I've always done, pushing myself to behave like everyone else without any regard for past or present feelings. This signals a new way of relating to people, and perhaps that's what makes me uneasy. I will, however discreetly, have to announce my inability to cope in advance of people even meeting me, and this will mark me out. It is the first day of the end of blending in. I don't like it one bit. My worst fear is that it will bring about some discreet attempts at kindness and understanding that I will not be able to bear.

So, I agree, gloomily, to allow H to pick me up every night (noting that this puts me back to the bad old days of him chasing me around Devon on his precious annual leave), sign up, and tell all my friends about it, so that I won't be able to back out.

And here I am. I sign up to the second-fastest walkers' group, and join the congregation for the opening blessing in the church. This is one of my many anxieties about the walk (alongside 'everyone will be fitter than me' and 'everyone will hate me'): I have not traditionally been the natural bedfellow of the devout. I was raised an atheist, and have remained one. The compulsion to tell people when I find their views ridiculous is strong with me. Or at least it was; I like to think I have a bit more of a lid on such things these days. I have learned – slowly, the hard way – that Christians don't really like it much if you constantly try to unpick the logic of their faith. I'm genuinely contrite for the amount I did this in the past. It's none of my business. Can we perhaps call it an outcrop of youthful vigour and agree to move on?

And, bizarrely for someone who doesn't really feel the metaphysical thing, I've spent a great deal of time in church. C of E primary school; Brownies; Guides; attending a secondary school that liked to march us down the hill to Rochester Cathedral whenever the opportunity arose. I had a brief career as the sole tenor in the school choir, and this somehow translated into a place in the far more serious chapel choir at university, where I was allowed to finally revert to being an alto. We performed a sung Eucharist twice a week, and I think it was there, finally, that I fell in love with the quiet, ceremonious routines, the candlelight, the hour of quiet contemplation that it all afforded. I came to love the patterning of it all: the *Magnificat*, the *Nunc Dimittis*, the whole arc of life between them. The rhythm of hymns, psalms, prayers, the reciting of the Creed. I resented the sermon for its intrusive variety. And I wished, fervently, that something would happen to make me believe in any of it.

It never did, or at least hasn't yet. But I took from it a love of church music, and today, in St Martin's, I can just about stretch that to singing 'You'll Never Walk Alone' with gusto. I like being part of a congregation; this is my kind of crowd. I just hope that nobody talks to me about God.

We set off as one big pack, crossing Waterloo Bridge before separating into our pace groups. This annual pilgrimage supports Connection at St Martin's work with the homeless, and service users are invited to join the walk too, with boots and walking gear provided. Here, in this group, it's hard to tell who's who. We're all just setting about the business of walking, boots on hard concrete, and worrying about the unseasonably warm sun. We hope it'll all feel better once we're out of the city, where the pavements are bouncing the heat back up at us.

Over the last few days, I have agonised over how to present myself to these people. They're a clean sheet. Will I tell them that I'm autistic (and if I do, will that be an advance apology, just in case I misbehave?), or will I force them to take me as I am? Will I chat, or will I walk quietly, hoping not to be noticed? All my instincts have been undermined. It's hard to resist the urge to excuse myself for future sins.

I try to take it as it comes. People chat as they walk, and so I chat back. I don't want to seem weird, or aloof. I fall back on the skills I learned a long time ago, and ask them about themselves, where they live, what they do. When they ask after me, I talk about working in a university and walking the South West Coast Path. I try to watch myself so that I don't talk too much, or interrupt, to speak so quickly that they can't understand me. I try to let the conversation move on, even when I have something left to say on the subject.

The best way to achieve this, I find, is to keep in mind that you're not very interesting, that no one wants to hear you go on and on. It's a bitter lesson to learn, and maintaining it is a labour in itself.

We stop for lunch at a church somewhere in south London, and I realise that I'm already disoriented, taken away from the train routes that I know in and out of the capital. I've been provided with a hand-drawn route map, but it's little more than a line through a silhouette of the South East; I wish I had the reassurance of an OS map in my hand. There is a bit of confusion around Beckenham – or Bromley, or Lee; I'm really not sure by that point – where we seem to spend an awful lot of time crossing busy main roads with railings around them, with the next slowest group suddenly hot on our heels. At that point we realise a group member is missing, and it seems that we are scuppered. But then the lost sheep appears from a corner shop clutching a four-pack of cider, and all is well again. Our group leader knows what he's doing; he's been walking this route for years.

After that, the terrain becomes leafier, and I'm told we're on the outskirts of Chislehurst. We're more or less in the countryside here, and in my own county again to boot. At the next stop for afternoon tea, there is a team of chiropodists ready to patch up sore feet. Mine ache, and my legs are tired, but I'm fine. The company has been pleasant, the weather kind, and the best parts of the journey lie ahead of us. I don't think I've shamed myself yet. I see a man struggling to tie up his bootlaces, and so kneel down to do it for him and then, afterwards, wonder if that wasn't an intrusion.

We start up again, and although the group begins to lose pace towards the back end of the afternoon, we eventually stagger, stiff-legged, into a churchyard in Swanley, where there is tea waiting for us and, crucially for me, H and Bert are running around the car park. There are no showers available until tomorrow night, and the pilgrims will be bedding down on camp mats in the church hall. Many of them are far older than me. The food is good and plentiful, and everyone's in high spirits, but it's clear that the walk is only half the challenge. It feels like a betrayal to go home. I knew it would. It's all the worse for the fact that no one knows the reason I'm disappearing for the night. As I pack my bags into the car, the urge to blurt out that I'm autistic is almost overwhelming. Instead, I blame it on Bert. *He'd miss me for a whole weekend*, I say. *This is his Bank Holiday, too.*

H is right though: I wouldn't get a wink of sleep, and by tomorrow morning I'd be nearly crawling out of my skin because it felt so dirty. I'm also far past the point when I can cope with talking to anyone. Arriving at Swanley station the next day, the difference is clear. I'm feeling refreshed after a hot bath and a deep sleep. Many of my companions from yesterday look pale and sunken, glassy-eyed. Nobody slept very much. A few people are feeling unwell. It's drizzling and grey.

I try to be cheerful. I'm in awe of everyone else's resolve. On days like this, I have given up over and over again. But they're all here, and there are only a few jokes about catching the train straight back to London while they still can. I'm particularly impressed by the slowest group, many of whom look unlikely to be able to make it to the bottom of their own garden. They walked, steadily, all day yesterday, and I can imagine how much they're hurting today because I've been there. Twenty straight miles. But they're back again, and they're probably the cheeriest of all of us, even though some of them are visibly limping.

Once we're out of Swanley, the walk is certainly prettier than yesterday, although the dual roars of the M20 and the

M25 are never far away. There are wooded paths and sloped fields. We stop for morning tea and cake in a church hall in the little village of Eynsford, where my mother used to drive me just for the wonder of the car wheels splashing through its shallow ford. I am pleased to be on my home turf, and mention to anyone who'll listen that they're collectively pronouncing it wrong. It's *Ay*nsford, not *Iy*nsford. Nobody seems particularly impressed by this.

We leave a couple of people behind in the village hall. They're exhausted and are going to hitch a lift to the next stop. We're walking through the beautiful Darent Valley now (which was Darenth when I was a child, but has mysteriously dropped its final 'h' since the millennium), and there are lush interruptions of cow parsley and the occasional hill to climb.

This is the landscape that Samuel Palmer drew in the 1820s, when he was barely out of his teens. After meeting William Blake and becoming a true disciple of his work, Palmer would walk the twenty-five miles from London overnight, into the west Kent landscape that, for him, encapsulated the wonder of creation. After a while, he moved to Shoreham, not far from Eynsford, and in a few short years produced the most extraordinary paintings of his life. In ink and sepia wash, we see a landscape that has been crafted by a benevolent artisan, in which buildings rise like cottage loaves and oak trees seem to reveal the imprint of the hand that set them in place. The Weald is populated by stolid labourers harvesting stout wheatsheaves, often under moonlit skies. They gaze dreamily at the celestial bodies above them, as if staring through time. It is impossible to see them without believing, even if just for a while, that all of creation is here in Kent, and that everything is just as it ought to be.

Few of them survive, because they were so hated by the art world of the time, which had previously believed Palmer to be a prodigy, the next Turner. He took to only showing his work to friends, and many of his drawings and sketchbooks were later destroyed by his son, who thought they were valueless. His later work became more conventional, but still offered views of the sublime. In Clovelly, Palmer was one of the first to see the beauty of perilous crags of coastline and trees mutated by prevailing winds. He died poor and forgotten. His work was rediscovered in the early twentieth century, long after his death, and there, suddenly, his vision of the world began to fit. Until then, he was simply a man who could plainly see things that other people could not – or would not – perceive.

If I'm honest I'm tired. Well, not tired exactly, just . . . odd-feeling. I can't quite put my finger on it at first, but my legs feel unsteady and my hands are shaking. My breath feels tight. I ask how far it is to the next stop; a couple of miles, probably a little less. This is fine. I will walk through it. I have probably hit the bottom of my glycogen stores or something, despite all the cake I ate in Eynsford. I don't break stride, but swing my backpack onto my chest and eat a handful of M&Ms. I glug down half a bottle of water, too, in case I'm dehydrated. It doesn't seem to get any better. I feel ever so slightly dizzy, faintly nauseous. Nothing to worry about. Best thing to do is to reach the next stop and then rest.

At Wrotham church hall (sadly, everyone already knows it's pronounced Root-am), lunch isn't quite ready, and so I lock myself in a toilet cubicle and try to steady myself. I'm shaking. My heart is pounding, and it won't stop. My ears are full of noise. I'm not dehydrated. I'm not hungry. I'm not hot. I'm not cold. I'm tired, yes, but I've walked through worse. I just don't understand it.

I go back out into the hall, fill a plate with food, and sit down. I eat. The people around me look weary, too. I'm not the only one. This is the moment when others find their resolve, and I'm not managing it. I don't feel like I absolutely couldn't walk. I just feel like I ought not do it.

My second-fastest group are gathering to leave. I don't feel as though I've had enough time. I don't feel like I have any words. My group leader comes over and says, 'Katherine, are you ready?' and I say, 'I'm not sure I am. I don't feel right.'

'Oh,' he says, 'I didn't realise.'

'No, no. It's not a big deal. I just feel a bit wobbly. I might sit it out for another fifteen minutes. I'll join the next group.'

I watch the news spreading through our team, and realise I've forgotten that this will matter to people. They feel like we've bonded, I suppose. I never did have much of a talent for absorbing the identity of the pack. All these perfectly nice people would be better off carrying on without me. It really doesn't matter. I desperately want it not to matter, for no one to be kind, and come over, and ask me if I'm all right, if there's anything they can do, if I'm really sure I don't want to give it a go.

I just need to make the shift into my head for a while. I sit on my bench, and watch the room empty around me. The second-slowest group gather and leave; then the slowest group. And then everyone is gone, except for people clearing the hall.

Someone asks me what I'd like to do, and I say I think I'd better call my husband and come back tomorrow. I think that's for the best.

I text H to ask him to pick me up. He says he'll be an hour.

I go outside and sit on the fence by the car park, because I want to disappear. I text Beccy to tell her I've dropped out. She rings back and asks me what on earth's going on, and then makes me take my pulse.

'It's still there,' I say.

'Well that's something, at least.'

And then I realise that I recognise the feeling I'm having. It's like a space is opening up between my shoulder blades, and my spine is floating away. Other people, I think, would feel dizzy at this point, but this is how vertigo feels to me; like my back is trying to fly. Like the floor is running uphill. Like everything is vibrating.

'Oh,' I say. 'It's a Ménière's attack.' I used to think I suffered from migraines, but they lasted for five days, none of the medication ever worked, and they were oddly painless. A couple of years ago, I realised, in the middle of the night – while I was stumbling nauseously around the bedroom banging into things – that I might have inherited Ménière's disease from my father. It causes pressure in the inner ear, leading to a feeling best compared to the worst phase of travel sickness. It's triggered, it seems to me, by stress, getting overheated, flickering light and long car journeys, but sometimes it just arrives. I suppose I've had too much light and heat over the last couple of days; I suppose I've been too anxious to fit in. I have tablets for the vertigo, but I've left them at home, being never knowingly prepared for any eventuality.

I endure the drive home with my eyes closed and my head pressed against the window. I swallow two pills as soon as we arrive, take off my boots, go to bed and fall into a black, featureless sleep. I get up, eat, and go back to bed again. The night is muddled and delirious, lurking somewhere between dreams and consciousness and darkness. The next morning,

I'm as fragile as an eggshell, thinly retaining my contents.

It's due to rain today. I swallow more vertigo pills and ask H to drive me to Detling, where the pilgrims are due to take their morning break. For once in my life, I am not going to simply disappear. The pills make the world more rigid again, but I keep my eyes closed in the car and pinch my nose to try to clear my ears. We arrive early to an empty church hall, but soon the walkers filter in, perhaps a little more road-weary than even yesterday, but full of cheerful noise. I feel like a pale ghost among them.

I have a purpose, though. I am determined not to vanish. Bert plays between the tables and steals food from the buffet table as I chat to my group, ask them how they're feeling, ask them how they've slept. I remember how good I am at this, acting like the most competent person in the room when actually I'm under attack from the noise and light, from the cloud of sensation that rises up from a group of tired, irritable people. Suddenly, it's a skill set, and I'm choosing to use it today, knowing that I can also choose not to at other times. I'm proud of it. I'm coping. I have identified the right thing to do, and I'm doing it. I'm discharging my duties, and saying goodbye. It's easier to say that you've been taken suddenly ill – and what rotten luck it is! – than to carefully explain that you were kidding yourself if you thought you could manage this, and that you've compounded the problem by trying to hide what you are.

We don't stay long. I wish everybody a good walk, and promise I'll try to make the closing service in Canterbury Cathedral tomorrow afternoon (knowing I won't; I'm holding my own closing ceremony here and now). Then I do the thing I came here to do; I seek out one of the men I've been walking with, and give him my cagoule. 'It's going to rain again,' I say. 'This is a spare we had at home.'

And that's it done. There's no point in me sitting at home and feeling miserable. We drive down the M20 to Hythe, so that I can teeter unsteadily around their famous ossuary in the crypt of St Leonard's Church, with its shelves of numbered skulls whose original identity was lost long ago. We are delighted by them, Bert and I; we are both morbidly curious about the stark mechanics of living things. H jokes that I prefer the skulls to living people: silent, plain, comprehensible.

No, no, I say. I'm pretty fond of the living, too. In moderation. I can match my pace to theirs most of the time. I think about the Harris hawk, as I often do lately. I like to imagine her sitting on my arm, showing me how to channel my over-eager senses into an alert poise. There's a term for a raptor raised by humans: an imprint. It may not recognise its community with other birds, and they, in turn, may not recognise it as one of them. The imprint is often dependent on humans for its basic functions, and can be tame enough, but it can also be needy and demanding, tending towards squawking aggression. Other birds are raised to retain their wildness, and yet are still persuaded to come back to human company through careful management. There is always the risk that you will lose these birds altogether, of course, but that's the risk you take for contact with the wild.

I've come to see myself as an imprint who is learning my wildness again. I don't know if I'll ever shake my unnatural compulsion to behave like other humans; but sometimes, I think I'm grateful for my mimicry.

4

The South Hams of Devon, June

On the train down from Paddington, I glance up at what I think is an entirely grey field, and realise it's the sea at Paignton. An expanse of silver water to my left, and a red cliff to my right. I am in Devon again.

H meets me at Totnes station. He has driven down with Bert, but I had to work this morning, so I had the luxury of a train journey alone, with a book. The drive, I gather, was far less pleasurable. Six hours in a car with Bert in the back, in various states of compliance. H is tired, hungry, and at the wrong end of a dispute about a parking space. Bert is petitioning to go to the beach. It's five o'clock; that isn't going to happen.

'Come on,' I say. 'Let's go home and try to start having fun.'

H groaned when I booked a farmhouse near Bantham in the South Hams of Devon; I had to remind him how much we used to love the South West, before I made it a chore. I have not walked far enough to deserve this, but we decided to break the rules. This is not a walk; this is a family holiday.

'Okay,' he said. 'At least you're not making me go to all the way to Cornwall.'

He's right; but I've hit upon an alternative plan for that. At the end of this week, H will go home using my return train ticket. Bert and I will keep the car, and go on a road-trip around the furthest tip of Cornwall. I've realised that I'm never going to walk it, and yet it's getting in the way, somehow, of me getting on with the rest of my life. I can't quite bear to let it go.

My first instinct was to buy a special trailer for Bert and to cycle the whole thing. I got quite far with this before H talked me down. His main point was: why on earth would you do that? But he also said – and I couldn't deny it – that I would inevitably get injured somewhere remote, or end up with sun stroke, or fall off a cliff. And also that I don't cycle very much, and so attempting to criss-cross half of Cornwall in five days would be basically insane. And that I really ought to stop making decisions driven by guilt, and based on the capabilities of the highly fit and deeply single-minded.

Old habits die hard, I guess. I make a show of thinking he's being excessively negative for a few days, and then quietly drop the subject. I'm not sure whether I'll ever learn, but perhaps that's no bad thing. Perhaps the cut-down versions of my grand schemes are the best possible outcome.

The following morning, Bert is beside himself with desperation for the beach. It appears that I have passed on my love of Devon after all; he's craving a sandy cove, or a rock pool, or a wade in the sea. The weather thinks otherwise: the air is damp and chilly, even in the intermittent moments when the sun comes out. I put on my shorts and a shirt, and then change three times. I wonder whether I'd be better off in jeans and a sweater. I want this to work. When I booked this holiday, I had a notion that we would walk everywhere, and would settle on Bantham beach every day, perhaps retiring to the pub in the late afternoon. It's already obvious that this was a pipe dream; by my estimation, the beach is two miles away, and most of the walk is along a narrow, pavementless road. Even if that were a safe option with a three-year-old in tow, it would be stupid to walk all that way in this weather. If it rained, we would have nowhere to go.

However, after waiting in all morning to see if the grey skies will pass, with Bert threatening to hyperactively spend our security deposit on the first day, the walk to Bantham suddenly seems to be a great option. We fill up our beach trolley (which is the kind of thing you own when you live five minutes from the sea), and set off on what quickly becomes an unmade path through fields of hostile-looking cows. Bert gets tired, and so I put him into my back carrier, where he promptly falls asleep. We pick through narrow paths, which seem surrounded by nothing but giant hogweed and stinging nettles, fussing over what his deadweight, bare legs might accidentally brush against.

It takes an hour to get there, which is longer than anyone should drag a ridiculous canvas trolley over rough terrain. Bert wakes up just as we're approaching the beach, and he gets down to run over the dunes onto a very beautiful, but utterly wind-whipped beach.

Everyone else is packing up to go home. Bert is desperate to play. I'm desperate to get out of the sand storm. We attempt to set up our beach shelter, but give up in favour of trying to weigh everything down. This is not usual for Bantham. It's usually the perfect family beach, where the Atlantic is uncharacteristically tame and shallow. You can usually see Burgh Island from here, but today it's more of a case of squinting through the bombardment of gritty wind and perhaps making out a grey shape in the distance. Bert tries to dig a hole, but even he has to give up as every mark he makes with his spade is instantly in-filled. It's cold, un-comfortable, and, frankly, I fear for our eyes. We retreat to the local pub while H walks back and fetches the car.

The next day starts overcast, so we decide to wrap up warm and drive to a rock-pool beach, perhaps Woolacombe or Prawle, we're not sure which. The sky begins to look so overcast as we reach the main road, though, that H suggests we go to Gara instead, where there is at least a cafe. Gara is my favourite; I wanted to save it for a fine, sunny day. But Bert is desolate at all our dithering. We park in a field and pack up the trolley for the long, steep walk down to the cove. If the weather's awful, at least we can huddle into our beach shelter and pull up the zip.

Reaching the cove at the bottom of Gara Rock involves a long descent on the South West Coast Path, followed by a steep scramble over some rocks at the very bottom, splashing through a stream as you go. This is just one small part of what makes it so magnificent: you truly earn your place there. It is in no way accessible to anyone who isn't physically fit. And that's just the climb down; getting back up again is actively horrifying. Less than a year ago, I didn't feel like I could quite make it.

If you brave the descent, though, this is what you find: a pristine, craggy cove that's jutted with crystalline green rock. There are little caves and valleys to explore, bulkheads of stone to climb on, and a scattering of white quartz and mica to pick up on the shore. Red birds of prey dart around the cliffs overhead. The waves are high, and cold, and won-derfully violent. I paddle in them and without meaning to, find myself swimming. The water is voluminous, potent; it's like being recharged with the purest elemental force this world has to offer.

I love the cockeyed view of the land you get when you're

floating in the sea. I watch Bert attempting to dam up the stream that flows onto the beach; the cliffs are unsteady above me. The water is so clear that I can see my feet, so cold my skin burns. The sky above us threatens to crack open any moment. It strikes me that all this imperfection is the best possible deal: the cold and the grey all to ourselves, with our little tent, and food, and water. Bert is having the time of his life, and H has joined in, the dam now built so high that they've formed a deep pool, and they're splashing each other.

A few moments later, the sun breaks loose and the sky turns bright blue, and we have the world's most perfect beach all to ourselves because we were willing to be there when it wasn't quite perfect yet.

We spend the rest of the week staying in places, rather than marching through them. We pitch our shelter on Thurlestone sands at low tide, and wade through the rock pools under its magnificent arch of rock. We stay on the beach at Hope Cove for hours, while Bert teaches his dam-building skills to a gaggle of other children, and then we retire to the village pub and stay for longer, playing draughts. We walk down to the lighthouse at Start Point and watch seals on the rocks through our binoculars.

At the end of the week, I spend an afternoon walking from Prawle Point back to Gara, deliberately following the South West Coast Path in the wrong direction. I spot tiny, yellowish cirl buntings flitting among the incredible tangle of bracken and bramble that surrounds the path. Everywhere I look, there are spikes of cerise foxglove. The bulkheads of green rock radiate the heat of the day. I had wondered if this part of the path would still astonish me after all the other incredible sections I'd walked through, but I needn't have worried. Here is my path, so lush and fragrant and busy with life. I couldn't hand on heart say that it's better than Exmoor or Hartland or the coast around Tintagel; I couldn't deny that the SWCP is a very different experience in the summer than the winter; but then, I'm under no obligation to be objective. This is my little bit of path, the part that set off a whole line of emotional dominoes that have sustained me through my adult life. I'm biased. I don't care. I'm dizzy with love for it.

Every night, beach-worn, Bert curls up in bed next to me, and I often wake to find two bright eyes on me, just savouring the glee of being close. He strokes my face and whispers, 'I love you, Mummy,' and then wriggles his little body nearer, insinuating himself under my chin. And I realise, quite unexpectedly, that Bert is the only person in my life whose electricity exactly matches my own, whose touch is as native to my skin as air or water. There was a time when I couldn't bear this, when I wanted to be separate from him. That has passed. We have negotiated, between us, some kind of balance. I admire his patience with me, his willingness to adapt. But then I admire, too, my own adaptations. I begin to believe that I'm not so terrible after all.

The roadside verges of Devon are one of the world's wonders. They rise ten feet high either side of narrow country lanes that are often barely wide enough to accommodate one car, let alone two. Driving through the South Hams is a process of continuous negotiation, sometimes requiring you to reverse several hundred feet to tuck your car into a passing space, and even then, you find yourself breathing in as the other motorist inches past you. Anybody who knows the area does this in a spirit of jocular goodwill; a willingness to reverse is a matter of personal honour. You can spot newcomers a mile off: we'll generously say that they find the experience stressful.

In high summer, the verges crowd into the road in great billows of bracken, vetch, cow parsley and mallow, evening primrose, dandelion, and daisy. In September, you could reach out of your window and pick blackberries as you drive; or in fact, if you drive along with your windows open, the blackberries will periodically ping into your car unbidden, leaving you in no doubt as to what keeps scratching the paintwork. On one occasion, a verge near Prawle Point disgorged two enormous dragonflies, which flew in through the passenger window and landed on the dashboard, where they proceeded to mate enthusiastically. H, whose phobia of insects I had failed to fully grasp until that point, screamed, stalled the car, and ran out into the road. One dragonfly followed him out and buzzed away over the high summer fields; the other remained in situ, carefully cleaning his compound eyes.

'Get it out!' shouted H from the middle of the road.

'How?' I shouted back. This thing was about the size of my hand; it wasn't like I could fit a cup over it, even if I had one.

'Kill it!' shouted H. 'Hit it with a book!'

'I can't do that! It's lovely,' and, I suspected, would not be all that easy to squash. The dragonfly and I eyed each other for quite some time, and then we engaged in a polite dance, involving a gentle shunting with a National Trust guidebook, until it gave in and flew away. But before that happened, I had to get into the driver's seat and pull the car over, because a tiny Devonshire traffic jam had formed behind me, and most of the drivers were asking H, quite politely, what on earth he was so afraid of.

I digress. My point is that the verges are the most

extraordinary ecosystem. They host merlins and kestrels; once, we startled a honey buzzard, which flapped up in front of the car, showing its speckled breast. This year, we follow swallows zooming low across the road at dusk to catch insects, looking for all the world like tiny X-Wings trying to follow the right channel in the Death Star; and we have to brake suddenly for a hare, which lollops along in front of us, before turning left at a farm gate. A whole universe is there, between one side of the road and the other.

One of the theories of what makes a brain autistic is that people with ASD perceive the world in far more detail than everyone else. Simon Baron-Cohen claims that this represents an extreme 'male' brain, because he thinks that men have a greater concern with detail in the first place, but I don't agree. For a start, Baron-Cohen makes it clear that not all 'male' brains under his terms belong to men; I would therefore suggest that he might wish to revise his terms to something a little more gender-neutral. Perhaps he has just never been at the wrong end of a dead-eyed bombardment of boy-band facts from a particularly obsessed teenage girl. Perhaps he sees this knowledge as somehow 'softer' than other kinds of knowledge. But even if we wish to stick to the assumption that men and women think differently – and I, with my male-ish female brain, find this incredibly crass – then I think that he ought to at least acknowledge that detail doesn't only lie in systematic knowledge of football cards or aeroplane serial numbers.

There are other kinds of detail, too. There is the detail of being in a room of people you love, and knowing who would like coffee, who would like tea (and the infinite, glorious ways they are taken), and who would really prefer a gin and tonic (me). There is the detail – quite mysterious to me – of noticing someone else's mood, and knowing what will draw them towards their equilibrium. There is the detail of knowing the names of all the flowers in those magnificent Devonshire verges, and there is the detail of knowing who will find it interesting if you speak about them, and how you should approach the subject. Detail has nuance; detail has application. Not all detail is iterative, blunt, competitive.

I don't deny that my brain holds detail. I don't deny that it sucks in more detail than other people's brains, making it difficult to navigate simple situations due to an excess of input. Being me feels – as Temple Grandin puts it – like being 'one big exposed nerve'. I'm just rebelling against the idea that the problem with that detail is that it might be a bit boring for other people, sometimes.

Let me tell you a story about the ledger of detail in my life. I went into labour on a Saturday night, while we were sitting around the TV, watching *The Voice*. Or, I didn't quite go into labour; I went upstairs for a pee, and it just didn't stop. After a minute or so, I realised my waters must have broken. It was three weeks too soon. We drove to the hospital, and we were parked in a delivery room that smelled of disinfectant and hospital food, where we sat for hours listening to the sound of other women giving birth all around us. I tried to use the bathroom, but the sink was smeared with someone else's blood. I wished I hadn't come in, but I knew, from my book, that I would now have to deliver my baby within twenty-four hours to avoid the risk of infection. I wanted to go home, where it was quiet and smelled right.

After a couple of hours, a harassed-looking midwife came in and told me, all in one sentence, that they were exceptionally busy tonight, and that my waters probably hadn't broken anyway because people were always coming in like this and it was always a false alarm. She examined me and said, 'Oh, they really have broken, haven't they?' and told me to go home and come back tomorrow. Then, as an after-thought, she took my blood pressure, frowned, and said I'd have to stay on the ward.

It was one in the morning before I went to bed. The whole place chattered with noise: groaning, shouting, shuffling. One woman repeatedly yelled that she would tear out her drip and go home. I ardently wished she would. I didn't sleep. Then the contractions started at three, and I knew it would be impossible after that.

I won't bore you with the detail. It's mundane, really: the dehumanising effect of exhausted, overstretched staff, and an underfunded maternity system that's still set up for women labouring alone, in crumbling buildings. I had to have antibiotics because nobody could induce me for thirty-six hours, instead of the necessary twenty-four; and even then it was grindingly slow. I had so much epidural that I couldn't feel my legs until the day after, let alone notice when my hip dislocated. I inhaled so much gas and air that I thought the foetal heartbeat monitor was talking to me. Even with drugs to bring on the contractions, the whole thing took forty-four hours. It was gruelling.

Don't let anybody tell you that they achieved something by having an intervention-free birth. That was just their throw of the dice. Nobody chooses a birth like mine. We just have to limp out at the other side, and thank God it happened in this century rather than the last, in the West rather than the developing world; that we survived it.

Bert was born at three in the afternoon. I held him, passed him around, was stitched, and taken back to the ward. Then H was sent home, the curtains were drawn around us, and we were quite alone. I put him down in his cot beside me, and I slept.

I awoke at four in the morning, because I could hear

him stirring. He didn't cry; he just clicked and squirmed and fidgeted in the expert swaddle the nurses had made. I heaved myself to the edge of the bed, reached over and picked him up. Two grey-blue eyes, watching me. 'Well,' I said, 'I think it's just you and me. We'll have to work out how this is done.'

I would be lying if I said it wasn't trial and error from thereon in. I would be withholding the truth if I implied I didn't spend the months – years – that followed in something resembling a blind panic that I would fail to keep him alive, or at the very least traumatise him with my complete lack of maternal skill.

However: *however*. Even in the darkest recesses of post-natal desperation, I always knew what he needed. I may not have known, always, quite how to provide it, but I heard the message loud and clear. It was all in the detail. He would click his little tongue – k-k-k-k – in the seconds before he would start to wail out his hunger; he would grow glassy-eyed if too many people handled him, and would relax again back in his Moses basket. I could see things that other people couldn't see. There was a wire running between us.

You want to know detail: there it is. Detail is the call-and-response by which babies are kept alive. Detail is the wonderful and terrible pull of motherhood. Detail is the way I can smell illness on him before he even knows it himself. I'm not claiming any special powers here; those details make me more like an ordinary woman than I've ever felt in my life before.

And if, in other circumstances, my brain misfires around detail, then there is also a counterpoise in which my level of detail is glorious. I have the privilege of walking through a wood, and hearing the song of every individual bird – of being unable to avoid hearing it, even if I tried. I have the privilege of being overcome by the scent of bluebells in May, by the deep mulch of damp leaves in November. I have the wonder of noticing every tiny, writhing, burgeoning thing in those roadside verges in Devon.

And this year, since I've been walking, I have been learning to name them, and notice how they change across the year. I have seen how the umbellifers throw up tight green stems with clumped heads in the spring, casting out white flowers in the summer, and then drying to rusty starbursts in the winter. I have watched how blackthorn bursts into white flower from indigo twigs, and then ripens sloes between its leaves. In my own street, I have finally noticed how privet hedges flower in the late spring, and have savoured its scent for the first time in my life.

Detail is not the problem. It is a life lived without it, among flat, modern surfaces and the eternal bright light of the warm indoors, that is making me sick.

5

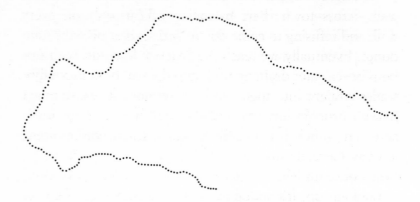

The far tip of Cornwall by road, July

Travelling with Bert completely subverts my usual walking plans.

There is no sense of moving forward, only a chaotic meander in all directions at once. He finds beauty in ring-road tunnels and the cobwebby corners of cafe toilets, rather than rugged coves and rolling country vistas. He sighs in delight at grey skies and prizes scraps of plastic that he's trawled off otherwise pristine beaches.

Lunches are tense; he'll spit out the freshest seafood and demand Mr Whippy over artisanal ice-cream, but most of all, he spills things. I get raggedly bad-tempered with him until I remember that I spill everything, too. At one point, I scold him for sloshing milk over the table, and in the process, tip the whole glass over myself.

We start our journey in Hayle, where we have taken a room in an Airbnb, hosted by a woman who is almost

absurdly kind to Bert. I stayed in Hayle once before with
H, during our one previous foray into Cornwall. We had
a static caravan on the towans (Cornish for 'dunes'), and I
remembered the fantastically expansive beach, and thought
that Bert would love it.

We arrive at about four, put our things in our room, then
walk across town (Bert balancing precariously on every
wall, and refusing to come down) and stagger over the high
dunes. Eventually, we reach the beach at low tide, with ribbons of seawater draining back into the sea. Bert, inevitably,
wades straight into them, and at that point I realise that I
haven't brought any spare clothes with me. I'm not really
sure how much it's possible to carry when you're alone,
anyway. I already suspect I'll be carrying him back from the
beach once his legs are tired.

Looking up, it's suddenly misty. I take some photos of
the greying sea while Bert darts around. And then I realise
that I can barely see the tideline anymore, and that my hair
is wet. We're in the thick of a dense, damp sea-fog, eerily
warm and sticky.

'Bert!' I call, and he ignores me, and so I have to chase
him along the beach for fear of losing him altogether.

'It's too foggy, Bertie; we'll have to walk back.'

'No!' yells Bert, furious.

'Look around you,' I say, and then, 'look at your clothes!'
The fog is swirling with droplets of water, and while it's run-
ning off my yellow raincoat, it has drenched Bert's T-shirt.
'It's raining,' I say, 'I think.'

At this moment, Bert realises he's wet and uncomfortable, and wants to be off the beach and back home, without
engaging in any of the processes that might get him there. I
end up piggybacking him over the dunes, pausing to knock
the sand out of our shoes on the stable concrete of the quay;

and then persuading him into slow progress through the town, step by step. We stop for fish and chips in a cafe, and then go home for a bath and bed. I am left with the haunting impression that I failed to strike the right note, somehow.

The next morning, we wake early and so leave early, because I can't face the thought of another trek over all that sand. The landlady shows me the local newspaper, with photos from a week ago, when Porthmeor was visited by a pod of dolphins who swam with the surfers for a while before disappearing again. 'You never know, Bert,' I say. 'We might get lucky.'

The sky is a beautiful, optimistic blue. We follow the coast around to St Ives, where we find the Tate gallery closed and the beach full of surfers, but no dolphins. The woman who sells me a coffee says she saw them last week, but seems strangely underwhelmed if that's true.

We park ourselves on the sand, and Bert starts a game of running up to the edge of the sea and then running away from the waves as they crash in. I'm left fussing over where to park my handbag and beach bag, while ensuring that he doesn't drown himself in the meantime. Parenting alone is an anxiety-ridden process. There is a terrible moment when the waves knock him off his feet, and I rush out to grab him, but he has absolutely no sense of the seriousness of the whole thing. I suppose that's lucky; I suppose I don't want him to be afraid. But I feel afraid, all alone, between the chaos of him and the chaos of the sea. I want to move on.

This takes some persuasion, but eventually we're back in the car, and I feel steady again. I am a little overwhelmed, but having him strapped into his car seat makes me feel safe again. I know exactly where he is, and I'm not juggling bags. The problem is that the far tip of Cornwall is surprisingly small, and so we're not in the car nearly long enough. We stop at Zennor, and I can't face getting him all the way down to the cove and back up again, so I take him to a cafe and watch him demolish a brownie while we talk, vaguely, about a mermaid.

Then we drive on to St Just, which is small and Sunday-afternoon quiet. We don't get out of the car, but instead head on towards Land's End. After becoming briefly stuck behind a lorry full of potatoes (which, I think, would attract a full five stars on the pre-school version of Tripadvisor), we come to Land's End. On approach, it looks worryingly like a theme park. There is a car park, and a long, white building with Doric columns blocking the view of the sea, and a man in a cabin waiting to charge you for the privilege. I wind down my window.

'Do I have to pay to get in?' I say, not fully controlling the disdain in my voice.

'We don't charge to get in; we just charge for the parking,' he says, and then, without me even asking, he adds, 'There's a lane over there where you can turn around and drive straight out again.'

I say, 'Thank you,' and swing back out onto the main road, muttering, 'What a bloody awful thing to do.'

'What is?' says Bert.

'That is. Building a shop at the furthest tip of the country.'

'Oh,' says Bert.

'We'll go to straight to Sennen,' I say. 'That's pretty near the bottom, anyway.'

We arrive in Sennen several hours earlier than our hotel booking should really allow, but we're shown straight to our room. Bert is beginning to say, 'Where's Daddy?' so we call him on Skype, only to find he's watching the tennis and can't really concentrate on us. Then we head for the beach, which is just across the road, and is full of interesting rocks to climb on and sand to dig.

I am determined to stay still this time. I have a carrier bag with tennis balls, and skittles, and a frisbee which we play with for quite some time until I begin to believe that Bert is deliberately throwing it towards the same group of people, over and over again. Their good humour is wearing thin. I try to distract him by collecting seaweed and shells in his bucket, and then we build a sandcastle for which I don't have the patience. He keeps demanding ridiculously over-ambitious designs, and then kicks them over for seemingly no reason. I end up yelling at him, raggedly, before realising that he's very much a chip off the old block.

Is Bert like me? I sometimes wonder. He's obsessed with the mechanics of things, and has a long-standing habit of tracing the beginning and end of every pipe in a room – and speculating where they might lead to – before he can settle. He will spend hours building complex train tracks, but then loses interest entirely when it comes to running trains across them and forming any kind of a narrative. When he's building his tracks, or tracing his pipes, he becomes so absorbed that he can't hear those of us in the outside world, trying to talk to him. His nursery wondered aloud if he might be deaf. And yet the hand-dryers in public toilets make him clamp his hands over his ears and squeal.

But then, I've noticed that every other mother around me worries the same thing. It's become part of the eternal vigilance of parenthood: we no longer just fear measles and meningitis; we're now looking out for autism, too. This sudden regression that comes on around the age of three: we're all alert to it, as if we'd know what to do when it happened. We've heard all about the fight you must put up for diagnosis and support. We're ready for it.

In actual fact, I think Bert is almost startlingly neurotypical compared to me and H. He's a party animal, craving social interaction to a degree that we both find baffling. I wonder what it means that, instead, I've turned that eternal vigilance in on myself. What on earth does it signify to seek a label as weighed down as autistic when I'm nearly forty? After all, I want nothing from it. I'm not seeking benefits or concessions or any special treatment at work. I'm not looking for medication, or a cure. I'm not craving membership of any special club.

Perhaps I am hoping to excuse myself. Perhaps I'm hoping that people will love me a tiny bit more for knowing that I can't help it, that I'll never be able to access the easy patience that I see in everyone else. Perhaps I'm hoping for a better life story, a coherent, tidy narrative arc that finally draws my scattergun life together into a kind of sense. I sometimes feel as though I'm asking for a privilege, to be allowed to say that I've watched my friends sail past me into competent adulthood, while I've stuttered and stalled, but that it's not my fault. It's beguiling to think that I could shake it all off that easily.

I have still not received a letter from the clinic that my GP mentioned, the one that specialises in people like me. I suppose I would chase it if I thought it was important. But I haven't; I don't want to. I'm a little bit afraid of it, if I'm honest. I'm a little bit wary of what it will bring.

As far as I can see, I live with a version of experience that clearly existed in the previous Diagnostic and Statistical Manual, but possibly not the current one. Some clinicians are still using Asperger syndrome as a profile within Autistic Spectrum Disorder, but a brief search on the internet will turn up people who have 'lost' their diagnosis altogether with the advent of a new set of criteria, sometimes with devastating financial and therapeutic consequences. These are not my own stakes; I have, mostly, been able to survive out there on my own so far, partly based on the good luck of finding a partner who can both tolerate me and earn a steady wage. But what I do have in common with these people is the fear of losing a crucial part of human dignity: the need to be believed. Saying I'm autistic allows me to assert a raft of experience that is otherwise mostly hidden. I fear I may have come along too late to have this privilege.

The DSM is, of course, not a neutral document. It is the work of human hands, and the very fact that it grows fatter with every edition points to a shifting understanding of the human psyche. That's the generous way of putting it. Some would suggest that, as a society, we're in the business of inventing psychological conditions to fit the times. Less than a century ago, we were still treating women for hysteria; nowadays, definitions of 'female sexual dysfunction' sail perilously close to pathologising the natural wax and wane of women's desire. In some cases it appears that we cast the diagnostic net so wide that we might all be caught in it; Jon Ronson's *The Psychopath Test*, for example, brilliantly reveals the blurry boundaries between 'normal' misbehaviours and a diagnosis of psychopathy. It seems very easy to step over an invisible line into a lifelong diagnosis.

Plenty would say the same about me. Why on earth would a happy, healthy, functioning person feel the pull of a neurological 'disorder' (don't forget that 'D' in ASD), when really I should be running as fast as I can to escape its event horizon? Why on earth wouldn't I want to accentuate the positive, and push the dysfunctional parts of myself as far away from human view as possible?

Well, here's the thing. When you have spent your entire life so far – childhood and adulthood – feeling as though you're continually circling the plug hole of not coping, you end up wanting to make sense of it. It really isn't so hard to understand. When you've made multiple attempts to pull yourself together, and to tamp down your own experience of the world, but it's still painfully evident that you're different from the people around you; when that difference, or the process of trying to ignore it, frequently makes you sick; when you realise it will probably shorten your life because you drink too much to cope, or your blood pressure runs high, or you wonder how many more times you can withstand the feeling of crashing out of the mainstream world and falling through the cracks; then you might just begin to think that it would be convenient to name the thing that's made everything so bloody hard. That's all. It's not actually that strange an instinct at all.

Right at the beginning of this journey, when I was driving in my car at night, listening to a woman on the radio tell out my experience of the world, I remember her saying that she felt definite commonality with people at the outermost reaches of the autistic spectrum. I wondered if I ever could, too, and I think, on balance, I do. I understand the way that the sensory world can scream at you so loud that you want to retreat; I understand the flashes of aggression that come from the threat it brings; I understand what it's like to inhabit a body that simply stops responding when it reaches its point of overwhelm. But at the same time, I realise I'm profoundly different. My bridge to the outside world is steadier, I think; I have the good fortune of an above-average IQ and a set of sensory experiences that are bearable. I could not, in all conscience, call myself disabled. I realise that other people like me do. I suppose I feel lucky, after all, to have gone for so long under the radar. I learned my life skills in the most brutal way possible, but I'm proud of them. They are worth it, on balance. They have given me so much.

The truth is that the label of ASD helps me to make a better account of myself, and to finally find a mirror in which I can recognise my own face. I'm proud of it, actually. It has given me many gifts. But, equally, taking on that label is the only way that I can remind other people of the spectrum of wonderful difference on which we all sit. Sometimes, a label is the only way of parlaying some compassion out of the world.

The next morning, in the car, Bert sleeps through Mousehole, Penzance and Newlyn. Eventually, we park at Marazion, and he wakes up in time to walk along a tiny section of the South West Coast Path to St Michael's Mount. On the way, he gets snagged on so many dandelion clocks that I begin to fear that our parking will run out before we even get there. And then, just as we're nearing the reassuring National Trust hut, he spies a river winding through the beach towards the sea, and before I know it, he has stripped down to his pants and T-shirt and is wading in. He crafts little boats out of twigs, grass and feathers, and shoots imaginary laser guns at the swallows as they dip down to drink.

'Shall we go across the causeway and see the castle?' I ask, in the most exciting voice I can muster. ('Shall we go to the *causeway* and see the CASTLE!!!?')

'No,' he says definitively.

My landmarks are not his landmarks. I realise, bitterly, that he's actually being terribly picturesque, even if it runs contrary to my plans. Several times this weekend, my brain has ached for the chance to disengage and sink into my own, internal world, and now I realise that he's needed a similar thing. His mind diverts naturally into play. I'm entirely ir-relevant. I talk to him about the gulls washing the salt off their wings in the fresh water, and he replies in boats, sails, captains and anchors. He's taken a lurch into imagination that is so absolute I can't break through.

I sit on the bank beside him and watch him wade through the water, making a tiny universe around him. I've spent a year trying to learn to feel the wonder that comes so naturally to him. It's like he exists on a different scale from me, an entirely new level of detail.

When we're finally allowed to leave, he says goodbye to every single ant in turn, regrets the loss of every blade of grass.

At the end of a long drive down to Lizard Point, Bert is visibly disappointed. I had definitely told him that there would be no actual lizards there, but he had evidently not believed me.

We have booked two nights at the Lizard's youth hostel, with the aim of immersing ourselves in the wild splendour of this most southerly tip of the country. Without H, though, everything is just endlessly difficult and complicated. It's hard enough to lug the suitcase in on my own, while simultaneously watching Bert, but in addition the hostel turns out to be a hive of fussy rules and petty omissions that leave me nearly tearful.

I don't think it's built with children in mind. In our room, the curtains do not fit to the bottom of the window, which means that Bert will wake at the first incursion of the dawn. The bathrooms are not en-suite, and I come to see this as an affectation rather than an economy; there are, after all, the same number of showers as rooms. Our nearest shower is adjacent to our room, and only lacks a connecting door. Instead, I must hang all our possessions on a single hook, and then attempt to wash a reluctant child in enough space for half a person. It's impossible for me to stay dry during this, so I have to take off all my clothes, and then, when I realise that I might as well shower myself, put up with Bert alternating between shouting that he's COLD and attempting to unlock the door. At the end of this unpleasant experience, I realise that all of my clothes have got wet anyway, and so decide that the easiest thing to do is to sprint naked back to our room and trust that anyone who sees me is probably German and therefore won't care.

There is no kettle in the room, so one must trek downstairs to the giant industrial kitchen, small child in tow, where there are copious signs ordering that all food must be name-labelled or else it will be removed. I have absolutely no idea why this is so important to them, but in any case I hadn't realised that I would need to bring all this stuff with me in the first place, so my chafing at the rules is merely symbolic.

This means we must travel up to the village to eat dinner and by this point I'm desperate for a drink, and so we walk. I realise it's mean of me to say that Lizard village is a little too popular for my liking, but there we have it. I'm in a mean mood. There are all kinds of restaurants, and quite a lot of cars, but the convenience store isn't open, and so we can't buy milk, or tea bags, or bread for toast. I'm not sure if I could bring myself to label it all anyway, to be honest. We'll just have to drink water and go without.

We find ourselves a nice little pub, where Bert sits with his colouring book and pencils, and I drink more wine than is probably considered dignified when you're the only adult. We spend longer there than we really ought to, and then go home to our bunk beds. Bert has to go to sleep without his usual glass of milk and so, with grim inevitability, he wakes at 5 a.m. as the sun blares through the absence of sufficient curtain, and says he's hungry.

By six thirty, we're on the road, trying to find somewhere that will serve us breakfast at this ungodly hour. We eventually find a Tesco in Helston where we order fried breakfasts with tea for me, and a glass of milk for Bert. Then we stock up on salami and pre-sliced cheese and soft rolls and grapes, crisps and apple juice and milk, and we drive back to the hostel.

As soon as we park, Bert wants to run along the path that leads to the cliffs, so I chase him down there. It's beautiful, as I knew it would be; the craggy rock drops down into a wild sea, and the slopes are rust-coloured, covered with little succulents and quivering thrift. I suggest walking right down to sea level, but Bert wants to play hide-and-seek instead. I have a tenuous relationship with play at the best of times, but I really don't have any left in me this morning. We dart about in the gardens of the hostel for a while, disturbing crowds of rabbits, and then I remember the shopping in the boot getting warm in the mid-morning sun.

I take the carrier bags into the big, empty communal kitchen and I am just fishing around in the bottom of my handbag for a biro to write my name on all of them when something breaks in me and I say, 'Oh bollocks, Bert, shall we just go home?'

Bert says, 'Yes,' and I say, 'Are you sure? It will take about seven hours in the car?'

'Yes,' he says. 'I want to see Daddy.'

As I'm hauling our giant case down the stairs and into the car, the hostel manager comes out and says, 'Is everything okay?'

'Fine,' I say, 'but we're going home a day early.'

'Nothing to do with the room, I hope,' he says.

'No,' I say, 'probably not. I just don't need to keep on going.'

6

Devon, late August

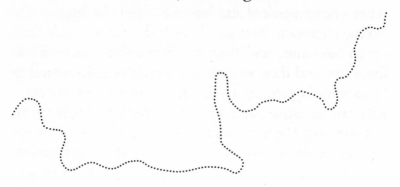

M ist hangs low over the fields around Whitstable, the memory of a marsh that has long since been pushed back. We set off at dawn with practised art, and by lunchtime we have our feet on the beach at North Sands, stretching our cramped legs.

Bert is running through a list of things he wants to do, and I am too: Thurlestone for rock pools and supper in the Beachhouse; a dash through the lush gardens at Overbeck's, followed by scones; watching the darting swallows at Prawle Point and clambering over the other-worldly landscape the tide leaves behind. But most of all, we both crave Gara Rock, where I will swim, and where Bert wants to see if he can dam up that stream once and for all. H is pretty much happy to do whatever we're doing, but, along with everything else we own, he's packed his Xbox too, just in case it rains.

I walk, too. I spend a lovely morning with my friend Lesley, striding across the headland around Noss Mayo, just along the coast from Plymouth. I feel as though I have almost joined up with Cornwall, except that I skipped the stretch of coast at the other side of Plymouth Sound, and I'm grateful that I didn't have to tackle the miles of industrial landscape around the city itself. Perhaps I'll walk it all another time; perhaps I won't. It doesn't matter. There are times when my lack of attachment is a real blessing.

One afternoon, Bert and I catch the South Sands ferry up to Salcombe, and then the Portlemouth ferry across the water, and then we walk the couple of miles inland to Gara while H races us in the other direction, driving up to Kingsbridge estuary and down the other side. He beats us, but only just. The next day, I walk, alone, from Thurlestone to Bolt Head, across wide-open Bolberry Down, where kestrels wrestle mid-air. Later in the week, I go back and take the long way around between East Portlemouth and Gara, feeling I missed out on an essential bit of coastline when I cut inland with Bert. I notice that the proud cerise spears that the summer foxgloves made have already dried to husks. I feel the autumn coming on in blasts of damp air and the barely discernible retreat of the bracken. It makes me crave Exmoor again, the heather and yellow gorse, the heady scent of Porlock Marsh at dusk.

These walks – five miles, maybe, or sometimes nearer eight – take a couple of hours now in the summer heat, and can be accommodated amid the bustle of other things. With a little planning, H will drop me off in one bay or another, and I will walk around the coast to where they're hanging out. Bert has become an expert at spotting me at the top of a cliff and climbing up to meet me. I wonder how many years it will be before we can set off together and walk all day? Perhaps never, if he inherits his father's feet, as looks to be the case. I have a feeling that he'll crave more daredevil pursuits than my stoical walking anyway.

Do I miss the longer walks, the fifteen milers that took all day and drew me into stuttering conflicts with my own soul? I do, actually. I mean, quite evidently, I shouldn't have undertaken so many of them in such appalling weather. But there are some places you can only get to by walking all day, and, probably, by walking all the next day too.

There is talk of an epidemic of autism. Some people (who are wrong) blame vaccines; some (who are also wrong) express a mildly eugenic concern about geeky people breeding in Silicon Valley. Some blame over-diagnosis by anxious parents who think ASD is the ticket to an educational upgrade. Well. If we will insist on running our education system to the advantage of such a narrow set of people, then we must not be surprised when people find ways to have their children's talents acknowledged.

I would lay a hefty bet that there's nothing remotely new going on here. We have, perhaps, acquired a different language through which to talk about it. We have perhaps started differentiating between varying qualities and causes of disability. We have even started to glimpse some of the ways in which we can improve lives that were formerly written off.

But for me – at my place in a very big spectrum – I think something else is going on. We've always been here, people like me, applying our detailed brains to problems that need precise solutions, and noticing things that would lay outside of neurotypical fields of view. We're not an evolutionary accident, but an adaptation. We are not what you think we are. We are useful, valued, loved. We're the scientists and artists, the dreamers and the engineers. We're vital to all of it. We've been pushing it forward and holding it together while the extroverts take all the glory.

I despise the modern habit of posthumously diagnosing

prominent figures from history with whatever psychological condition is currently piquing our interest. That's why I would never dream of suggesting that my great, impossible heroine Jean Rhys, or the belligerent vicar of Morwenstow, or the visionary Samuel Palmer shared any traits with me. But I will unashamedly say that difficult, complicated people can achieve great things if they're allowed to create their own conditions, and if they're allowed their time alone by the sea.

Perhaps Asperger syndrome is only meaningful in a certain time and place after all. Our ways of seeing in this world are profoundly contingent on the eras in which they occur. The competing urges for solitude and social contact, and the angry frustrations that made Jean Rhys a marked woman would be almost ordinary now, their extreme edges blunted by a society that would have allowed her to be clever, and given her a Twitter account on which to share her acerbic thoughts and incoherent rages. Well maybe, anyway.

Meanwhile, I would not have been so strange in a previous era. In a quieter world, a less hurried one, without the whine of mobile phones and the ceaseless electronic drone of voices from the radio and the TV; without the noisy surges of hand-dryers and the bleeping of train doors; without the flat plastic unknowable surfaces and the dry-air containment of office life; without pulsing lights and the ceaseless sense of personal availability.

Without all of these things, I might have been different. Walking would have been a part of ordinary life, like learning the names of the trees and flowers, and identifying birds by their song. I would have written with ink on soft paper, and read in the evenings, and heard music only when somebody sat down to play it. I would have seldom encountered the chaotic press of too many bodies in one place, and perhaps my nerves would have been steadier for it.

As a woman, of course, there are few points in history when I would have felt the advantages of this greater sensory freedom, and so I must content myself with the noisy, demanding present day, and be grateful for it. But that is why we need diagnoses like ASD; so that people like me can explore the strange ways that we might fit into this brave new world.

At the end of our week in Devon, we have lunch at the Riverford Field Kitchen, as we have many times before. Set on an organic farm, the restaurant invites you to sit on long tables and share plates of food – whatever's currently in season – with the other guests. It's something I ought to dread, and I usually do, but I have never once left regretting the people I've met and the topics I've roamed through. Today, over slow-roast lamb, we talk to a couple from Cambridge whose four children have now grown up, and who spent the last three summers walking the South West Coast Path in sections.

'We stayed at the Camelot Castle in Tintagel,' says the man, conspiratorially; 'we couldn't resist it.' My lack of recognition must show on my face, because he adds, 'You know, the Scientology hotel.'

I remember being told about this when I first started the walk, that it's a curio along the path that everyone has to see once, just for the experience. I'd quite forgotten it by the time I got round there, concerned as I was with putting on miles rather than experiences. Now, as the couple list this little country pub here, and this wonderful cafe there, I realise how much I missed along the way. I hardly recognise the places they mention, although I must have walked through them. They were just scenery for me, another crinkle at the edge of the map.

It goes without saying that I regret that now – or perhaps regret is too strong a word. It's just that I've learned something, that's all, about the value of being in places that you love, and knowing them, and coming back to them.

We spend the final night of our break in a yurt at the mid-line of the Cornish border, as far from the sea as it's possible to get. We explore the long grass and Bert finds a series of black beetles, all of which are called Alexander, and he lets them roam around his hands until I can persuade him to repatriate them to their wood pile. Then, we light a bonfire and eat our supper outside as the stars come out. After Bert has gone to sleep in the centre of our king-size bed (I am no more keen on roughing it than I was when all this began), H and I sit outside and drink warm gin and tonics, and talk about the year to come with some gentle kind of optimism.

As we set off home the next morning, Bert watches the trees rush by at the side of the road and says, 'Bye bye Devon, see you soon.'

And we will: over and over again, every time we need to be set straight again.

Epilogue

There's a high, artificial perfume in here. I can taste it on my glass of water. The room is painted the kind of yellow that I think is supposed to be soothing.

The man opposite me has a file in his lap with my name on it, and he's taking notes.

'Where shall we start?' he says.

'Anywhere. I don't know.'

'How about the here and now?' he says. 'What's your situation at the moment?'

I tell him about going to work, and the bombardment I feel from all the people I encounter there. How many jobs I've given up after getting sick for mysterious reasons. About hiding in the toilets at parties. About being the child, alone, in the playground, listening to the mothers of other children gossiping about me. About breaking down at seventeen, and then again, and then again. About being overwhelmed by the touch of my own baby. About the shame of that; the shame of all those things. About being apparently so un-likeable when I try so hard. Never being able to solve that. Never being able to quite see it, somehow.

He listens, and he writes. He tells me when I've said enough about one thing, and moves me on to another. I can feel the heat radiating off my cheeks as I voice one mental glitch after another, a litany of missed transactions with the outside world.

Eventually, he says, 'All right. I think that's all I need,' and there is a taut moment when I wonder if he will now close that file, and laugh at me, and tell me to go home.

'From everything you've told me,' he says, 'you certainly fit the narrative of someone with ASD.'

I do have a narrative, then. Finally. I do have a life story that makes sense when you put it all together. I smile. 'Great. Thank you.'

'It's funny,' he says. 'People are always so pleased when we diagnose ASD. Everything else tends to be bad news.'

'It's a relief to make sense of everything,' I say, 'and to have someone else see it too.'

'We'll do more tests,' he says. 'We'll get a more accurate understanding of exactly where you lie. Have you thought about what you want from this? I mean, treatment, medication . . .'

'Nothing,' I say. 'I can't think of anything I want.'

'You know there's no cure.'

'I know.'

'But we can help. There's lots that can be done.'

'Just tell me I don't ever have to go to a party again.'

'No,' he says. 'I'd never suggest avoidance. But adjustment, certainly.'

Adjustment, I think. Now that really is the story of my life.

THE END

Acknowledgements

Thanks, first of all, must go to my adored H for driving me down to the West Country and back again month after month, and only sometimes wishing aloud that we could go somewhere sunny for a change.

To Emma Brownridge and Beccy Scott for walking with me, literally and metaphorically.

To Lucy Abrahams for saying, 'This is a book, surely?' and making damned sure it happened.

To Emma Smith, for commissioning the book when it was just a few pages and a vague intention to walk the whole way around. Only a fellow walker could have understood. Thanks also to the team at Trapeze, especially Katie Moss and Leanne Oliver for getting this book into people's hands.

To Madeleine Milburn for taking such great care of me and my book. A good agent is like the best kind of mother: nurturing to you, fierce to everyone else. I'm so grateful for this, and to her superb team, including Hayley Steed and Alice Sutherland-Hawes.

To Peggy Riley, Sarah Barton and Liv Bays for reading early drafts, and for being as wise and perceptive as I always knew they would be.

To Andy Miller for making my subtitle his personal mission.

To my colleagues and students at Canterbury Christ Church University for putting up with an awful lot of walking talk, and for supporting my project with crucial grant-funding.

To the good folk of Connection at St Martin's for accepting the world's most rubbish pilgrim.

And, perhaps most vitally, to the astonishing community of autistic people I've found online, to whom I am very grateful and proud to finally belong.

A Note on the Walking Routes

Both the South West Coast Path and the North Downs Way have excellent waymarkers along their routes. However, I also always use an Ordnance Survey Explorer map and a compass to get a more detailed understanding of the terrain.

Here are the maps I used:

Minehead to Ilfracombe: *OS Explorer OL 9*
Ilfracombe to Peppercombe: *OS Explorer 139*
Peppercombe to just north of Bude: *OS Explorer 126*
Bude to Tintagel: *OS Explorer 111*
Tintagel to Mawgan Porth: *OS Explorer 106*
South Devon: *OS Explorer OL 20*

Dover to Canterbury: *OS Explorer 138/OS Explorer 150*
Canterbury to Chilham: *OS Explorer 150*
Chilham to Charing: *OS Explorer 137*